MY GIRLHOOD

MY GIRLHOOD

TASLIMA NASRIN

Translated from the Bengali by
Maharghya Chakraborty

PENGUIN
An imprint of Penguin Random House

HAMISH HAMILTON

USA | Canada | UK | Ireland | Australia
New Zealand | India | South Africa | China | Singapore

Hamish Hamilton is part of the Penguin Random House group of companies
whose addresses can be found at global.penguinrandomhouse.com

Published by Penguin Random House India Pvt. Ltd
4th Floor, Capital Tower 1, MG Road,
Gurugram 122 002, Haryana, India

First published in Hamish Hamilton by Penguin Random House India 2020

ISBN 9780670093922

Typeset in Adobe Caslon Pro by Manipal Technologies Limited, Manipal
Printed at Replika Press Pvt. Ltd, India

www.penguin.co.in

This is a legitimate digitally printed version of the book and therefore might not
have certain extra finishing on the cover.

To my mother, Begum Edul Wara

Contents

The War

1.

War was afoot.[1] There were rumours spreading from one neighbourhood to another, like wildfire, bringing people out on to the courtyards, the fields and the crossroads. Shock was written all over their faces, their eyes bulging wide, and the tremors moving restlessly across their faces, painting their noses, the insides of their mouths, their cheeks, their ears, their heads. Everyone was alert. Scores of people were running helter-skelter, dragging after them their children, their bundles, their belongings. They were running away, escaping the city in favour of the provinces, heading away from Mymensingh to Phoolpur, Dhobauda, Nandail. Houses and courtyards, shops and businesses, the school, the Amarabati Drama Centre, everything was abandoned as people crossed the river and the paddy fields, traversed the unending plains, to go hide in the forests. Even those who were never the first to leave their homes were beset with a terror that drove them to feverishly begin packing their belongings. Vultures were flying in with the smell of carrion on their beaks and one could hear distant gunshots whenever the pigeons flapped their wings restlessly. In a bid to run for cover people set out on foot, on trains, on boats, leaving behind their homes, the small plants in their yards, the familiar pew, kitchen utensils, the odd black cat, everything.

One evening, two three-wheeled machine-run cars turned up at our house to take us to the village of Madarinagar, south of Panchrukhi market. Barely had we left the city and crossed the Brahmaputra by ferry to reach Shambhuganj when six young men with *gamcha*s tied around their waists ambushed us on the road. Clutching Mother with both my arms I saw in horror that all six were carrying guns on their shoulders. That was perhaps when I first realized what war was, a time when you could waylay someone suddenly on the road and slaughter them. One of the six, a sharp shiny moustache adorning his upper lip, peered into one of the cars and spoke. 'Where are you going abandoning the city? If all of you go away who are we going to fight with? Go back home.'

Mother flipped aside the veil of her burka and, with a slight hint of pleading tempering her simmering anger, snapped back: 'What are you saying? The car ahead of us has gone through. My sons are in it. Let us pass.'

It failed to soften the stiff black moustache. He tapped his gun on the ground and began to yell, warning us against advancing even a fraction further. Forced to retreat, we had no choice but to get back to the ferry, when the middle-aged driver, having struck a match to his beedi, remarked, 'They are Bengali. They are our people. Not like them, these men don't wear kurtas. There's nothing to fear.'

My nine-year-old heart was beating in a steady nervous beat as if the six guns had been fired at me all at once. Accompanied by the steady prayers of the two women in black burkas I was wedged between and the mechanical whirring sound of the car, we started on our way back past

Jubilee Ghat and Golpukur. There were no other sounds except the beating of my heart, the whirring of the machine and the ceaseless prayers on my either side. The rest of the city had wrapped the dark night around itself, turned down the lights and gone off to sleep.

That very night Father sent us off again, this time to the west instead of the east, to Begunbari instead of Madarinagar. My sister Yasmin and Chotku[2] spent the journey sleeping, with Mother too dozing from time to time. This left only my grandmother and I awake alongside the blue plastic basket held firmly in her grasp.

'What's inside this, Nani?'

'Cheera, muri, some jaggery,' was the rather cold reply.

The house shaded by a grove of plantains that our beedi-addict driver finally took us to belonged to the in-laws' of Runu *khala*, Mother's younger sister and my aunt. A horde of people spilled out of the house and the shades around the yard were raised for everyone gathered to get a good glimpse of us.

Us, the relations from the city . . .

'Go throw the bucket into the well . . .'

'Put some rice on the boil . . .'

'Get some paan . . .'

'Make the bed for them . . .'

'Get them a fan . . .'

At night we huddled into the makeshift bed, the relations from the city, the dead-to-the-world Chotku with his leg flung over mine, which I was left unable to move lest I get kneed in the stomach by Yasmin. Flattened between the two I whined about my bolster without which I could never sleep.

Incensed by her spoilt daughter's complaints as she tried to fan her prickly-heat-speckled feet, Mother growled under her breath, 'You don't need it! Just sleep!'

The scolding managed to shut me up. Nani was huddled
in one corner of the bed, her black-bordered saree protecting
her face, her head, her basket and the food and the jaggery
inside. A small lamp burning near the threshold was throwing
the shadows into sharp relief on the tin wall, it seemed a
demon with many hands and feet was dancing and making
a shushing noise. Dipping my head between my knees in
fright I cried out:

'Mother, I'm scared.'

No sound from her. She was sleeping like a log just as
Chotku.

'Nani, Nani can you hear me . . .'

Not a peep from her either.

My introduction to the spectral world had happened
via Sharaf mama, one of Mother's younger brothers and
my maternal uncles. One night he had returned home out
of breath and told us how he had been waylaid by a white-
clad *petni*, a marsh witch, by the pond. She had apparently
thrown her glamour at him; he had dropped everything and
made a run for it. Shivering, he had hastily slid inside the
covers that night, as did I, and we spent the night hiding like
snails. The same thing had happened again the day after.
While returning through the bamboo grove Sharaf mama
had been stopped by a *mamdo*, a male ghost that had asked
him to tarry a little there in its atypical nasal twang. Sharaf
mama had made a run for it again and on reaching home
he had taken an ice-cold shower to calm his nerves. These
incidents, however, resulted in a noticeable surge in Sharaf
mama's popularity within the household. Felu mama, Tutu
mama, me, all of us would gather around him till late into the
night. Hasem mamas's wife Parul, our mami, would be there
beside us fanning him incessantly while he waited for Nani

to bring her traumatized-by-sprits son a plate of steaming rice and catfish curry, with a pinch of salt on the side.

Kana mama used to be a great fisherman and the size of his catches too used to be immense. But he could never return home with an entire fish. One night he was on his way back home when he noticed a cat following him. The fish he had caught that day was slung over his shoulder and he was walking back. As he neared his home he felt as if the weight on his shoulder had become considerably lesser than before. He turned around to discover half the fish had been eaten and the cat too was nowhere to be seen. It had not been a cat of course. It had been a fish-eating ghost that had appeared as a cat to get to the fish. Sharaf mama would eat and regale us with such tales of Kana mama's exploits.

Fear, as a result, had sort of crept under my skin, so much so that I would not even venture out to the bamboo grove behind our own house, not even in stark daylight, let alone after dark. As soon as it would get dark, I would be indoors, unwilling to even go out to the bathroom to answer nature's urgent calls. If it ever got too much to bear someone had to show the way with a big kerosene lamp so I could run out, check carefully if the coast was clear, do my business and then run back in promptly.

I was around seven and a half or eight when we shifted from Nani's place to our house in Amlapara. Father had asked both his sons to suggest possible names for the new house. Dada, my eldest brother, came up with 'Abakash' while Chotda, the one younger to him, wanted 'Blue Heaven'. Although I was not asked, I declared I wanted it to be called 'Rajanigandha'. Dada's name stuck, was etched in marble and put up on the wall by the big black gate. It was a huge house with ornate pillars and tall doorways.

Looking up at the ceiling it would seem as if one was gazing at the sky, one with green crossbeams and iron plates neatly arranged at ninety degrees, a rail waiting for a train to chug on it. Outside, winding stairs starting from the base of a bael tree led to a roof with a set of ornate railings around it from where one could see the entire locality spread out around us. The field beyond the house had a row of coconut and betel-nut trees along its edge. Our courtyard itself was lined with trees ranging from mangoes, jackfruits, guavas and custard apples to baels, pomegranates and Ceylon olives. Giddy with delight my two older brothers, my sister Yasmin and I would run around the house playing gollachut. It sort of drove out from our minds the memory of yet another house, my Nani's, tucked away barely a couple of miles away in a hole-in-the-wall lane. A modest dwelling, a pond full of tiny fish, a spot to wash the dishes where we used to press holes into the ground with our fingers to play with marbles, the dirty ashen rags we used to clean the glass chimneys of kerosene lamps before lighting them every evening, the cool reed mats we used to sit on with our mamas in the evenings while swaying back and forth as we recited 'Amader Chhoto Nodi',[3] fresh date juice tapped from the trees at dawn, my Nani's steamed rice cakes, everything that we left behind. The only thing I got to carry along to the new house was my fear of ghosts, which was not ready to abandon my side even at our temporary shelter in Begunbari.

Sharaf mama used to say the spectral always return to their realm at the end of the night. When I awoke in the morning the phantom with the five legs and feet was gone. The sun had found its way through tiny holes in the tin walls and the room was fairly warm. Mother, Nani and Runu khala's mother-in-law had pulled out seats in the courtyard and were chatting away. I had never really gone away from the city before, unless one considered the train journey from Mymensingh to Dhaka as a child to visit my Boromama, Mother's eldest brother, at his house at the edge of a vast meadow of red earth that stretched right up to the horizon. All I wanted to do was fly around the sky as a kite and play tag with the girls in the clouds. While standing in the yard brushing my teeth with ash, the thought crossed my mind that war was perhaps not a bad thing after all. The schools had suddenly shut and I had been spending my days playing with my dolls on the roof of Abakash. We only had to rush downstairs whenever planes passed overhead, when Mother would stuff cotton into our ears and make us duck for cover under the bed while she sat praying nearby. Later a shelter had been dug in the field where we would take refuge in case bombs fell. It was only after the hospital was bombed that Father packed us all into the two cars, Dada, Chotda, Sharaf mama, Felu mama, Tutu mama in the one which was allowed to pass to Madarinagar and us in the other one. Father himself decided to stay back at Abakash, having come to an agreement that if things went further south he too was going to lock up and leave for safety.

Rinsing the ash in my mouth with water from the well I took a deep breath, the air around me heady with the smell of lemons. Father wasn't there, there was no one to stare me down with fiery red eyes, no one to scold me at every turn or slap me around at the slightest pretext. To me there could be no better news. So elated was I that I could dance like the wind on the village roads and under the listless shade of the forest. Whichever direction I turned there were broad beans growing and I could hardly wait to roast and eat some and invite the farmers to share with me.

'Chotku, let's go to the shop. Let's buy tamarind.'

Chotku did not require much persuasion. I was salivating at the prospect of tamarind and it did not take long for us to slip under the fence by the banana tree that partially hid the courtyard and find our way down the narrow strip of earth that separated two paddy fields, determinedly walking towards the main road, with me in the front and Chotku bringing up the rear. We would have reached too had it not been for Hasu, that scarecrow! A short dhoti wrapped around his waist and twirling a dead branch, the hefty boy declared:

'Chotku can go, you can't. You're a girl. Girls shouldn't be going to the shops.'

'Why not? I go all the time!' I pursed my lips attempting to disregard the village bumpkin.

'That's in the city. This isn't the city. It's the village. Here women stay indoors, they don't go out.'

The scarecrow had begun to advance, his eyes like tiny rats with their snout out scouting for grub. I had always read about the bucolic, verdant and pastoral village in books, had always wanted to see one. Here I was finally in one such place but I was not being allowed to dance in the fields, or lose my way and chance upon a young shepherd playing his flute in some shaded bough by some stream or lake deep in the forest somewhere. No, instead, my morning met with rat-eyes, that too of a person in whose house I was a guest. Dejection clogging my throat, I sidled up to Mother back in the courtyard. She was wearing a pale saree, some of which covered her head, the hair she had left untied. I grabbed hold of the edge of the folds slung over her shoulder and, beginning to twirl the piece around my finger, let the sorrow spill over in earnest. 'He won't let me go to the shop?'

She didn't answer. Turning her face around towards me by her chin I insisted.

'That Hasu, he won't let me go buy tamarind.'

Snatching her face away Mother replied in huff. 'No tamarind. Too much sour makes the blood turn to water.'

This had always been her one argument against tamarind. Just so she wouldn't find out I used to hide on the stairs leading up to the roof of Abakash with tiny globules of tamarind that I would proceed to smear in salt and nibble on bit by bit with my thumb, all the while making a slurpy *tcha-tcha* sound in my mouth. I would only be done once my tongue was white, my teeth were sour and my blood was perhaps entirely water. I would be deathly scared of cutting myself anywhere for fear of getting caught. What if, instead of blood, water gushed out? Obviously whenever I did manage to cut myself, on snail shells or bits of glass or rose thorns or the odd piece of brick, it was blood that came out. And Mother would dress the wound with Dettol and wrap a rag around it while I half smiled about my blood having not turned to water yet.

There were too many people in the house at Begunbari. All the girls were named after fruits—Dalim (pomegranate), Peyara (guava), Angoor (grape), Kamala (orange)—while the boys were all Hasu, Kasu, Basu or Rasu. Rasu was my aunt's husband, my second khalu. He used to live in the city and none of us knew in which village he had gone into hiding after the panic about the war spread. His mother, Runu khala's mother-in-law, had a mouth full of paan at all times, her cheeks swollen, often some red juice trickling past the corner of her lips, the tips of her fingers white from the lime. Using a still non-white finger to scoop a tiny morsel of lime into the already bulging cheeks, she leaned in towards Nani

and whispered, 'Who knows where Rasu is! Who knows if
he's even alive! They are saying the Punjabis are wiping out
entire cities.'

My grandmother's tiny frame resembled a small cloth
bundle huddled over the small seat. The white bundle with
the black border did not respond to the news. There was
another bundle inside this one, the blue plastic one with the
food and the jaggery. Her eyes too remained transfixed like
tiny jewels as she stared away unseeing at a distance. It was
as if she could see her second son again, my Hasem mama,
knocking on the door of their house at the dead of night. As
soon as she threw open the door the rumbling of the passing
train drowned out whatever Hasem mama was trying to say.
'Ma, I'm going.'

'Why are you calling me so late in the night? What's
happened?' She turned up the wick of the lamp as she stepped
down on to the steps.

'I'm going.'

He had begun to walk towards the pond. She began to
run after him. 'Where are you going so late in the night?
Stop!'

Without turning around Hasem mama replied, 'I'm going
to war. I'll only be back once the country is independent.'

'Hasem, wait!' Nani kept calling after her errant boy until
he was no longer visible past the darkness. She stood still.
Her heart was beating, the heart whose warmth had kept the
tiny Hasem alive back when he had born during the famine
of the '50s. Parul mami, Hasem mama's wife, stood with
one foot on the threshold and the other on the step beyond,
weeping. People used to say she looked like a fairy and that
night in the dark Nani could swear she saw Parul mami glow
in the moonlight. She was indeed the moon and Nani did

not know where to hide such a moon any more. Their six-month-old daughter was sleeping inside! What sense did it make, this abandonment?

Nani did not know where to turn in the darkness, where to look for Hasem mama. She had not just seen war, she had seen *the* War when the Japanese had bombed the country, but even back then the family had not been torn apart. So she left her tin house at dawn, dropped Parul mami off at her parents' house and came to Abakash to her daughter's house, with her four other sons and the blue plastic basket, to seek advice. Father instead suggested that the city was no longer safe and that we should all move to the villages. The move had separated her from her three sons, leaving only the infant Chotku, the one younger than even her grand-daughter, near her. As Runu khala's mother-in-law sat weeping over the whereabouts of her missing Rasu, my tiny bundle of a grandmother could only sit silently by her side, her back to the sun. She knew her son had gone to war but she could hardly say anything. Did anyone ever return from war?

Her gaze did not waver.

2.

Runu khala's father-in-law brought news that the military was on its way to Begunbari; six severed heads had been found in a jute field about a quarter mile away. As usual there was a group of people running to see the heads and another running away from them. For us, the relations from the city, it was decided that we were going to be shifted to villages further within the wilderness. In the middle of the night we set off on bullock carts towards Haspur with Kasu, Hasu's younger brother. A little later, amidst a symphony of buzzing flies, howling foxes and the occasional scary hoot, we found ourselves abruptly coming to a halt. I was already curled into a ball, almost under Mother's behind. Sharaf mama used to say that ghosts came out in the darkness, to grab hold of unsuspecting humans and pop them whole inside their mouths. They usually nested on the highest branch of the tree for better vantage and our cart had stopped under a shaora tree on a new moon night. I could hear footsteps approaching us. The driver's whip could be heard swishing through the air and landing on the bullocks but they still wouldn't budge. The driver yelling. More swishing. And then just as suddenly the animals broke into a run, speeding through the forest, the sudden movement tossing us about inside the cart, our heads hitting the cover above as the tiny infant with us, no eyebrows, no hair on his head or his body, his tiny body already weak from repeatedly falling sick, began to squeal in protest. More yelling, more swishing whips. Chotku held on to Nani tightly with his emaciated hands; she in turn held on to her blue plastic basket with the cheera, muri and jaggery.

The house at Haspur belonged to the in-laws of Dalim, Kasu's sister. Leaving the bullocks and their driver to catch their breath in the compound of the house, Kasu led his city-bred relatives inside. Time and again he would turn around and glance at us, but his eyes not at all like his brother's rat-like gaze.

Two rats in Hasu's eyes I spied,
And now off I am to Haspur
Past the bamboo grove.

Everyone at this house wanted to please us, the educated people from the city who rode cars and lived a proper big house.

The biggest room was set up for us to stay in and the best china with the pretty flowers and leaves was brought out from the cupboard. A feast of koi and catfish was prepared and we were all called to flock together in the kitchen and dig in. Once we were done eating, as were the children and the menfolk returning from the fields at the end of day, only then did the women of the house sit down with their meals. The cosiest hand-stitched and embroidered *nakshi kantha* adorned our beds along with pretty pillow covers that had 'Forget-Me-Not' stitched on them in red and blue, one for each of us. Since there were no bolsters, the pillow had to take its place between my legs; a habit was a habit whether we were at war or not. I dreamt of floating like a duck in the ponds of Haspur or drifting in the breeze like Chotku and Kasu's red kite.

Women my age in the house wore proper sarees and some I found were already married. They woke up at dawn to let out the chickens and the ducks, get the fires started, get all the spices, etc., for cooking in order, thrash and clean the rice and perform a myriad other chores. I called some of them to come and play with me. It only made them laugh though none of them came forward. The boys were scampering up the trees to pluck mangoes, mabolos and green coconuts, and seeing them I wanted to follow suit. What I got was a stern warning: women die if they climb trees. They pulled up their lungis and played *hadudu* but when I wanted to join in, I was told it was not something girls did. They flung their gamchas over their shoulders and went to the ponds to fish but when I followed them, I was informed that women weren't allowed to fish either.

'Not even fly kites?'

'No, not even that.'

'Who says?' I shot back, hands on my hips and back arched.

'Repeat after me,' said one of the boys, dark as coal, caked in mud and with a mouth full of yellow teeth, retreating a couple of steps, 'and you have to say it very fast.' It was a tongue twister involving the mabolo and, hoping they would take me with them if I could do it, I launched myself at it earnestly, only to be stopped short by an incomprehensible litany of twisted sounds slipping off my tongue. The yellow teeth parted wide in a sneer as did the other boys' with him. Leaving me behind, the city girl in the ready-made frock, the boys turned on their heels and continued on their way.

In the afternoon, when the women went to swim in the pond, some crossing the entire stretch in one stroke while others swimming to the shore from the middle in one breath, I could not help but sit by the bank and watch them in fascination, my feet dipping just below the surface of the water. I could hear them talking about me: she's just tall; look at her, no breasts yet!

Whenever he would go swimming, Sharaf mama used to gather water lilies and bring them to me and ask, 'Do you want to learn how to swim? Eat ants, a lot of them and you will be able to swim.' I cannot count for sure the number of times I did try such a thing, eating ant-ridden sugar and jaggery before going to swim in the pond. The water would invariably drag me down into the mud and that would be it. In Haspur even the naked young boys could jump into the pond head first and swim perfectly and all I could feel was shame for not even being able to wade past waist-high water despite being much older than them. In my heart, though, I was swimming like them, crossing the pond back and forth again and again. Is there anything more joyous than swimming in cold water during scalding hot afternoons? Word arrived from Mother asking me to get out of the water and get back to the house lest I caught a cold. The city girl had no choice but to leave the refuge of the cold pond and wade back to the furnace ashore.

Meanwhile, lots of things were happening on land. The Punjabis were burning down houses and the women of these charred homes were going around the other remaining houses of Haspur begging for aid. The air was tense as if bombs were to begin falling any moment. Only two houses in the village had radios, the one we were staying in and Kasem Sikdar's. In the evening a crowd of people gathered at the two homes to listen to the news.

The men who came to listen to the radio spread reed mats on the floor and a hookah was passed around as they sat and talked. One of them, a bald man with round cheeks wearing a green lungi, had heard on the Swadhin Bangla news channel that the Mukti Bahini[4] was on its way and freedom was almost at hand, or so he had been saying over and over for a couple of months. Dalim's father-in-law was sitting on a low stool, occasionally swatting away flies off his gleaming dark back with a gamcha. Stroking the strip of white beard on his chin with his fingers he shot back, 'How will they fight the military? Apparently they have trained in India. Why, didn't Jamir Ali, Turab, Jabbar, Dhanu Mian, didn't all of them go to war too? They are infants, not soldiers. They will fight wars! Dhaka is a place of death now. Village after village has been torched. Do you think the military is even human? They are nothing but animals. The other day at Trishal Bazar this one soldier caught hold of me and starting asking my name and such. I asked him immediately what business my name was to him. The imam of the Chan Tara

Masjid was following the chap around. I didn't like the look
of the man.'

Taru Khalifa sighed a fairly loud 'hmm' in response. His
sight compromised by old age, holding a walking stick and
in a completely tattered undershirt, rumour had it that Taru
Khalifa was actually a fairly rich man. He used to be a tailor
in Trishal Bazar but after losing sight in his left eye, he had
tidied his affairs and come to stay with his son in Haspur.
Quite often he would disappear from this house too, without
a word to anyone, and stay away for months on end. Ever
since the war had started he had not left the village and came
over every evening to the house we were in to listen to the
radio. A man of few words, he used to mostly listen to others
with his head resting on his right shoulder and whenever he
didn't like something he was hearing he would sigh audibly
with a 'hmm' and then succinctly put forward his own
opinions on the matter. His 'hmm' resulted in an immediate
silence in the surroundings, broken only occasionally by the
gurgling of the hookah. The man in the green lungi had been
sitting with his back to Taru Khalifa and he turned around
towards the old man. After a few more 'hmm's, Taru Khalifa
declared, 'The Mukti Bahini will bring us freedom. Our
guerrillas are marching forward. If required, India will send
in its forces too. This will be our land. Sheikh Mujib will run
the country and the time of the Ayubs and the Yahyas will
be over for good.'

Once Taru Khalifa was done talking, the man in the
green lungi called out loudly to someone called Siraj to get
him a fan. Siraj, the boy with the yellow teeth, appeared
instantly out of nowhere with a palm-leaf fan in hand.
Gone was the boy caked in mud; he had clearly taken a bath
after their fishing expedition. The man in the green lungi

proceeded to scratch himself with one hand and fan with the other. The women of the house, in the meanwhile, had their ears pressed to the walls trying to discern what the men were talking about. My tiny bundle of a grandmother remained steadfast on the bed, her eyes constant like twinkling stars.

I could feel my newly discovered fear of the military jostling for space with the ghosts already nesting deep inside my heart.

Taru Khalifa was correct. Eventually the Mukti Bahini did bring freedom to Bangladesh. We were in another village called Dapuniya at the time. One winter morning I was sitting in the sun just outside the living room of the house and blowing smoke out of my mouth. All of a sudden loud cries rang out. Children were running towards the main road to see what it was and it soon became evident that the source of the commotion was gradually moving closer. Everyone was justifiably curious; it was not as if sudden arrivals were common in Dapuniya! What if it was just more news about burning homes and corpses? For the entire week, prior to that, the sound of ceaseless gunfire had effectively made our ears go numb and the village had been holding its breath in anxiety. The noise was obviously a source of new worry and the first thought was if it was the military again. Since the sound didn't particularly resemble anything related to the army people were left glancing at each other in bewilderment. The women, of course, were inside the house and trying to peer through the curtains to see what the matter was. I could care less about such subtleties; besides, I was still young enough and since I didn't have breast yet I could still fall in with the other kids. The scream was different from anything else I had heard and hope flared at once in my heart, as if a hundred doves had taken flight together.

The sound was approaching Dapuniya market. Soon we were greeted by the sight of about twenty–twenty-five young men on a truck, many of whom resembled the men who had held up our car in Shambhuganj, shouting slogans of 'Joy Bangla'. There was such intense energy in those slogans, such a paralysing feeling of excitement that in an instant it seemed to shatter the tense gloom that had the village in its grip. As if a group of men who had been allowed out of a cave after eons had met with a burst of sunlight. Or men drowning in an icy-cold deluge had caught sight of distant sails. Thus far the people of Dapuniya had only been able to whisper Joy Bangla to each other, if at all, and here they were being greeted by loud slogans! Shaking off long-held shackles of terror the villagers as well as I joined in the chorus, fists thumping in the air. People were running after the truck, running after freedom so to speak, an independent nation at long last. I ran into the house to tell Mother and found her standing by the window.

With a little pirouette in my step I cried out, 'Ma, say Joy Bangla! We are finally free!' I noticed she was laughing and crying at the same time; she was wiping the tears away with her saree from time to time but the smile did not dim one bit.

Nani's eyes, however, remained unmoving. Save for the tapping sound you could make on an actual stone, Nani's wasn't much different. Why did she not smile widely with her brown paan-stained teeth? Was it because of the blue plastic basket, the one she no longer had to protect or curl around to keep safe?

There were so many people on the road, some were still running, chants of Joy Bangla reverberating across Dapuniya. Gunshots and wails of despair had been replaced with laughter, joy and slogans overnight. No houses were going to burn any more, no one else was going to get shot, no other bombs were going to fall, no one was going to blindfold anyone and take them away, the stench of death would no longer permeate the air and neither would vultures circle above us. We were going to go back home, to the city, and I was going to go back to my old room and my bolster and my family of dolls who I had left sleeping on their tiny beds that night before we had gone on the run.

So excited was I that I did not quite know where I physically ended and where exactly that feeling of excitement began. Without even trying to make sense of it, I ran off to join the crowd that had gathered outside. At the head of the procession outside was Khaled holding a flag on a bamboo branch—green with a giant red dot and a crumpled yellow cloth in the centre of the red—followed by a veritable deluge of young men and boys of the village. In the crowd I could spy Chotku waving a similar flag and, seeing him, I knew I wanted one too. This was a new flag. Earlier in school we used to have to stand in front of the old green flag with the moon and the stars and sing '*Pak Sar Zameen Shad Bad*'.[5] When Chotda used to hold meetings calling for the fall of Ayub Shah, one day he had taken one of these old flags with him from under the mattress. After returning from the protest march in the evening he had told us how he had burnt the flag that day.

After the procession came to a halt Khaled climbed atop a jackfruit tree by the road and, perched on a branch, informed us that the new flag he was waving was the flag of Joy Bangla. 'This is going to be our state flag henceforth. All hail the glory of Joy Bangla! The green is for our green fields, with the red sun at the centre and our map in its middle.

After a nine-month-long battle we have freed our country. This new state will no longer be called East Pakistan; it's Joy Bangla! All hail the glory of Joy Bangla!'

As the crowd erupted in a chorus Khaled dropped off the branch. He was a dark-complexioned man in a white lungi and shirt, with jet-black hair, tiny red pimples on his cheeks and large black eyes like two plump hornets. That night I was lying awake on my bed near the fence, staring fixedly at a gun that was propped up against it. Everyone else was sleeping. All of a sudden I heard footsteps and hurriedly pulled the cover over me. I peeked out at the sound of bullets being loaded into the gun and my eyes met two dark hornet-eyes.

'Do you know what this is?'

'It's a gun,' I tilted my head too for effect.

Passing his hand over the gun he pointed out to me the butt, the trigger, where the bullets went, and mechanism of how it was used.

'Do you kill people?' I ventured, my voice dry as paper.

'I kill enemies,' he said through a laugh.

The gun had been kept hidden under the straw for a long time, in fact right on the stack we used to sleep on. Who knew! Khaled had turned up one night and retrieved it from there. Then deep in the night he had wrapped a black shawl around himself and disappeared into the darkness with the gun. That was the first time I had seen Khaled after arriving in Dapuniya and this was the second. He resembled my Hasem mama in many ways and the two of them were like brothers. They had studied in the same school, eaten off the same plate and followed each other to war.

I wrapped the blanket snug around me, the straw promising warmth against the wintry night. Chotku was fast asleep beside me just as he had been sleeping that fateful night not so long ago. Had he not been asleep he would have probably screamed the house down and they would have shot him too, him as well as us who were in bed with him, me and Yasmin. I had not slept, I had only been pretending to, as if I was soundly sleeping and lost in my dreams. As if I was not aware of the many boot-clad feet walking about the room, guns hoisted on their shoulders, laughing and joking and willing to shoot anyone whenever and wherever. If they were to sense someone was awake, the guns would have bellowed at our heads or we would have been dragged from our beds to the camp, to be whipped to shreds or crushed to pulp with bayonet butts. Whatever the booted men did, we girls had to stay perfectly still and pretend to sleep, make sure our eyes did not stir, that not a finger moved, that even the heart did not tremble. And if the heart did quake we had to make sure the men did not sense it even when they raised the mosquito net and flashed their torches on our sleeping faces, our breasts and our thighs, speaking in an alien language that I didn't recognize. One could sense the lust pouring off their eyes and fire on their tongues but we could not let them know we were aware, that we were awake. And if they did figure it out, one could only hope that like others they would leave with the rebuke that since we didn't even have breasts yet we were just tall girls, not women, not even adolescent.

A cold snake had slithered up my body, wrapped itself around my throat and was making it nearly impossible to draw breath. But I managed to breathe somehow. My eyes desperately wanted to tremble under the torchlight's beam that was trained on them but I was at war with myself, trying to keep them shut, Chotku's leg over mine, one hand placed over Yasmin's tummy, back resting awkwardly on a bolster. The men in boots stood there for a long time, the net raised and torch in hand, their fiery and drooling tongues and eyes trained on our sleeping bodies. The cold snake had slithered off them and roamed all over our bodies, sniffing our backs, our tummies and our vaginas. Finally, it seemed to crawl inside me, inside my flesh and bones, burrowing within my blood. The night Khaled came for the gun in Dapuniya, the snake visited me again. I could not sleep for a long time afterwards, expecting to hear boot-clad feet again, heads covered in helmets and wearing olive-green uniforms. Nothing, neither the straw nor the kantha, could bring me warmth and the snake too refused to leave me alone.

That first night I didn't know how long I stayed in that manner, how long I pretended to sleep. It seemed years passed but the torchlight remained unwavering and the net remained half-raised. I was dying and becoming cold as ice, my body lightening like a feather. I was no longer sleeping between Yasmin and Chotku; instead I had been swept away by the north wind, beyond boots and roving gazes and far beyond anyone's reach. I was on the moon and the old woman there was spinning her yarn and waving at me to come closer. I was thirsty and I wanted water but there was no water on the moon! My mouth was dry with thirst and my chest about to explode from the exertion when I heard, at a distance, the fading sounds of boots walking away and entering another room. I could hear the woman on the moon whispering to me to open my eyes, asking me why I was sweating on a winter night. I didn't wish to open my eyes, didn't want to meet those lustful eyes, or the cold snake slithering all over me. So I stayed still as before, Chotku's legs over mine and one hand placed over Yasmin's tummy.

I heard a flute in the distance. Who could be playing a flute so late in the night? Who wanted to wake me up at such an odd hour? I didn't want to wake, wanted everyone to go to sleep like me and leave the night peacefully quiet, wanted others to travel to the moon like me, where even the old woman would have wrapped her spinning for the day, rested her head on the clouds and fallen asleep.

It had sounded like a flute but it was not quite one. It was the sound of Mother weeping. It seemed to me the sound was not coming from the house but from somewhere outside. I found Mother bent over in the courtyard outside, crying over the prone form of Father. Rasu khalu was there trying to pacify her, trying to tell her that Father was alive, asking her not to cry any more. But Father looked as good as dead. Rasu khalu reached out and untied his hands from the base of the coconut tree and the unexpected release propelled his motionless form forward. His head slipped off Rasu khalu's shoulder and he fell forward face first on the grass. Khalu dragged Father's unconscious body inside. His unconscious form was laid out on the floor, blood dripping from his mouth, chest and stomach.

Rasu khalu was not supposed to have been there; he had only turned up that day to find a hiding spot for himself somewhere in the large house. We were not supposed to have been there either; we ought to have been in Dapuniya. Once the fires had reached Haspur we had fled in the middle of the night to Hasem mama's friend Khaled's house, right on the main road, south of Dapuniya market. When news had arrived from the city of things settling down it had brought my nana (grandfather) along. He had explained to us rather animatedly, his thin white beard swaying ever so slightly in the wind, that we should all head back home. We had been convinced enough to immediately return to the city bag and baggage, Nani,

Chotku, Mother, Yasmin and I. Nani had returned to
her small house and we to Abakash, only to be greeted by
Father's anguished cry, 'What have you done? Why are
you here? The war isn't over yet!'

That fact we had figured out at the first sight of our
locality. My friend Archana's house stood empty, as did
Prafulla's. At Bibha's, her family wasn't there but there
were other people living there who spoke an unknown
tongue. Father informed me that it was the Biharis who
had taken over many of the Hindu houses. At Abakash the
grass had grown taller than us, as if no one had lived in the
house for a thousand years. It was like something I had
once seen in the zamindar palaces of Muktagacha: lime and
plaster falling off walls, snakes slithering through reeds, the
wind playing with the resident ghosts in the empty halls
and making an eerie moaning sound. Father had anxiously
informed us that the city was not in a good state and that
the military had taken over the dak bungalow. We had
decided to only spend the night and go back to Dapuniya
the morning after.

At least that had been the plan. Dada had gone and
fetched Nani back to Abakash. We had been afraid that
the ramshackle house she lived in was not safe enough, that
at the very least there was a threat of dacoits. So Nani too
had tucked her plastic basket under her burka and taken a
rickshaw to the safety of Abakash. Since we were meant to
head back to Dapuniya again the very next day, Nani had
spread the *janamaz* in the dead of the night to sit down to
pray, with her precious blue plastic basket propped nearby,
her gaze often getting distracted from her prayers and
straying to the cherished object instead. While living in
Haspur, I had put my hand inside the basket one day for

cheera and jaggery. Nani had been praying then too but she had frozen mid-bow, abandoned her sajda and snatched the bundle away from me. I had made a fuss about wanting food but she had snapped at me and sent me away.

That night, she had almost finished her prayers when, all of a sudden, we heard a loud commotion at the main gate, as if a herd of wild elephants were charging at it. Rasu khalu had rushed in. 'Run! The military is here!' Mother had been reading the Quran sitting in the room where Chotku, Yasmin and I were sleeping. Hearing his cries she had dropped the Quran there and then, left behind the bangles she had taken off before prayers and placed on top of the holy book, and made a run for it. She and Nani had run across the dark courtyard and escaped through the sweeper's exit to Prafulla's abandoned house.

Father lay on the floor. Having returned to the house after the boots had marched away, Nani was searching near her janamaz, trying to figure out in the dim light where her blue basket was.

'Rasu, Edul, where is my basket?'

'We have been robbed,' Rasu khalu replied in a hushed voice.

Mother was walking from room to room with a candle. There was no money in the cupboard. The Quran was still there but not the bangles she had left on top. Nani's basket was nowhere to be seen.

'It happened in an instant! They have half-killed the poor girl's father and taken everything away. Oh, why did I come back to the city! How could this happen!' Nani was becoming hysterical.

As she began to turn the room upside down for her basket a faint sound suddenly burst forth from Father. 'Water . . .'

Rasu khalu rushed to give him some water; he was still
motionless but at least his lips were moving. Khalu was still
trembling in fear just as he had been trembling in his hiding
place. He had sent the women of the house away and taken
refuge under the bed. The military had an insatiable thirst for
female flesh, be it middle-aged or adolescent it never failed
to give them a hard on. Rasu khalu had wrapped a bedsheet
around himself so as to resemble a heap of quilts, slithered
under the bed and begun to pray so that his soul remained
steadfast even at the moment of death. He had only emerged
after the booted feet had walked out of the black gates of
Abakash.

Mother dropped to the floor with a thud. 'It's a
catastrophe. Ma's basket had nearly five hundred grams of
gold and about twenty thousand taka. It's all gone.'

'Where did grandma get so much gold?' Rasu khalu
could not conceal the astonishment in his voice.

'It belonged to the women of the house. Plus, some of
it belonged to a couple of neighbours, Parul, Fajli, Runu,
Jhunu, Soheli's mother, Sulekha's mother and Shahab's wife
too. They had given it to Ma for safekeeping. She has not
slept, not even for a night. She has been guarding all of it
all this while.' Mother's voice sounded nasal, like that of a
poltergeist.

The candle was about to go out. Mother was sitting on
the floor near Father's senseless form, crying. Rasu khalu
sighed and said, 'Many people have buried their jewellery
and stuff. Why was grandma carrying it all around? What
is more important, duty or your life? You women were all
spared, that's a lot already.' Nani was still searching, under
the bed and the sofa, even under the janamaz. The basket
was nowhere to be found though.

3.

Nani rummaged through the bones. Thousands of bones had been retrieved from the well of the big mosque. Numerous people were gathered among the bones trying to find their lost sons and husbands in the heap, a mass of skeletal feet, ribs, arms, even skulls. Nani was rummaging for Hasem mama's remains. The day darkened to evening after a while and many turned back, wiping their eyes and heading home. Nani sat beside the well of the mosque, rummaging amidst the mountain of bones, looking for her Hasem.

Birth, Aqiqah, etc.

1.

Mother had had two sons before I was born. At least that had been a saving grace, or else who would have carried on the family name! Women were not suitable for such a task; their function was simpler and more ornamental, helping their mothers around the house and keeping the hearth in order for the pleasure and satisfaction of the menfolk.

After two sons my father declared his desire for a daughter. So it happened. The daughter was born upside down though, she was born feet first.

The makeshift nursery was a tiny shed beside Nani's run-down home with its pond full of small fish. After her marriage to Rajab Ali, my father, this was the place they had shifted to in exchange for five hundred taka. Earlier, he used to live in the pleader's house and work, teach the children, etc., in exchange for rent while studying medicine. They had shifted to my Nani's place after getting married to my mother Begum Edul Wara, with the prior understanding that they were going to move out after he finished his degree. He finished his degree, got a job, became father to two boys, got his wife pregnant the third time and still there was no talk of moving out. When the neighbours began to talk about Rajab Ali wanting to become a live-in son-in-law, Mother couldn't tolerate it any longer. She began to pester him every chance she got: he was a doctor, earned well, couldn't they live separately with the children, how much longer were they going to stay there, people were gossiping, etc.

The midwife Sarojini had spread a piece of rag on her stomach and was softly pressing her distended belly with the warm earthen pot. Mother was clutching Sarojini's hand in pain, the smell of onions wafting off her grip, turmeric visible under her fingernails. She had been eating in the kitchen when the contractions had started. Pushing aside the plate she had crossed over and headed straight to the bedroom, the pain starting even before she could lie down on her back. Nani was sitting near her head fanning her and trying to talk her through the pain. Women had to bear the pain, they had to learn how to. Nana had walked to Sarojini's house to fetch her at once. It was barely three months that the midwife had come to the house for a similar occasion: the day Nani gave birth to Felu mama. In her case it had been a quiet birth, let alone the neighbours even family members had barely got wind of my infant uncle's arrival. In Nani's case, when the contractions had started, she had merely spread a mat on the kitchen floor for herself. Sarojini had arrived, taken some burning coal from the oven in an earthen pot and begun massaging her belly. Nani did not need to be told to bear the pain any more because she had learnt it well and could do it all by herself. After having sixteen children giving birth was a breeze for her. That did not mean she liked doing it though, year in and year out. Her grandchildren were growing up and the family was growing rapidly anyway. It was time for her married daughters or daughters-in-law to get pregnant and there she was visiting the nursery herself every year much to her chagrin. Sarojini was telling Mother that the warmth was meant to help with the pain, that it helped the child move down. Just a little longer and it was going to be over, she cooed.

Father returned home and brought out his scalpel and scissors from his leather box. He had birthed both his sons and this time he was going to do the same for the daughter he wanted. With Sarojini sitting near her head he parted Mother's legs and put his hand in; in moments murky water gushed out from between her legs. 'Her water's broken. It shouldn't be much longer,' exclaimed the old midwife. Father pushed his hand in further, almost up to the amniotic sac, sweat dotting his forehead and his hands trembling. Suddenly he got up and walked to the well. Drawing a bucket of water, he began to wash his hands much to the astonishment of my grandmother.

'Amma, Edul has to be taken to a hospital. The birth can't happen at home.'

'What are you saying? She's had two here before!' Nani exclaimed, deliberately lowering her voice.

'This one's upside down. An operation is the only way. We might have complications if we don't get her to a hospital immediately,' Father replied, wiping the sweat of his brow with his sleeve.

Mother was lying there screaming like an animal being slaughtered, waking the locality, the neighbours and even Nani's three-month-old infant Felu. Returning to the nursery from the well, Father became aware that one leg of the baby could be seen. 'What if it dies on the way to the hospital?' Sarojini anxiously inquired. The anxiety, contagious as it was, did not take long to appear on his brow too.

He tried listening to the infant's heartbeat to see if everything was all right, his white shirt sticking to his back like skin. A doctor of anatomy, he was a teacher at Lytton Medical School where he used to dissect dead bodies in the mortuary to teach his students the circulatory and nervous systems. He would demonstrate hearts, livers and vaginas preserved in formaldehyde, which he would bring out in trays like tea while teaching. Obstetrics and gynaecology were not his area of expertise. But there was no time to dilly-dally and a chance had to be taken. Having coached himself thus, he inserted his hands between his wife's parted thighs again, fingers trembling in hesitation, to pull out the other foot that had folded at the knee and got stuck, leaving both feet of the newborn dangling outside. A makeshift nursery, a pair of scissors, a couple of knives, some gauze and thread for sewing wounds, this much was not enough for safe childbirth! Father took off his sweat-soaked shirt and stared helplessly at the dangling legs, the screaming woman and the folded hands of the midwife. If the umbilical cord was wrapped around the baby's neck then death by asphyxiation was certain. He could hear his own heart beating furiously and he did not have the courage to check if the newborn's was beating too. Sarojini edged closer and whispered, 'Pull by the leg, doctor saab.'

What if something bad happened? Father had read in books how newborns died at such a stage from a sudden blow to the head or getting choked by the umbilical cord. Instead of taking a risk the best recourse was an operation, not a forceps delivery but a C-section. Rushing out of the nursery he instructed Nani to send someone to get a rickshaw for the hospital. Back in the room he could do nothing but pace to and fro nervously. The vest he had on was wet with sweat too. He had read in books that pulling by the legs helped in pulling the back out safely. As he began to pull, he could see the back slowly appearing.

'Push downwards. Push with all you have got,' he bit out through gritted teeth. The entire body except the head emerged.

'It's a girl! You had wanted a girl and here she is.'

The girl was yet to see the light of day though. Ever the good student of medicine, a thousand ideas were jostling for space in Father's head. The renowned anatomy teacher proceeded to use one of them on his struggling wife. Pressing the tube of the stethoscope on the tiny girl's chest he could hear her steady heartbeat indicating there was still hope. Inserting his hands into the birthing canal he began to manoeuvre her neck free of the cord twisted around the neck. 'Think of God, Edul,' advised Sarojini from the side. 'Call Allah, call His name,' came Nani's response from where she had been standing beyond the door. As if on cue Mother too began chanting His name.

In the end I was finally born, but only after a bout of severe trouble breathing and with my tiny heart threatening to give up. Mother's chants of 'Allah' were drowned out by my cries as Sarojini lowered me into a tub of lukewarm water to clean me up.

Before long Runu khala had snatched me away from the nursery; I was passed on from her to Jhunu khala and then to Boromama who exclaimed on seeing me, 'Oh, she's a princess! A princess has been born among us.'

It was dawn and the eastern sky was just beginning to bleed red when a deluge of joy crashed on to the courtyard of Nani's rickety old house. A daughter after two sons! Hasem mama, Tutu mama, Sharaf mama, everyone lined up for a glimpse of the new princess. Fajli khala peeked inside the nursery and told Mother, 'What a day your daughter's chosen to make an entrance! Twelve Rabiul Awwal is the birth date of the Prophet. This girl will be very virtuous. You're lucky, Edul.' Later in the morning Nana brought home an entire case full of sweets as neighbours and acquaintances began to pour in to meet the new princess who had been born on the auspicious date of 12 Rabiul Awwal.

As I was growing up, whenever I used to press Mother to tell me stories from back then she would only tell me that she had slipped and fallen near the well while she had been pregnant with me. The impact had apparently jerked me around and that is why I was born upside down. 'They lay you down on the round table. Such a huge table and you were about half its size. No one had seen anyone like you before. Ma used to ask me to keep you wrapped up in blankets and draw a black dot on your forehead to ward off the evil eye. Two days old and Soheli's mother asked in astonishment how many months old you were. Manu's mother felt your round head and observed that even bael fruits had more ridges and curves on them.'

One day, while listening to her reminisce as she lay on the bed, I rested my chin on her belly and asked, 'How are babies born?' Mother had moved aside her saree pallu in response and pointed to her soft belly, 'From here. Your father's a doctor, right? He cut you out of me with a blade.' She had pointed to the white marks on her lower abdomen one by one and said, 'This was Noman, this was Kamal, this was you and this one was Yasmin.' I had stared at the white marks pitifully, rubbed my hand over them ever so softly and felt terribly sorry for her. 'Ish! Didn't it bleed?' Touching my chin with a laugh she had replied, 'It did. But then they sewed it up and I was OK.' A little later she had dragged me closer towards her and whispered, 'Will you cry if I die?' I had tilted my head to the right and replied, 'You won't. If you die, I will die too.'

Mother had to do household chores with her upside-down daughter attached to her hip, quite literally, washing and cutting the vegetables, stuffing the clay oven with fuel, her eyes watering from the fumes, and a host of other things. Her daughter, asleep on her lap, would awaken from time to time, assaulted by the smell of onions, turmeric, pepper and her mother's sweat, or the cries of dogs and crows. When Mother had to go to the bathroom I would crawl around in the yard, in the dirt and her own pee, occasionally picking up and putting the odd piece of brick, a grain of sand or an odd dry leaf in her mouth. My older brothers would come back from school, pick me up and walk about to keep me occupied. On one such occasion, Chotda made six-month-old me sit on the ledge of the well so he could tie his pants. A slight tilt to the side and I could have fallen into the well and died. Of course, I could have. But for a girl whose birth had been so risky, how would falling into the well and dying have looked like! The princess began to grow up ensconced in a lot of love and warmth, as well as some occasional disregard.

When the princess turned eleven one day her mother picked up a sewing machine and made her two pairs of pyjamas. She was informed that she was a grown-up and thus no longer allowed to wear half pants.

'It was a bad phase. I used to cry all the time.' The afternoon was languid and deeply melancholic; Mother was staring out past the window as she spoke. 'Your father was in love with this woman called Razia Begum. Chakladar's wife. Every other day I would find letters in his pockets while washing his shirts, the ones she'd written to him. You used to roll over and fall off the bed, it happened so many times. You got hurt but I had no mind for anything. I could not concentrate; it just would not happen. And your father too had begun returning home late.'

Razia Begum was a beautiful woman. In my mother's definition, 'beautiful' meant fair. Razia Begum was fair with large, bovine, black eyes, lips like two perfect slices of an orange, and she had a cascade of dark tresses that fell past her waist, a mane so thick that when she tied it in a knot it seemed something had been put inside to make the bun appear bigger. To top it all, in a manner of speaking, she had rather large breasts. Now, I must confess, I have never seen this Razia Begum with my own eyes. But from my mother's vivid description I always nurtured the image of a giant dairy cow, the udders making it difficult for her to walk. In short, Razia Begum was a fairly ample and well-endowed woman. When she walked the earth trembled. My mother, on the other hand, was a tiny, dark woman, fine strands of hair like the dry husk of a coconut, tiny eyes, a flat nose, a frame as delicate as a dragonfly's legs. The conclusion was foregone: my father had lost interest in her. Whoever she met she would catch hold of and talk about the disaster that had befallen her.

'Your father was going to marry her. Where was I going to go with the children?'

At such a time of catastrophe, just as I turned eleven months old—entirely ignored all this while, my erstwhile perfectly round ridgeless head slightly dented because of all the falling off the bed, half-fed on barley and leftover milk or perhaps sucking on Dada's little finger—Father was transferred. To Mother it was as if an angel from heaven had descended upon her hearth, extended a hand to pull her out of the hellfire she had been burning in and offered her the path to paradise instead. She had long dreamt of a separate home of her own and, finally, proving all the naysayers wrong and removing the cursed tag of a live-in son-in-law off her husband once and for all, Mother bid goodbye to Nani's doddering old house, consigned the name Razia Begum to the pits forever and set off for the city.

They had a very beautiful house in the middle of the prison. The convicts worked in the house of the prison medic, doing all manner of jobs and chores, taking the doctor's daughter out on strolls, etc. Even though I spent most of my time with them, there wasn't much cause for concern, not even for the gold necklace around my neck. In her free time Mother would sit and braid her hair, line her eyes with kohl, powder her face and then neatly wear a saree, pleats and all. In Pabna, where they had been transferred to, there was no Razia Begum-shaped threat looming over them; Father had no reason to be late and letters too stopped falling out of his pockets. Mother went around making acquaintances with the neighbours who invited her to their house, a small pool of influence that she gradually built around her in which she revelled in the role of the prison doctor's wife. However, despite her myriad attempts to firmly wrap this newfound happiness around her finger, she could not push back the uncertainties festering within her like a disease infecting her joy and her life. Her husband was an extremely handsome man, one in a million, a doctor on top of that, and she herself was a dark and disagreeable woman who had only studied till class seven. At thirteen she had been pulled out of the schoolroom and pushed straight up the altar. So when her eldest son had started going to school she had decided she wanted to attend too. Father had taken her to school on his

Hercules cycle too for a while, that is, until Nana had played spoilsport and she had to quit. He had issued a dictum. My mother was a married woman with children to raise and a husband to please; besides, a woman had no use for too much education. Consequently, as my father went ahead in life at lightning speed, my mother remained in the well she had been consigned to. She would dust his fat medical volumes, arrange them in order, and relearn through every moment of it how insignificant she was compared to her brilliant husband. The anxiety that Father was going to leave her one day would not let her be in peace even though she tried her best to mask it with more powder, or put more kohl so her eyes appeared bigger, anything to make her not look hideous.

Paradise, however, had an expiry date; in this instance, one year to be precise. Yanking her out of her blissful pool by the hair and tying it firmly in a knot with the dead weight of reality, Father declared one day that her dream of a separate life, free of the Razia Begums of the world, was over. He had applied for and been granted transfer back to Mymensingh. Sweeping aside the unvoiced dreams of an inconsequential woman like reeds in a dust storm, the entire family packed and moved back to our old life and our old house. Not for free this time though, and neither for a joint kitchen. Father paid Nani cash for two small rooms in the eastern corner of the property for our own place and our own set-up. Nevertheless, despite the fact that no one was ever going to call her husband names again because he lived in his wife's old house, Mother could not feel an iota of happiness. She had returned to an actual prison, the prison in Pabna having been the most free she had ever been in her life. She entered the house and broke down in tears, tears that everyone interpreted as those of joy. Nana only sighed with relief that his daughter was back where she belonged. Runu and Jhunu khalas were both very excited to see me. The fact that I was walking, running, talking was especially amusing to them, as if they had expected me to come back looking, feeling, acting exactly how I had left!

As expected, Father got busy the moment he returned to Mymensingh and it was not possible for him to comprehend the feeling of loneliness that assailed Mother. Neither did he have the time. After he was done teaching at Lytton for the day, he used to sit at a chemist's called Taj Pharmacy in Swadeshi Bazar, in a tiny cabin inside the shop where he would attend to patients till nearly 9 p.m. I still remember the pharmacy clearly, especially the curtain with 'Doctor' written on it that one had to part to get in. At six I had to go to the pharmacy fairly frequently for some time to get injections in the stomach after getting bitten by a mongrel in the neighbourhood. It had not been my fault entirely. The boys of the locality used to pelt the dog with stones whenever they saw him. So one day, having just returned from school and seen the dog in our yard, I too had decided to emulate them. Unfortunately, after doing the deed no sooner had I brushed my hands and turned around to climb the stairs than the dog, a wound-infested mutt with patches of missing fur that had been glaring at me angrily all this while, ran up to me and bit me on the thigh. I was taken to Father's chamber and given three injections on the first day—one in each arm and one beside the belly-button—followed by one injection every day for the next fortnight. Every day after the injection, Father used to take me to Sri Krishna Sweets and feed me rosogollahs. Taking a rickshaw on beautiful breezy afternoons to the chamber to get the injections, swinging my feet off the chairs of the sweet shop as I bit into succulent rosogollahs thereafter, all these attractions were too great for the injections themselves to matter that much. I would sit inside the pharmacy as I waited for him, surrounded by the smell of medicines, as he examined patient after patient and scribbled on prescriptions. It was a different side of Father that I got to see during that time, not the tired, irritated and aloof stranger who used to come back home at night. It used to make me want to love my father. And trust me when I say that it was not an easy task for any of us.

At times Father would emerge from his shell quite suddenly. After we had settled down in our new home with all amenities required to run a house, he asked Mother one day, 'Happy now? No one will call your husband names any more!'

'As if I care! They will still call me names because I'm dark and ugly. An uneducated simpleton,' she replied through a pout, her lips glistening with cheap lipstick, the colourful glass bangles around her wrists chiming in support.

'You're a mother of three. Your responsibility is bringing up the children. Educate them well and it will bring you peace, you'll see. Even if you are dark and ugly and what not, I still married you, didn't I?' he said poking her in the waist a few times. His overtures and words, however, failed to placate her. Her old fear, Razia Begum, had reappeared in her head and she was afraid Father was going to leave her for the other woman. She would stay up waiting for him to come back home no matter how late it got, afraid of even breathing too hard lest it drown the sound of a knock on the gate. One new moon night when he did not return home till very late, she could stand it no longer and walked up to Nani's room to wake her up.

'Ma, he hasn't come back yet. It's almost eleven. Who knows where he is! Or he must be staying the night over at that woman's!

'Stop talking,' snapped back Nani in irritation. 'Go sleep. She's standing here crying! Look after your own interests for once. Think about yourself. How does crying help? Will tears bring him back?'

Mother couldn't help but recall a similar incident many years ago when Nana had brought home a new bride suddenly. He would go off to sleep with his new wife, leaving Nani to cry her eyes out the whole night on the next bed. Mother had asked her back then why she kept crying and Nani had said she was too young to know such things. That once she was older, she would understand how bad men were and how they could never be trusted.

That night Father returned home at about two. When pressed he confessed to have got delayed at a patient's house, a serious case that they had had to rush to the hospital eventually.

The next night Father was late again. Unable to wait any longer Mother woke Chotda up and asked him to accompany her. Holding him by the hand she took the torch and walked out the door, taking the path by the pond to the main road. From there she took a rickshaw to Razia Begum's house. By the time they reached it was midnight. Hearing the knock, a bare-chested and lungi-clad old man who had been sitting on a chair in the veranda enjoying the breeze called out in a shrill voice.

'Who's there so late?'

'Is this the Chakladar house?'

'That would be me. Who are you?' the shrill voice retorted.

Walking up to the porch Mother asked him directly, 'Bhai saab, is my husband here? Dr Rajab Ali?'

In the darkness Mother could make out the bones on the old man's chest shifting. He was blocking the entrance. 'No. he isn't here.'

Pushing the skeletal frame aside Mother barged into the house and walked past the living room into the bedroom beyond. The room was dark but a mosquito net could be seen in the shaft of light filtering in past the window from the lamp-post outside. Pulling the net up she flashed the torchlight inside. Father was sleeping on the bed with Razia Begum, her huge naked breasts unmistakable in the torchlight. Father woke up with a start. Without a word he swiftly put on his clothes and shoes.

'Come,' said Mother.

Walking behind her and Chotda, Father followed them to the rickshaw. Neither spoke the entire way. Throughout the journey Chotda lay in her lap, switching the flashlight on and off again and again.

Back home I had woken up and begun crying for my mother by then. In order to calm me down Dada had had to spare the little finger of his left hand for me to suckle and that had calmed me down. The torch was still switching on and off.

2.

Father was born in a farmer's family in the little-known village of Madarinagar, south of Panchrukhi Bazar under Nandail Police Station. The farmer Janab Ali, my boro dada (grandfather), had some land where he grew rice and a few cows. He used to be a hardworking young man who tilled his field with his own yoke and bullocks. My father had to accompany him to the field to do various chores or run errands, with the understanding that being a farmer's son he was going to follow in his father's footsteps. Till the land, plant seeds, grow paddy, harvest rice. A farmer's son was going to become a farmer. One night, Jafar Ali Sarkar, my great-grandfather, while sitting on the porch puffing on his nightly hookah, revealed he had other plans.

'Let your son go to the pathshala, Janab Ali.'

'Pathshala! And what about all the chores he has at home!' exclaimed the assiduous farmer, swatting mosquitos off his back with his gamcha.

'He will become a learned man if he goes there. People around him will show him respect and try to please him. He can get a job if he's educated. Haven't you seen Khushi's father? He is educated, he has worked in the city and now he has begun buying off all the land in the village.' A teacher at the pathshala of Madarinagar, Jafar Ali Sarkar's voice had softened at the end of the argument.

His eyes trained on the run-down cattle shed, Janab Ali replied, 'I was a sharecropper. We could barely make ends meet. I worked day and night to buy some land of my own. Rajab Ali is learning the ropes. In a few days he will be ready to take up the reins himself. If we worked together, father and son, we will be able to buy more land.'

'Janab Ali, the times are changing. Sashikanta, Rajanikanta, Nirad, Jyotirmoi, they have all gone to Calcutta to study. Educated people are held in high esteem. If your son becomes a learned man people will respect you too. Let him go to the pathshala and he can come back after noon and take the cattle grazing or do his chores. You're not sending him to Calcutta yet!'

Jafar Ali had passed the hookah to his son and was patting the latter lightly on the back. 'Think it over for a couple of days.'

In the moonlit courtyard Rajab Ali had been pouring saline water into the troughs for the cattle and keeping watch over the entire conversation through the corner of his eye, his heart dancing with joy. As soon as he heard his grandfather calling, he appeared, wiping his salt-coated hands on his lungi.

'Do you want to go to the pathshala?'

'Yes!' he nodded vigorously, the gurgling sound of the hookah punctuating the conversation.

Jafar Ali bought his grandson a white shirt, a new dhoti and a copy of Ishwarchandra Vidyasagar's *Barnaparichay*[1] from Panchrukhi Bazar. The day after, post a heavy breakfast of paanta-bhaat and after having milked the cow and leaving her some straw, the young boy took a bath in the pond, put on his new dhoti, picked up some banana leaves and a reed pen, and walked to the pathshala, bare-chested, through the field. There he met the other students and recited tables with them in chorus. At night he would spread a mat and sit and read the *Barnaparichay*, wanting to finish the whole book at one go. He smeared jackfruit leaves with mustard oil, held them over a tiny oil lamp to catch the soot in the oil and then dissolved the oily soot in water to make ink. He would dip his reed pens in the ink and practise his alphabets on banana leaves, excited about the morning after and the pathshala. Time to time his father would snap at him to douse the lamp and not waste oil.

Jafar Ali, whose monthly salary as a teacher was five taka, bought a big bottle of kerosene from Panchrukhi Bazar, telling all and sundry that his grandson was studying in the pathshala and needed the oil for the lamp at night. He was confident the child was going to grow up and become a clerk in a multinational company. Aided and abetted by his own grandfather, my father's education went ahead smoothly and he soon graduated from *Barnaparichay* to slightly more advanced primers with the morals and the life lessons. Jafar Ali would sit in the yard listening to his grandson studying, all the while resolving to send the boy to the local school once he was done with the pathshala. As planned the young Rajab Ali joined Chandipasha School three miles away where he soon surpassed the Kalicharans, Balarams and Nishikantas he had always heard of. Eventually, while handing him his matriculation certificate, his teacher patted him on the back and strongly advised him to never turn his back on education.

Rajab Ali did as his teacher had said. When it seemed like he was not going to be allowed to go to the city for higher studies his headmaster came to his house to talk to Janab Ali, successfully pleading with the latter that his son was going to become an extremely successful man and bring fortune to the family if he was allowed to study further. Rajab Ali arrived in Mymensingh from his remote village with two shirts, a pair of pyjamas, a pair of black rubber shoes and a bottle of mustard oil tied in a bundle. He barely had four paisas on him and his first act on arrival was to look for places where he could stay as a tenant and work in exchange. While his results ensured an easy entry into Lytton Medical School, an acquaintance arranged for a set-up at a pleader's house and just like that Rajab Ali graduated to being medical student living as a working tenant in a friendless, remote, unfamiliar city. One day he ran into Maniruddin Munshi, my nana, at Notun Bazar. Munshi was a benevolent man, the kind that used to feed the fakirs for free regularly. Had his acquaintance made Rajab Ali greedy? As per Mother it definitely had.

'He always wanted money. He came to the city with nothing. It was my father who put him through medical school; a favour he all but forgot. And look how he bothers me now!'

Could it be that my father had realized that pursuing his acquaintance with Maniruddin Munshi would mean he wouldn't have to pay for medical school with the money he got from the village?

'Of course not! Your father didn't get anything from home in the first place. Rather, he used to send money back home to his family. Not that he had too many expenses. He was a scholarship student and had no addictions to speak of.'

That meant all his expenses were met by his stipend and he lived and worked at the pleader's house! So he never had to borrow money from anyone!

'And what about his other expenses? So many times, my father fed him. Father had bought a barbershop and the entire proceeds from it would go to your father. After we got married Father took him to Dhaka to get him a suit and he would frequently give your father pocket money for food, etc. The stipend used to go to his family in the village. Even all his books were bought by my father. Your father used to touch your grandfather's feet twice a day to seek blessings and even asked permission to call him father since his own family lived far away from him.'

Maniruddin Munshi was not averse to the idea of Rajab Ali calling him father. Ali got invited to Munshi's house for rice and fish and the latter would even slip him some money at some point to spend on whatever he liked. As the relationship grew deeper Rajab Ali became a frequent visitor

in Munshi's household. In the evening, when Munshi's
daughter Begum Edul Wara used to study with her private
tutor, young Ali would stand by the window and watch her.
The tutor too would put paper on the chimney of the lamp
so that the young man could stand in the darkness of the
window and stare at the light glazing the girl's face to his
heart's content. Although, while Ali took advantage of the
situation, Edul Wara herself, deeply invested in her studies,
usually paid scant attention. She liked to read, could do it
very well and practised her lessons in large round handwriting
in her exercise book. It was Rajab Ali who made the first
overtures about his interest in marrying the wraith-like girl,
directly to her father. Maniruddin Munshi was glad that
his prospective son-in-law was a handsome, courteous and
soon-to-be doctor; he readily agreed to the match. One day
soon Edul Wara was dressed in red silk, neighbours were
fed pulao and meat curry to their heart's content and a stub-
nosed dark girl was wed to a sharp-nosed, fair boy.

After the wedding Rajab Ali wrapped up his accounts
at the pleader's and shifted to the single-room shed in the
Munshi household, the one where I was born. The room
they moved to was where Munshi's own working tenants
used to live—they used to teach his daughter but since that
chapter got over after her marriage—they too were shown
the door. For Rajab Ali it was a definite upgrade, not least
because of the differences in the food situations of the two
households. At the pleader's he used to teach the man's son
and get food and boarding in exchange; it was functional
but hardly satisfactory. At the Munshi household, since
he was the new son-in-law, his mother-in-law would cook
delicacies especially for him and fan him as he ate. Given
the amount of pampering he got from his new family, it did

not matter all that much to him how his wife was. All Rajab Ali had been looking for was relatives in the new city, a family to take care of his physical as well as emotional needs. That tiny shed was where my older brothers were born too, whose arrival Nana celebrated by singing an azan of 'Allah hu Akbar' standing at the door of the house, loud enough for the entire locality to hear. No azan was sung when I was born; women's birth didn't require joyous announcement. Seven days after my birth a grand *haittara* was held, a birth ceremony where Mother finally abandoned the shelter of the nursery, everything was cleaned and sterilized and she could finally rejoin the outside world. My older brothers did up the house with candles while many of Father's friends came with gifts for me and partook of Ayna Bawarchi's sumptuous food.

The *aqiqah* followed soon after haittara. For both my brothers a cow had been sacrificed; since I was a girl it had to be a sheep. The ritual involved the sacrifice of a sheep if a girl was born and a cow if it was a boy. If it wasn't possible to sacrifice a cow, then two sheep were sacrificed. Before the ceremony a meeting was called in the house to decide my name and people came up with their suggestions. Boromama, Usha; Runu khala, Sova; Jhunu khala, Papri, etc. While this was happening, Dada had been standing by the door fiddling with his toe. He had not liked any of the names and the others had failed to notice that he was getting annoyed. Of course, one couldn't exactly blame them for not noticing! The duty of thinking of a name rested on the adults and none had considered that he wanted a say in the matter. Dada had been seething and munching on a bag of peanuts. Finally, unable to bear it any longer, he opened his beak wide like a stork and let loose, words and peanut bits shooting out of his mouth with equal force. With the already existing soundscape in the house of barking dogs, mewing cats, cawing crows, crying children, screaming family members and boys yelling in the field outside, it was not easy getting oneself heard, especially if said voice was coming out of a mouth stuffed with nuts. Eventually it was Runu khala who managed to notice the distinctive sounds of outrage coming from the direction of the door. Grabbing him by the arm she pulled him from the threshold and dragged him to the wooden pillar at the centre, all eyes and ears suddenly on him.

'What is it? Who hit you?' began Runu khala, holding up his chin.

Wiping the tears off his cheeks with his palm Dada stopped sobbing. 'My sister's name has to be Nasrin.'

For a moment there was tense silence. Then, just as abruptly, everyone burst out laughing as if at the circus.

Pulling him further within their circle, my uncles and aunts let loose a volley of questions.

'Why Nasrin? Where did you hear that name? Did someone tell you to say that?'

Along with the litany of questions another packet of nuts too was passed to him. Picking one out from the packet and biting into it, Dada revealed the real reason behind his inspired choice. 'There's a very pretty girl in my school. Her name is Nasrin.'

The circle wanted to submit to another laughing fit but they also wanted more information. The latter impulse won when Hasem mama casually asked, 'Where does this Nasrin stay?'

Even before Dada could answer, Boromama stepped in. 'No, this Nasrin and all will not work. It has to be Usha.'

Flinging aside the packet of nuts, Dada ran out of the room. He went straight to his room, packed some clothes in a bundle and called out to Mother, telling her he was leaving.

'Wait! Where are you going?'

'Wherever I feel like!'

Dada did run away from home that day. Assuming he would be back before he could even reach past the pond, my uncles and aunts did not go out to look for him immediately. Once it was past evening and there was still no sign of him, and Mother had begun to have a nervous breakdown, Boromama and Hasem mama had to go out to find him, with Nana joining them once the news reached him. It was around ten that Hasem mama found Dada in the jungles of Hajibari and brought him back home. Through her howls, as she hugged him tight, Mother promised Dada that he could choose any name he pleased for me. Since his son wanted it, Father declared the next morning that my name was going to be Nasrin. My uncles and aunts were not impressed; they could not understand how a princess could have such a provincial name. When Dada returned from school, he couldn't help gloat, sucking on his thumb and staring them down.

Jhunu khala was plucking mangoes with a hook from the tree on the south side of the well. 'Oi, shit cart, what'll be your sister's full name?' 'Nasrin Jahan Taslima,' Dada's face split into a beatific smile and he slipped the thumb out of his mouth. Jhulu khala broke into a peel of laughter. Runu khala, who had been slicing mangoes sitting on the porch to make into a mash later, chimed in. 'This Nasrin girl in your school, do you fancy her?' 'Yes!' His teeth had parted in glee. 'Do you want to marry her?' Dada put the thumb back inside his mouth again with a shy smile and tilted his head to the right, the laces of his half-pant swinging past his knee. Throwing the hook aside Jhunu khala tapped him on the head and teased, 'That girl won't marry you! You used to shit your pants in school, and your beautiful Nasrin must have already found out.' Dada ran into the house to Mother, his eyes brimming with tears of heartbreak. She put her hand on his head and cooed.

'Why are you crying, love?'

'Jhunu khala is calling me a shit cart.'

'Don't make the poor thing cry. He has had the shits since birth. So many medicines we have fed him but nothing works. It's been years he's not taken a stiff shit.' Mother had to come out into the courtyard and mock-scold Jhulu khala.

However, after all the drama over my name, the aqiqah was postponed. The harvest of rice hadn't been that great in Madarinagar that season and Father was feeling quite low. A few months later when the new rice turned out good and the talk turned to the aqiqah again, Father got transferred to Pabna. Father was sad again and the ritual was delayed yet again. By the time we returned from Pabna and a date was finally chosen for my aqiqah, two years had passed by. On the day of the ceremony, my aunts covered the floor with pristine white alpona and hung colourful paper chains from the pillars, as people streamed in for the feast laden with gifts: gold chains, rings, brass pitchers, primers, clothes and shoes, copies of the Quran, plates and bowls, suitcases and suchlike. Ayna Bawarchi dug holes in the fields to make giant clay ovens on which he cooked massive containers full of pulao and meat, the aroma wafting throughout the house and making the air heady. Nana brought in pitchers of mishti doi (sweet yogurt). Dada was the busiest on the day of my aqiqah. He got dressed in nice clean clothes and new shoes, his hair nicely parted and brushed, and went strolling casually through the mingling guests. Whenever he managed to catch someone's attention, he would smile indulgently and reveal to them his secret, that he had chosen my name over the myriad other suggestions that others in the house had made, all of which he had rejected.

Mother packed away four small suitcases I had received as gifts above the cupboard. The brass pitcher was transferred to the kitchen while the clothes, shoes, plates and bowls, and the copies of Quran, went to the cupboard. The gold was put inside the drawers and locked; the key usually remained tied at the end of the drape of my mother's saree. The only thing I was left with was the book, the primer *Sabuj Sathi* (Young Companion). Back then everyone in the house used to be my teacher. If they were to catch me poring over the book, they would not let me go without making me recite my alphabets. Whatever they asked me I had to say. Before I could learn writing all the alphabets properly on a slate, I was taught to pronounce words, just like a cuckoo kept in a cage can be taught to say new words. Long before my Sharaf mama and Felu mama picked up their first books, I had finished my primer.

A few days after my aqiqah, entirely out of the blue and without consulting a single soul, Nana sold the house to a man called Basiruddin. When Basiruddin turned up to take possession of his new property it seemed the sky had fallen on Nani's head. An odd enough expression, isn't it, especially for a child? I had looked up that day to check if the sky had indeed fallen; what would have happened to Nani if it had? Regardless, we never found out what Nana did with the money from the sale. Nani sat Basiruddin down on the nice chair, served him tea and snacks and tried reasoning with him.

'Bhaijaan, one person's crazy whim, how can an entire family be made to suffer for it? I have so many children; I'll have to live on the streets with them. I will pay you back your money. You sell this house to me and I will pay the money back to you in instalments.'

'No instalments,' Basiruddin coughed. 'Since you're asking like that, fine, I'll sell the house to you. But no instalments. You have to pay up all at once.'

'Where do I get so much money all at once? I am a helpless woman, try and understand my predicament. Give me a few days,' Nani implored from behind the curtain.

Sipping on his tea Basiruddin shook his head. 'No, no! How can I do that? I can't make time. Allah sends each of us with a fixed amount of time to spend. If you can pay me by tomorrow or the day after, I can sell you the house. Or else you will have to excuse me.'

Having finished his tea Basiruddin took a paan from the plate Nani had sent out with Sharaf mama, picked up a pinch of extra lime with it and, staring at the hens and ducks in the yard, said, 'So I'll see you tomorrow?'

Nani emerged from behind the curtain after he left. A thorough search of the house ensued and after she had broken the bamboo piggy-bank too it was revealed they had just about five hundred taka. She put on her burqa and went to her neighbours—Sulekha's mother, Manu's mother, Sahabuddin—and then finally ended up at our door that night. Father had just returned from the chamber.

'Have you heard? What can I do?' Nani made no effort to suppress the anxiety in her voice.

Father had heard the news; my mother had made sure of that as soon as he had returned. She had told him how Nana had sold the house, how Basiruddin wanted the entire money at once and only then was he going to sell the house back to Nani. Nevertheless, Father pretended as if he knew nothing and asked, 'What is it? What's happened?'

They were seated on two corners of the bed. Nani replied, 'He's sold the house.' Beginning to swing his bare feet sticking out from under the lungi, Father continued his charade.

'Which house? Whose house?'

'What do you mean which house? This house!' Nani sounded annoyed.

'Why? Why would he sell the house?'

'How do I know why? As if he's told me anything! He's crazy, that man. Not an iota of sense in him! Who knows what he's done with the money!'

Father remained silent, his feet still swinging.

'I offered to buy the house from Basiruddin . . .'

'Who's that?' he interrupted.

'The man he's sold the house to!'

'Where does this Basiruddin live,' he asked, scratching his swinging knee.

'Near Notun Bazar, I think,' she replied, taking out a paan from her handkerchief and popping it into her mouth.

'What does he do?'

'I don't know. He came home and asked for money. I offered to pay in instalments, begged him to sell me the house,' Nani confessed hesitantly.

'That's good! Pay in instalments.' Father did not appear too perturbed.

'But he doesn't want to listen. He's asking for the entire money together,' she bit out, the anxiety back in her voice again.

'Then pay it in one go!' he smiled sweetly.

'Does money grow on trees? Where will I get six thousand taka now?'

She was looking at Father helplessly as she finished. He stopped swinging his leg and called out to Mother. 'Edul, get some tea for amma. Amma, have some tea before you go.' Seeing Nani shake her head in refusal he continued. 'Then what will you have? Have something at least!'

'No, I don't want anything.' Nani was annoyed again.

'Edul, get biscuits or some munchies at least.'

'No, no, don't,' Nani turned to Mother and raised her hand in refusal.

Father and Nani remained seated on two corners of the bed, my mother on the other bed with me. Not a soul spoke. Finally, Nani said in a broken voice, 'Can you lend me at least five thousand? Where will I go with the children if I lose the house?' But Father remained steadfastly quiet; Nani continued, her anguish mounting. 'In some way or the other I will return the money to you in portions every month.'

Father's silence was too much for my mother to bear as well. 'My father's done so much for this family too. And during such a time of crisis there's no one to stand beside my mother! When you went away to Rajsahi for studies, there was not a drop of milk to feed the kids on so many days. Father used to get giant tins of milk. Much of my life after getting married was spent at my parents' house.'

Wiping her glasses with the drape of her saree Nani tried again to get a response out of my father. 'Say something at least! Basiruddin will be back again tomorrow.'

Father did not say anything to anyone that night. When Nani finally gave up, sighed and got up to leave, he only rubbed his neck with his hands a couple of times and said he was going to talk to her the next night. He did lend her the money though and Nani too repaid the loan in three years as she had promised. When Nana heard about it, his sole reaction was to laugh and admit that he had never had doubts about his wife Khairunnisa, my Nani, being able to move mountains if she tried.

My nana was a careless but fun-loving man. He loved to eat and feed others and that was what made him the happiest, although if my Nani had not taken up the reins of the family who knows what would have happened to him too. Originally from Bikrampur and always a vagrant at heart, Nana had broken into his father's safe when he was thirteen years old and run away from home with a lot of money. By the time he had finally reached Mymensingh after travelling from one city to the next he was already broke. He used to sleep and eat in the mosques and catch hold of fakirs and madmen on the road and regale them with tales of Arabia. The devotees visiting the mosque would throw coins at him at times and he would pick them up and feel as if he was nothing less than Emperor Babar. He used to catch hold of beggars on the road and inquire where they were from and if they had eaten anything. Beggars are never not hungry and he used to listen to their tales and be overcome with grief. With tears streaming down his cheeks he would turn his pockets out and give them whatever he had to buy food with.

The new imam of the Chan Tara Masjid near Zilla School crossing did not fail to notice the large number of beggars who my nana would bring along for the jumu'ah prayers. One day he called the young man.

'Miyan, what's your name?'

'Maniruddin,' replied Nana with a smile.

'Where are you from?'

'Nowhere.'

'What's your father's name?'

'I don't remember.'

'Where do you live?'

'There is no dearth of places in this huge world.'

'Are you educated?'

The question was greeted with a wide smile and little else.

There was something in the vagrant that made the imam want to domesticate him. The man had a twelve-year-old daughter at home, of perfect marriageable age. That day onwards the imam began to stay on guard hoping to catch hold of young Maniruddin at an opportune moment. One winter night, noticing the young man curled up without a blanket on the cold floor inside the mosque, the imam called him.

'Maniruddin, come home with me. There's a bed, there are pillows and you will be able to sleep better.' Seeing no response forthcoming from the young man the imam pressed further. 'There's warm rice too, with some meat stew.' That caught the vagabond's attention and he got up and stretched. 'How far is your house from here, imam saheb?'

That night the imam took young Maniruddin home, fed him warm stew and rice and put him to sleep under a warm blanket in the outer quarters of the house. Maniruddin slept till noon the next day. He had not been spoilt in such a way for many years, having left home early to escape his stepmother's abuse. He could faintly remember his own mother who used to feed him milk and rice and put him to sleep. He got up, stretched and went out to the courtyard where the imam was washing his feet in the water kept in a pitcher. The action reminded him of his father who used to tilt the pitcher similarly to wash his feet. Maniruddin took the pitcher from the imam's hand and began to pour water on the old man's feet as if he was washing the feet of his father who he had not seen in years. Suddenly he burst into tears.

'What is it? Why are you crying Maniruddin?'

Instead of answering the young man covered his face with his hands and walked out of the house. He wasn't back until about a month later when he suddenly turned up one day with a ton of sweets. Smiling he spoke to the old man, 'Imam saheb, these are wonderful sweets, please have some. Warm rosogollahs from Calcutta.' Everyone in the house shared the sweets and once the imam was finally alone with the young man in his living room, he asked the boy to marry his daughter Khairunnisa.

'Marry!' Maniruddin could barely hide his shock. 'Where will I put up my wife? At the mosque?'

'Don't worry about at all. I have a lot of land, I will figure something out,' the imam had assured him.

Maniruddin had been in a good mood that day and he did not take long to give his consent to the union. Without further delay a qazi was called to read them their vows, rice and meat was cooked for an impromptu feast, and before the night had deepened, the two were husband and wife. Khairunnisa did not get to know what he looked like or what kind of a person he was. She was educated, could recite the scriptures well and yet she was married off to an unlettered man, even before she had managed to digest the rosogollahs he had got for them. She could have done better, obviously, but the imam was convinced that even if Maniruddin had nothing else to offer, he still had a huge heart. His experience throughout life had taught the old man that it was this last bit which was the most important.

The imam had a son too, but mostly in name. The boy was addicted to jungles and travelled across the jungles of India as a hunter, usually returning home once a year for barely a month or two. His health having taken a turn for the worse and having lost all confidence on his own son, the imam made Maniruddin responsible for all his property and declared that his young son-in-law was also his son. While this first bit was easy, changing someone's nature was a task easier said than done. Within a year the new son managed to sell off more than half of the imam's property to help those in need of aid. Of the bit that remained, a part was taken over by the government for a school boarding house to be built on it while Khairunnisa took over the rest, erecting a few tin huts and planting a garden to set down roots so to speak, or more accurately, to hang on to the last bit of whatever she was left with. She was tired of her husband's large heart, especially when the children started arriving every year and the number of hungry mouths baying for food only began to increase. They had a roof over their heads, true, but who was going to provide for so many people?

Maniruddin, busy hopping from one port to another, had barely a care in the world, only returning home when he needed money. He would come and ask for food, call the children to gather around him and eat together, blowing some life into the household by sheer force of will. Khairunnisa usually fed them without a word. Only once did she tell him no, there was no food at home; Mother was three or four at the time. Nana was shocked. 'What did you say? There's no food?' Nani was sitting on a stool beside the cold hearth and nodded. 'No, nothing. No rice or dal. I have been gathering water lilies from the pond for the past few days and boiling them for the children.' Nana was so crestfallen by the news that he went to bed and stayed there for two days. In the meanwhile, Khairunnisa gathered coconuts that had fallen from the tree in the yard and made sweets. She wanted Nana to go and sell those and bring back rations from the market. As directed, Nana picked up the wooden box packed with sweets and went to the government offices. This soon became a routine; every day he would keep some money from the sales aside for himself and hand over the rest to his wife. She put aside whatever she could until one day, when Mother was around five, Nani handed over a bundle of money to her husband, taken out from the bamboo bank she had been saving in, and asked him to start a small hotel selling rice, fish, etc. Yet again, like the ever-obedient boy, Maniruddin listened to his wife and opened a small shop in Notun Bazar, complete with a new set of tables and chairs, as well as a new cook. This was the time of the British and the shop took off almost immediately and began to do very well.

At the time people were terribly angry with the British. Nana, on the contrary, had no complaints against anyone. To him every person in the world seemed to be a good soul, even his stepmother for that matter. Anyone who came to the shop, he would sit and chat with them. Thieves and scoundrels were his friends; cats and dogs gathered in his kitchen whenever hungry, feeding off rubbish and leftovers. Mad beggars, anguished souls, he was immune to no one's sorrow and gave away money from his cashbox to people who asked for help. Everyone was welcome under his roof and weary travellers would come in to rest for a while, often managing to get free stuff like a cold drink or something from him. Everyone knew Maniruddin's was not a business, it was a guesthouse. Khairunnisa used to send Edul Wara to clean the eating house along with one of her sons, Siddique.

While the young girl swept and did up the place the boy would sit with his father gorging on jalebis. Around evening their father would feed them rice and fish and send them back home. Maniruddin was usually late and Khairunnisa would wait up for him, the dim glow of the kerosene lamp by her side. Every night when he came back home late, she would give herself up to his boundless sexual appetite, hoping to tame and domesticate the wild bird with sex, prosperity and progeny. She was a woman and it was not possible for her to take care of the business. So she planted bamboos in her room within which she saved money and, at night, with her hair spread out beside her satisfied husband, she advised him financial caution. Maniruddin did not know how to count money, he managed it by the fistful. So no matter what else was possible for him, becoming careful with finances wasn't one of them.

There was a terrifying famine in the '50s. Numerous people died of hunger and there were many who could be seen going from door to door begging for starch. Maniruddin closed his shop and opened a community kitchen where he began cooking food for the hungry masses. He had money to buy rice for the kitchen but try as he might there was no rice to be found anywhere in the city. In desperation he went to the mosques, praying and in tears, asking Allah for help. The year of the famine was spent like this and it was only after rice and milk was airdropped as part of foreign aid that he could find a measure of relief. Khairunnisa did not let her children feel the famine though. She had hid away some rice in the house and she kept a strict tab on how much she was cooking. Thankfully, her infant had not been weaned yet. If she had not been there the entire family would perhaps have been swept away by the ravages of the famine. She had never managed to tie Maniruddin entirely to the family but had at least succeeded in creating certain lasting ties. So she was always terrified that the bird would fly away one day.

Everyone was so busy with the aqiqah that for a long time no one realized that Nani's mother had quietly breathed her last in the kitchen. After her husband's demise she had moved in with her daughter, preferring Khairunnisa over her hunting-obsessed son. As it is, social rule dictated that a woman had to be under her father's rule as a child, under her husband's as an adult and, finally, under her son in old age. Seeing her lifeless form on the bed, Nana fell to the floor and wept as if he had lost his own mother yet again.

Life has its share of sorrows, it has a lot of want, but it also has its moments of joy. No time lasts for long. The bad ones passed just as the rains washed away months of grime and dirt. One day, amidst a symphony of the rain beating down on the tin roof and leaves falling into the pond, the darkness that had gathered in the house somewhat dissipated. As Jhunu khala stood by the window watching it pour outside, Runu khala began humming a tune. Tutu mama, Sharaf mama and Felu mama were running around the courtyard playing in the rain. Kana mamu, sitting on a low stool leaning against one of the pillars of the roof, stirred himself from his grief, preparing to face the world again after his mother's passing. Looking at the courtyard, he spoke to Runu khala. 'Why just sing? Do a twirl or two!' It was on the tip of Jhunu khala's tongue to point out how futile that would be, since he was blind; but she didn't say anything. Rather, as asked, Runu khala wrapped a pair of *ghungroos* on her feet, tucked the pleat of her saree near her waist and danced, a beautiful dance echoing the beautiful song she had been singing, of a beautiful forest of mahua beside a blue

mountain where someone was playing a plaintive tune on the
flute, a tune so heart-rending that it echoed with the song of
the birds in the forest and made one's eyes well up. As she
danced, Kana mamu began tapping his walking stick on the
ground to keep the beat.

Only Father was not happy. He seemed tired and
annoyed, a man to whom both the drought and the rains
were synonymous. During drought the land went barren and
crops suffered; during the rains the fields got flooded and
crops suffered. He made arrangements to send his entire
salary to his father back in Madarinagar with a letter asking
my other grandfather to buy the patch of land south of
their house from the present owners as soon as possible and
promising to send more money the following month. My
father used to earn a lot back then, as an LMF doctor who
had graduated to an MBBS. He had sort of risen through
the ranks, made evident by the shiny rubber stamp he had
got made with his name and designation: Dr M. Rajab Ali,
MBBS. He lent Nani five thousand taka to buy the house
back from Basiruddin and then took five rooms on rent
from her, including the central courtyard—a living room, a
bedroom, a kitchen, a bathroom and a spare room—concrete
floors, tin and slate roofs and brick walls. A few of the new
rooms were entirely of tin too; the two previous rooms we
already had were repurposed as separate singles for my two
older brothers.

For my father, dancing, music, having fun, all of it was
a waste of time. Seeing me dancing in the rain he forced me
inside by the throat, I was unable to utter even a single protest
out of abject fear. I could ask Mother to tell me fairy tales;
with my father I had to swallow it as soon as the thought
occurred before they could slip past my lips by mistake. I was

so afraid of him that I could barely look him in the eye, the
chasm between us unfathomable and ever-widening.

I have always been told it was not always like this between
us. Before he moved to Rajsahi for his studies, apparently, we
used to be quite close. This was right after we returned from
the prison in Pabna. As soon as he returned home, I used
to jump on to his lap and make a fuss about taking me on
a stroll by the river. Father would always defer it with some
excuse or the other and Mother used to pinch my cheeks and
tell me kids were not supposed to go by the river lest they got
taken away by someone.

'No, no kidnappers will come get me. I'm a girl,'[2] I would
insist, burrowing deeper into my father's lap while he laughed
out loud in response.

'There's Foting Ting by the river! Three people, joined
together but with no heads and with mouths on their feet!' I
tried scaring him one day with a story I had just heard. Instead
of delving deeper into it, he kissed me on my forehead and
cheeks and asked, 'Tell me love, who are you to me?'

'I'm your Ma!'[3]

Father had taught me this and my response drew another
kiss on the cheek while he proceeded to tuck my errant hair
behind my ears. Back then I knew nothing other than my
father; he had wanted a daughter after two sons and I was
my father's little girl through and through. And yet, in just
two years, all of that changed once he was back from Rajsahi
after completing his MBBS. I could not recognize him as
my father at first; he appeared so unknown and peculiar. He
beckoned me to climb on to his lap like old times but I turned
tail and ran, refusing to call him or address him in any way
whatsoever. Nani, Runu khala, Jhunu khala, Hasem mama,
Sharaf mama, Felu mama, even my drifter Nana, I thought

of each and every one of them as family except him. As if it would have been best had he not returned from Rajsahi and left the three of us, my mother, my brothers and I, alone. As if a sudden cataclysm had thrown our peaceful lives into disarray, as if a vicious Foting Ting had come and laid our playhouse to waste.

The distance that suddenly cropped up between my father and I never quite went away. He would call me by the old affectionate 'Ma' but I would freeze in my tracks and not respond. Even when he embraced me, the invisible barrier between us held fast.

Growing Up

I was born on a sacred day, 12 Rabiul Awwal, at dawn on a Monday. Such a girl was meant to start chanting the name of Allah from the very moment she saw the light of day, because that is what blessed children were meant to do. Fajli khala had apparently said my face resembled a rare gem, so holy was my occasion of birth.

In time, however, burnt and tanned by the sun, the gem lost its sheen considerably. All it took was running after my uncles, especially in the evenings when we would play cops and thieves around the trees in the courtyard. Whoever the 'thief' managed to tag automatically became the next thief and on and on it went. My uncles, none of them much older, were still older than me. Ergo, they could run fast, leaving me to be the unfortunate thief in the melee most of the time. No matter how fast I ran, they always managed to outrun me. It was the same when we played *danguti*; I would throw the short stick and one of my mamas would hit it straight past the field. I wanted to be the one doing that, hammering the short stick with the longer baton, and even though that did happen from time to time, I would hardly get a chance at it before someone or the other was there taking it away from me. Whenever we played with marbles, I ended up losing all of mine to my mamas. Sharaf mama had a large glass jar full of his and he would turn it over on the bed, often, to take stock of his spoils. I would sit not too far away, staring in wonder, because that was all I was allowed to do: stare and not touch. I did it once and got soundly whacked by him. In fact, I lost everything to them when we played, even the cigarette packets we'd gather—Baga, Caesar, Bristol, Capstan—to use as bets. We would mark a circle in the yard and then stand within it to throw targets; we called them 'chyara'. Then you had to grab as many cigarette packets as you could and hide them under your thighs, with the challenge being anyone who managed to land a target anywhere four fingers away from yours got everything you had. Suffice to say I rarely got to keep anything.

Despite my beautiful gem-like precious face losing much of its lustre under the combined assault of cops, thieves, danguti, jars full of marbles and abandoned cigarette packets, not to forget the sun under which all this happened, it nevertheless failed to move Fajli khala from her belief that I was going to grow up and follow the path of Allah. Her convictions strengthened after I returned from a visit to Nandibari. Runu khala's friend Sharmila lived in Nandibari; one had to take a left turn on the way to the jungles of Hajibari. I had accompanied Runu khala when she had gone visiting her friend. Sharmila lived in a dilapidated old house, its plaster missing in many places giving it the appearance of these fabled houses where one could turn a corner and come across hidden treasure being guarded by snakes. It appeared almost haunted, as if you could expect to see a beautiful spectral girl in the middle of the night dancing in the shadows on the roof, disappearing as soon as one approached her with a light. The building itself had almost been overtaken by trees and foliage, while it was a surrounded by a grove of litchi trees. The trees with their fat, red low-hanging fruits were well-known in the area for the quality of their litchis, but I could not dare touch any for fear of snakes lurking somewhere. Not too far from the main stairs there was an odd pond, its bottom clearly discernible, the water clear as glass. Even when I didn't want to smile, the rippling water made it seem I was. In the fading light of the kerosene lamp Sharmila had served us sweets which I refused no matter how much they tried to make me change my mind. I was much too petrified by the idea of snakes, djinns and ghostly girls to put even a tiny morsel into my mouth.

Sharmila was a stunningly beautiful girl; she almost appeared like an apparition that could be dancing on their roof in the middle of the night, like a lost twin or a pale memory of another lifetime. A wave of thick black hair snaked past her waist and fell almost to her knees. When she was alone at home, lounging on the cane seat in a white saree with her hair untied and blowing in the evening breeze, I could spy a sense of desolation in her dark eyes in the dim glow of the evening light. When she spoke, it was as if a flock of pretty white birds had flown in with the words.

'Such a sweet girl! What's your name?' There were tinkling bells in her words, at least I could hear them.

'She's Shobha,' replied Runu khala.

'Have some sweets, Shobha,' Sharmila was smiling at me.

I wanted to say that was not my name but I couldn't do it. 'Shobha' was better than my actual name but it still wasn't mine. When someone called me Shobha it made me uncomfortable; whenever I had to answer to it, I felt like a liar, as if I had stolen someone else's name and taken it for my own. In her white saree with her long hair kept untied, Sharmila did not seem like Sharmila to me. She seemed someone else, her own dead twin or perhaps a memory from a past life. When she spoke, it was like a tiny bird flapping its wings or the tinkling of bells. The room we were seated in smelt of bel, or something sweet like that since there were no flowers in the room and nor were there any bel trees in the garden. Who knew where the smell was coming from! Was it from her? Who knew, could be. I grabbed Runu khala's hand and whispered.

'Let's go home.'

Barely had the words escaped my house when abruptly the kerosene lamp went out, plunging the room into darkness. There seemed to be a glow coming off Sharmila that formed a potent brew with the smell of bel in the air. 'The moon's going to be out soon. It'll be beautiful. We will sit in the moonlight and sing *"Aaj Jyotsna Ratey"*.[1] Won't you join us?' Sharmila broke into a peel of laughter as she finished, her words were directed at me. I edged ever so closer to Runu khala and could only croak my earlier request yet again. 'Runu khala, let's go home.'

While returning home I realized the moon had been just above Sharmila's house that evening. It followed us home and when I said that to Runu khala she didn't seem the least bit surprised. Once we were home, I repeated my observation to Mother and she didn't seem astounded either. Instead she asked what we had eaten while we were at Sharmila's. 'She ate nothing! Because it's a Hindu household obviously.' Runu khala seemed to swell with pride as she revealed to Mother that I had chosen to not eat anything because it had been a Hindu house. I never used to let Mother put kumkum marks on my forehead, would always turn my face away whenever she tried. She was convinced that this was due to my auspicious date of birth. Not even two days had passed after our visit to Sharmila's house that she broached the topic to Fajli khala. 'You know, it's because she was born on such an auspicious day that she doesn't eat anything in Hindu households, or lets me put marks on her forehead.'

Fajli khala would often cross the jungles of Hajibari to come over to Nani's house. As soon as she would arrive, she would take off her burqa and come out to the courtyard, making her way to the kitchen to inspect what was being cooked. Whatever it was, *ilish* or *chitol*, she would promptly scrunch up her nose in distaste, as if the smell was too offensive or the thing itself was too distasteful. When we sat down to lunch—and Nani used to give her the best pieces of fish, rice from the middle of the handi where it was just the right consistency, perfectly shaped eggplant pakodas with fried onions sprinkled on top—even then her nose remained curled. As if she was missing the exquisite food at her husband's house and was only having lunch with us just to be polite, because she had landed up and it was already lunchtime. Occasionally she would speak too.

'Who cooked the greens? So sandy!'

'Did someone forget to put some garam masala in the meat?'

'There wasn't enough oil when this fish was fried.'

Fajli khala had just stretched out on the bed after lunch. She was chewing paan and Mother was telling her about the piety she suspected I had in me. That day too she had had a complaint about there not being enough garlic in the pigeon curry. Nani had picked up a few cloves of raw garlic and put them on her plate asking her to check again. Unable to counter that move khala had grumbled about the raw garlic and then swiftly changed the topic to how it was enough that the meat was cooked through and edible, how Allah did not like lavishness in food and wished for his believers to make do with as much as is necessary and no more, and how the Prophet too used to be a light eater. Fajli khala was extremely fair and with a few stray locks adorning her forehead she used to look like the goddess Durga. Chewing on her paan some more she made a stunning revelation to the others who were also resting there.

'I knew it, that this girl was going to be pious. See how she did not touch any food at the Hindu house. She doesn't even like marks on her forehead like the Hindus put. No one's taught her these things, so how did she know? It's Allah who is teaching her these things. When she was a child she used to smile in her sleep. She must have been playing with the angels! You are indeed lucky.' This last bit was directed at my mother.

No matter who said what, Mother could not believe she was lucky. She had always wanted to study, used to be a very good student too, but she had not been allowed to continue. She used to go to school in a burqa because Nana wanted her to, despite the other girls laughing at her. Then she got married and had to quit, much to the chagrin of her teachers who had been convinced she had a bright future. Even after her marriage she had wanted to continue. The first time she had tried was of course when Dada started going to school, which Nana had put a stop to. Later when Father moved to Rajsahi for his higher studies, she got admitted to school again without telling anyone at home. While Dada was in class seven of Zilla School, Mother was in the same class in Mahakali School. The teachers knew that she was married, that she had children, and they had kept the news secret so that she would not be uncomfortable attending class with the younger girls. In the first trimonthly test she had the best results. But in the end, all of it had been in vain. When her secret was finally revealed to the family, Nana had firmly reminded her once again that women did not need to be too educated. Her primary responsibility was staying at home and taking care of the children. Unlike the previous time, Father too had written from Rajsahi, telling her almost the same thing. Invisible shackles were placed on my mother's feet and her dreams were wrecked yet again. Try as she might, she could not consider herself lucky.

Had she been lucky, would Nana have had to slip into her room in the dead of one night, away from all prying eyes, to hand her a can of fairness cream wrapped in paper? Would he have had to tell her to hide the thing from everyone and diligently rub it on her face at night? He had given the can to her so she would not appear unattractive to Father, so he would not abandon his wife and children again. Mother used to rub the fairness cream on her face every night but her skin remained as dark as ever. Her eyes sank into their hollows, bags formed beneath them and the nose remained the same stub it always was. She would reassure herself that even though she wasn't pretty at least she was talented; she could sew, she could cook. But was she really talented? She could never shake off the feeling that there were women who could do these same things better than her. So she turned to other reassurances, that at least she was an entire human being without disabilities, physical or otherwise. Soheli's mother, for instance, had one daughter who was completely insane who had been married off to a guy under false pretences. In her mind at least she was superior to a mad woman!

Even though she wasn't mad, madness often struck my mother. Once, while Father was working in Rajsahi—the first time he had moved there, before I was born—she left the children with Nani and set off all by herself to go see him. She was afraid he didn't love her any more, a feeling that had intensified after Nana had brought her the fairness cream. As a child when Nana bought red frocks for her, and the blue ones only for Fajli khala, she used to cry. Later, when Father used to take her to buy sarees and tell the salesperson to show sarees best suited for dark people, she used to be too terrified to cry. Mother never managed to get rid of this fear and on her way to Rajsahi this fear made a sudden comeback. She had never left Mymensingh on her own but she quashed down the fear bubbling inside her and told herself that she was not doing anything wrong. She was going to see her husband, the father of her two sons, and not any other man. This was the man whom she had lawfully wedded and she had every right to want to see him. Although Father had not asked her to visit, she felt a deep longing to see him. On his last visit, he had left a large drum of rice and enough money with her to run the house but she could barely concentrate on anything. Rations weren't everything! A wraith-like, silly, dark girl had feelings too, feelings which would not let her be, and it wasn't possible to explain this to anyone.

Father had a transferrable job and he used to travel all over the country. Ever since his transfer to Rajsahi he too had been trying to move back to Mymensingh but his superiors did not care. One fine day he was shocked to discover his wife standing at the door, a garish shade of red on her lips and her face chalk-white with powder. She was carrying a leather suitcase with her, packed with colourful sarees, the face cream Nana had brought for her and a can of Tibetan face powder. For my father it was as if he had just sighted a ghost.

'Why are you here? How did you come? Who's come with you?'

'I've come alone,' Mother replied with a dry smile.

'Alone? So far? How is that possible? How are the children?' Father inquired in one breath.

'They are well. How are you? You don't write at all. Have you forgotten me?' her voice choked on the last question, tears threatening to spill over.

'Have you gone crazy!' Father asked, pacing to and fro in agitation and then walking to the old iron chair of the doctor's quarter to sit down. 'You left infants in someone else's care?'

'They won't have any trouble. There are people to watch over them.' She began walking towards him tentatively as she replied.

'Do you still have the money I gave you before I left?' Father asked finally.

'No, it's over. Bajaan or Miyanbhai[2] have been buying their milk.' She put her hand on the arm of the chair, close enough for him smell the sweet fragrance coming off her.

'You should have sent me word! I would have gone home with some money! Go back to Mymensingh tomorrow at the earliest with some money,' Father said, getting up all of a sudden and plunging his hands into the pockets of his pants.

'Who cooks for you? What do you eat? You've lost so much weight!' She placed a hand softly on his back, her hands smelling as sweet. Father remained quiet, brows pursed, tired and annoyed.

When Father moved to Rajsahi the second time to do his condensed MBBS course he told her explicitly to not leave the kids behind and go looking for him again. Ignoring her pleading tears, he firmly told her that he was leaving behind enough money and would come back in four to six months with more. The few letters he wrote during this time usually went thus.

> How are Noman, Kamal and Nasrin? If you've run out of rice ask your father to go and get some more from the mill in Notun Bazar. Make sure to get the groceries from Manumiyan. Keep an eye on how Noman and Kamal are doing. Tell them to concentrate on their studies. Will send you the sum you owe Sulekha's mother next month. Don't waste money, don't buy unnecessary things. Be safe.

> *Rajab Ali*

My mother's letters were altogether different. She was from the city, had seen a few Dilip Kumar–Madhubala movies with her husband after getting married and she wrote back in large bold letters:

> Beloved, how are you? When will you come back? I can't live without you any more. I feel like a bird that has been shot down from the sky. Take me there with you, we will live together happily with our children and be a family again. You will become a big doctor in Rajsahi. I keep telling people that and my chest swells with pride whenever I do. I know I'm not good enough for you, I am not smart enough or educated enough. No matter what I don't have, I still have you. You are my happiness, my peace of mind and there's nothing more I want of this world.

Father's replies hardly ever went off course either.

> Don't spend more than 2 to 2.5 taka on daily essentials. If
> you run out of money get stuff from Manumiyan's shop
> on credit. Take care of the children. Whatever you spend,
> maintain a ledger.

Mother didn't maintain a ledger; she didn't want to. She would keep money tied in her pallu and whenever her children wanted to eat something, munchies or ice cream, she would untie the knot and take it out. In the mornings she usually sent Dada to the shop to get piping hot dal–puri for breakfast. When she ran out of groceries, Nani was the one she turned to. If it so happened that the lamp needed a wick or oil, she would borrow some from Sulekha's mother for the night. This one time, Chotda left with money to buy groceries and never came back, which meant no food. When Sharaf mama found him later sitting by the road, we discovered that he had lost the money. He had thought the money in his pocket to be useless scraps of paper and thrown them away.

I have previously mentioned how, when Father returned from Rajsahi after finishing his degree two years later, his relationship with his family could never go back to the way it used to be. I rarely ever went near my father and with my mother too his relationship sort of mutated into one of groceries and essentials. Mother gradually stopped rubbing snow and powder on her face and her interactions with him transformed into her extending lists towards him, of things required at home or in the kitchen; Father would simply glance at the list and head out shopping. Mother cooked for him and fed him lunch and at night she usually kept his dinner aside for him to come back and have. He came back, freshened up at the well, ate his dinner and went off to sleep. He was tired and exasperated all the time. Not only did he have a family of his own to feed, he could also not forget he was a farmer's son from Madarinagar. After his grandfather Jafar Ali Sarkar had passed away, no one had shown much interest in getting his younger brothers Riyazuddin and Iman Ali educated. My grandfather had promptly got them involved in farming. Father wished to at least have his two remaining brothers, Amanudaulah and Motin, move to the city and get a proper education. He wanted to do for them what Jafar Ali had done for him. He had many dreams involving Madarinagar too, at least Riyazuddin and Iman Ali visited their city-dwelling brother often enough for him harbour such dreams.

'We should buy the land north of the pond, bhai saab.'

'Khushi's father is selling their land. If we don't make a move, Jamir Munshi surely will.'

'Father was saying we should buy two more pairs of bullocks for the field.'

Whenever they told him such things, Father would find himself transported back to the lands he used to roam when out grazing the cows and he could feel himself running across the same green fields again. So he usually bid his brothers farewell with a thick wad of money with which to buy all the things they had made him dream about.

His generosity did not escape Mother's eye. Once, just after he had given some money to Riyazuddin to buy land, she handed him a list of some things she required:

1. Two sarees for use at home
2. One petticoat (white)

3. One blouse (red)
4. A pair of sandals (Bata)
5. A pair of earrings (danglers)
6. Fine glass bangles
7. Soap
8. Jabakusum oil
9. A 570 detergent bar
10. Soda

'What is this? I bought you sarees barely two months back,' Father had shot back in astonishment on glancing at the list. With a cold stare Mother had replied, 'They're torn. I wear the same ones while cooking, cleaning and doing all the household chores. It's not as if they're made of straw.' 'Where? Show me where it's torn,' he hadn't been convinced. Mother had gone inside, torn the saree from a two-finger tear to an arm's width and produced it in front of him as evidence, with her eyes cold as stone and a knot of pain lodged in her throat. 'I bought coconut oil just the other day. It's over already!' Father hadn't been willing to give up on his suspicions. 'It's been over for some time.' 'Where is the bottle? Show me the bottle,' he had taken off his glasses and thundered. 'I've thrown them away,' Mother had replied a tad vaguely.

Putting his glasses back on Father had glanced at the list again and said, 'Here, I'll give you some money for detergent soap. The rest you don't need.' The one-taka coin that father had placed on the table that day at the end of his decree had stayed right there for a long time. Mother never even touched it. But she would often glance at the thing and feel herself reduced to someone whose presence within the family was entirely superfluous.

So it was not easy for my mother to consider herself lucky and neither was she convinced that her auspiciously born daughter had managed to change her luck in any way whatsoever. She sighed and replied to Fajli khala's pronouncement, 'The less said about my luck the better. My luck's rotten.' Fajli khala rubbed a hand on her back and tried to placate her. 'Take Allah's name. You'll find peace. Tell Dulabhai [brother-in-law] to read the namaz regularly.' Staring at Fajli khala's fair hands Mother sighed and spoke. 'Your Dulabhai keeps calling me dark and ugly. How is his reading the namaz going to make me fair?' 'No,' Fajli khala sat up with a start, not a mean feat considering her heavy frame, and snapped, 'Allah gave us our colours. We should be happy with what He has given us.' More than anything else it was this new realization that managed to perk Mother up a little bit. Our skin colours were ordained by Allah himself; looking down upon someone's complexion would be like looking down upon Allah's will itself!

I was still four when, after two successive miscarriages, Mother announced that she was expecting again. Father was transferred to Ishwarganj around the same time and we packed and set off for the new posting. Nani had just given birth to Chotku; in fact, she and my mother had both been pregnant almost around the same time.

In Ishwarganj a jeep was provided for Father by the hospital where he was posted. He usually dropped my brothers off at school on his way to work; I wasn't old enough for school yet and spent my time at home learning my alphabets and conjuncts from Mother.

Around her due date Father drove the jeep to Mymensingh and brought Jhunu khala to Ishwarganj to take care of Mother. On arriving at our house khala's joy had to be seen to be believed. She immediately sat down to chat with my brothers, as if she wouldn't be able to finish talking about all that had happened in six months even if they had six years. She stayed up late, telling us about her new tutor, Rasu, who used to gape at her like a catfish. Within no time Jhunu khala also managed to do up the large house we had in Ishwarganj rather prettily, so much so that Father took one look at her handiwork and told her to teach the same to my mother before leaving. A jibe to which Mother could only reply saying he didn't like anything she did, almost as if he was trying to find faults in everything because he didn't like her. Father too would do things like pull Jhunu khala on to his lap and tell her how pretty she was and how whoever was going to marry her was indeed a lucky man; she would in turn blush at his words, unable to find a suitable response to anything he said. In fact, Father used to take even more liberties with Fajli khala, would even pull her to the bed, telling her in seeming jest to come near him so he could find a measure of peace. He would say he could sacrifice his life for her only for her to laugh and dismiss his excesses as jokes. For men, taking such liberties with their wives' sisters and female relatives was perfectly all right, it was halal even, and they could sexualize their comments as much as they wished without any eyebrows being raised. Mother, however, could never shake off the feeling that Father often didn't recognize his limits. He never resisted the temptation of touching fair female flesh, irrespective of whether it was his own sister-in-law or Chakladar's wife, Razia Begum.

Six days after Jhunu khala's arrival, Mother went into labour. On receiving the news Father returned home early with equipment and a nurse from the hospital and declared he wanted another son this time. With the house swooning

under Mother's screams and the smell of Dettol, we stood
outside her bedroom door with Jhunu khala's eyes pressed to
a hole on the door. She had her hands over her mouth and
she was laughing at something she was seeing inside while
I stood behind, bobbing up and down in excitement and
asking over and over again how babies were born. Time and
again khala would look away from the hole through which
she was spying to blush and give in to laughter and to tell me
she could not answer my question.

Jhunu khala was still laughing when suddenly the sound
of an infant's cry rang out. Since I could not reach the hole
on the door, khala held me up so I could take a peek inside
too. I saw Father and the bloody gloves on his hand and the
nurse dipping the baby in a tub of warm water and washing
it. There was an array of knives and scissors laid out; Father
had cut her stomach out and she was bleeding and screaming
in pain. It was only for a few seconds but it was enough to
send a shiver down my spine. Jhunu khala was waiting to
hold the baby with a small kantha that Nani had sent over
for the newborn. As soon as the door opened and Father
stepped out, she lunged at him, 'What is it Dulabhai? A boy
or a girl?'

'What I didn't want. A girl.'

'Fair or dark?'

Father lost his temper. 'Dark will produce dark, what
were you expecting, it'll be white? I've left tons of work at
the hospital. I have to get back.'

After he was gone, we wrapped the baby in the kantha
and took turns taking her in our arms. We massaged her
tiny body with mustard oil and laid her down on the bed,
her tiny head on the tiny pillow, a tiny mosquito over her,
a boat-shaped milk feeder near her head and us by her side.

Mother stayed in bed crying softly; my brothers came back from school and were faced with the astonishing sight of the new baby.

After Father returned home that night Jhunu khala served him food; he ate and then promptly went off to sleep. When the child cried out, he screamed and asked everyone to be quiet so he could sleep. Khala cooed and whispered to the baby to keep her quiet, changed her kantha, fed her some milk. I lay there listening to the silent house sighing in despair, feeling deeply sorry for khala, my parents and my infant sister.

Father was transferred back to Mymensingh from Ishwarganj, then to Thakurgaon, and then back to Mymensingh again, all in fairly quick succession. After a year and a half of travelling around we moved back to our old house again, the one I was born in. This time Father decreed that so much travel was causing havoc with the boys' studies and henceforth we were no longer going to be accompanying him when he got transferred. I was quite tall by that time and there was talk in the house that I was going to be put in school. My younger sister had been named Yasmin by Father, to rhyme with mine. She was still very much an infant and Mother would feed her, bathe her, massage her with mustard oil and leave her outside to sunbathe. In the evenings, by the light of the kerosene lamp, Dada would teach us. By then I could recite poems and rhymes nonstop and had even moved on to short stories, especially the ones for children written by Rabindranath Tagore. But all it took was Dada sitting down to teach me for everything to start unravelling in my head.

When was Rabindranath born?

Who wrote the poem *Kajla Didi*?

Spell 'momentous'.

I was afraid to answer any of his questions. What if he slapped me, or worse, what if he made everyone gather around to listen to my mistakes?

Once, before we shifted to Ishwarganj, while trying to test his amateur teaching expertise on me, he had made me sit with a book and asked me to read the spellings out aloud. Around the time I had just about moved on from the alphabets and slowly begun to foray into the conjuncts. Instead of the words all I noticed were the sketches accompanying them. Following his order, I had picked up the primer and tried in earnest to spell.

'T-U-R-M-E-R-I-C'

'So what is that? Say!'

The photo I had been staring at was that of a piece of ginger. Well, sort of. 'Ginger,' I had replied confidently. In my defence I did successfully spell K-O-I and identify it as FISH. Nonetheless, my thirteen-year-old teacher couldn't wait to call our entire family on me. Everyone—my mother, grandmother, uncles, aunts, everyone—sat around me in a circle as Dada proceeded to demonstrate in front of them my newly acquired reading skills. For my life, though, I had failed to understand what the fuss was all about! It had soon dawned on me that perhaps they were all there because I was reading well. Convinced that if I could do it again I would be showered with love and treats I had wasted no time in launching at it again: 'T-U-R-M-E-R-I-C', and then with a pause, 'Ginger.' The room had exploded into a fit of laughter, people sitting down, clothes flying askew, rolling on the floor in mirth. I had stared at the laughing faces around me and my face had split into a smile too; laughter was terribly contagious after all. Besides, the spotlight was on me, I was the one on stage while my family was my audience, so how could I not! In the end Nani had pointed out my mistake of having swapped the two related things but what could I have done? The pictures were stuck in my head, not the words! I read images, not the alphabets naming them! Even before I could write I used to draw.

Chotda had got me admitted to the PTI School in Thakurgaon. Ignoring my screaming and yelling, he had even taken me to school on the first day, right up to my classroom. The master had sat me down on his lap and sang, 'Khoya Khoya Chaand, Khula Asmaan'[3] to make me stop weeping. Once I did, he had put me with the other kids and asked us to draw a pitcher. I had boldly drawn one in two-three strokes and proceeded to decorate it with a garland of flowers. The other children had stopped their work to peek into mine and stare. On the very first day itself I had made quite a name for myself in the PTI School, enough to warrant the master raising me up by the waist and showing me off to the others, telling them I was going to be a big artist one day.

While teaching me Dada would ask me to recite poems, like Nazrul's 'Chal chal . . .' for instance. Even before I could finish the first stanza, he would shoot a question at me. When I invariably failed, he would take the pencil and, tapping me hard on the fingers with it, reproach me for learning things by heart like a monkey without understanding their meaning. Whenever teaching me caught his fancy the evenings usually passed amidst tapping pencils, smacks and blows, until Mother called us for dinner. The other evenings we usually sat together—Tutu mama, Sharaf mama, Felu mama and I—on a mat spread out on Nani's veranda and studied together like in a pathshala, as in studied out aloud so that all the grown-ups could hear us, with one kerosene lamp each between the two of us. Sharaf mama and I read out rhymes while Felu mama was still with his primers. At some point in the evening, Tutu mama would read out aloud the story of a crashing storm—a usual and regular ritual among us— with tin roofs being blown away, trees being uprooted and people falling flat on their faces. By this point they would all be giggling, while I consistently failed to fathom why a person falling over was so funny. Often Nani would emerge from within and scold us for talking while we were meant to be studying. At eight we would be called to the kitchen for dinner. No matter what we ate, it inevitably ended with a huge bowl of milk, wrist-deep. Since Yasmin slept with my parents on their bed, I had to move in with my Nana, Nani and my two younger uncles, sharing the three beds that had been put together to make one long space in Nani's room.

Two months after we returned to Mymensingh from Thakurgaon, Nana got the three of us, Sharaf mama, Felu mama and I, admitted to the Rajbari School, me and Sharaf mama in class two and Felu mama a class below us. He also bought us identical black umbrellas to take to school, with our names written on each in white. We ate rice with ghee and sugar in the morning and walked to school, umbrellas over our heads. There was tiffin at school during recess and returning home in the afternoon meant having lunch and then going off to play in the fields adjacent to our house. Once it was evening, we usually washed up and sat down to study with kerosene lamps. My early life was spent mostly flitting between two courtyards: my Nani's and my mother's. My clothes, books and things would be strewn about in both places and my daily routine was never fixed to one place. That time too was like a parade of tiny joys and sorrows, one following the other in rapid succession as if they were all neighbours and lived close by. Since starting school my singular obsession became the coloured plates they used to set out during recess for us. There were brightly ornate ones with fruits and flowers as motifs and plain white ones as well. During recess someone would come by and place a plate in front of each pupil, followed by a staff member who served the food, ranging from egg–bread–banana to khichdi. Poppy, the good girl in the front row, whose mother was also a teacher in the school, usually chose a flower-fruit patterned plate for herself. The perks she had because of her connections were not something I, the idiot in the last bench, could hope to enjoy. So it was only once in a while when someone missed their chance at a colourful plate that it would end up in front of me. My eyes nonetheless were evidently more interested in the plates than the food served on them.

The Rajbari School used to be the palace of Raja Sashikanta. When the king, the queen, the princes and the princes, everyone was gone, the building was refurbished with desks and chairs and turned into a school. It was an old house ensconced by banyan trees. There was a nude Meera Bai sculpture in the front and a pond of water, dark as the eyes of a duck and its edge paved with marble, within. Steps from the house led deep into the surrounding gardens. The doors were so high that even the tall gatekeepers with their long sticks could not reach them, the ceiling even higher, nearly like the sky. The windows were stained glass, beautifully etched. Stepping into the school I was regularly assailed by the feeling that I was of royal birth. The feeling was fleeting though and barely lasted till I reached my classroom where I promptly reverted to my meek and daft self among the crowd of my classmates. I could never stand in front of the blackboard and recite poems; I would stand there with my head hanging in fear and shame, my throat choked and voice barely audible. The master would give me a rap with the duster and send me off to the last bench. I was a nobody in school; all the adulation went to the beautiful Poppy who resembled a fairy. While my hands would shake during our drawing classes, no matter what the subject given to us, Poppy would get full marks irrespective of what she ended up drawing. I was simply the niece of Sharaf, the school hellion. One afternoon after school, Sharaf mama and his friend Nasim, their hands tied behind their back and black cloth wrapped around their eyes, were made to stand on the steps and given a sound beating while Felu mama and I, along with the entire school, stood in the garden and watched, pale and petrified. It was soon revealed that Nasim had stolen money from his father and given it to Sharaf mama in exchange for magnets. That day Sharaf mama was held back in school after the beating, forcing Felu mama and I to return home by ourselves. Later in the evening the severely beaten and exhausted Sharaf mama was brought back home by Nana, tied up against one of the pillars and given another round.

The girls in school used to keep fern leaves within the pages of their books. They used to call them 'leaves of knowledge'; apparently keeping them in books ensured knowledge. Taking a cue from them I too began keeping the invaluable leaves in my books, but try as I might I could still not manage to solve a mathematical problem on the blackboard when called upon to do so or recite a poem when asked to. My head would bow automatically and the lines and tunes in my head would collapse to the ground and get smeared in the dust and grime. Thus, even the ones I knew by heart, the ones I had read a thousand times, I forgot—

Our little river winds along
Running knee-deep all Boishakh,
The banks high and inclined,
Letting carts and bullocks through;
No dirt or mud but a sliver of shiny sand
Along the edge, while along the other,
A plain of soft white grass in full bloom,
Where birds chirp at day,
And foxes howl at dusk.

All I could remember, however, the only image that kept popping up in my head, was a river and shepherds crossing over from one bank to the other. What if they had given me the scene to sketch? Instead, I got my ears boxed and had to endure the added slight of the entire class laughing at my ignominy. When the bell rang and they ran off to the grounds to play, no one remembered to call me. I was relegated to a corner of the stairs of the palace, awkward and alone, as if I had had a falling out with everyone else at school and hence no one spoke to me or looked at me twice. As I had no one else I could play the games of friendship and falling out with, I mostly ended up playing them with myself.

Not that I was any less alone at home, despite the many people I lived with. Sharaf mama usually picked me for his team only when he had no other choice. Besides, I could barely keep up with them at their games. They climbed trees, swam the ponds, while I mostly stayed on the sidelines as a silent spectator. Dada had grown out of his cricket phase and moved on to a new area of interest—photography—having even managed to borrow a camera from a friend. Dressed in teddy pants and shoes he roamed about beside the river and in the parks looking for new subjects to shoot; he cut paper and made an album on his own to keep the photos he had taken. We were not allowed to touch the album; we could only see it from a distance. While everyone remained preoccupied with their own games, I had the task of cleaning the kerosene lamps out with sand, lighting the wick and placing lamps in each room. It was a job I volunteered for in fact, because of a game I had devised for myself. Swinging the kerosene lamp from my arm I would go out of the room yelling 'Ice cream!' as if I was a vendor out with my wares. Someone or the other, Runu khala perhaps, would stop and ask me prices and generally play along much to my delight. I would go on and sell them make-believe ice cream in exchange for make-believe money. It was my game and mine alone, without loss or victory; my uncles predictably failed to see the real joy behind it and would often advise me, obviously making fun of me, to go play with Chotku who was then around two and a half.

Such were my earliest years, growing up without an ounce of intelligence or a shred of wisdom. While Sharaf mama and Felu mama were moving on from cops and robbers to more mature sports like football and cricket, I remained behind in the yard with Chotku, playing the same old childhood games. I was still cutting paper into circles and roasting them over the kerosene lamp pretending it was bread, or filling pages after pages with absurd and colourful sketches instead of memorizing and writing my tables: a reed hut in the midst of a grove of plantain trees, the wide open sky in the background, birds in flight against a bright red sun, a river winding past the hut with a tiny boat sailing on it, the boatman sitting at the stern and a woman in a red saree making her way to the water's edge with a pitcher against her hip. Fajli khala could not fathom why a girl born on such an auspicious day as 12 Rabiul could be so obsessed with drawing things. When she saw me draw people, she couldn't control herself any longer and asked me why I did it despite being who I was. Would I be able to give life to the image I was drawing? Then why draw it? Not that I understood anything of what she meant, so the only recourse I was left with was to stare at her in bafflement whenever she asked me such things.

Not that I was the only one who was doing things one wasn't supposed to do back then. One day Mother chanced upon a new letter from Razia Begum in Father's pocket. It left her a little mad and utterly devastated, made her forget herself, her meals, her chores and just about everything else. Abandoning everything she locked herself up in her room. After a few days passed like this, Soheli's mother came over to counsel her against wasting her life crying over her husband. Advising her to divert her attention elsewhere Soheli's mother did her hair, helped her put on a new saree and took her to Alaka Hall for a film. Initially Mother would go with Soheli's mother but as time passed, she began going for films by herself, without waiting around for anyone else. She would stand in queue for tickets, munch on nuts while the movie was on, all by herself, the dark woman in her cheap saree and cheap sandals who no longer cared about jewellery and fine clothes and such things. Father had jewellery, etc., made for his wife and daughters but she left them behind at the oddest of places, in the bathroom, under the pillows, or beside the hearth, uncaring and unfeeling about such possessions any more. She who had been wearing a burqa since she was twelve eventually began going for movies without one, once even with mismatched sandals on her feet. All she cared about back then was Uttam Kumar[4] and at night she dreamt about the matinee idol approaching her with a garland of flowers and sweeping her off her feet.

I had never been to see a film before. The first film I saw was one winter afternoon when the bioscope-man had come over with his wooden box that one had to gaze into to see the images moving inside, as the man narrated the story in a sing-song voice. Hardly had the memory of the bioscope-man faded when news arrived that there was going to be a screening of a silent publicity film in the field adjacent to Sahabuddin's house. On the day of the screening, children gathered at the field as soon as it was evening as bricks were laid out on the ground for us to sit on. The film was played on a large projection screen and I sat there watching the spectacle unfold with my mouth gaping open, scarcely understanding anything that was happening on screen. After I returned home, I could hear my mamas' jibes: 'The foolish girl has her head full of shit.'

That wasn't entirely untrue. Had it not been so would I not have told everyone about the incident? Only I couldn't say anything, I had to stay quiet, and not a single person got any wind of the incident that had happened in the house one day in broad daylight. It was 16 August 1967, two days after Pakistan's Independence Day celebrations. I had just returned from school and was waiting for Mother to come back and give me food. Like other days there was a book club in session in Nani's room: Kana mama was leaning against the bed, Nani was on the bed chewing on paan, Jhunu khala too was half-sitting and half-reclining, Hasem mama had his feet up on a chair and was fanning himself while Runu khala was reading out exploits of the bandit Bahram. Such scenes were very common in Nani's room during those long and languid summer afternoons, right after a post-lunch siesta.

Runu khala would read and everyone would gather to listen and intermittently make appropriate noises of appreciation or distaste. Kids were not allowed inside during those hours lest they disrupted the proceedings. So that day, alone and waiting for my mother to return, I went and stood at their door. Hasem mama noticed me and immediately said, 'Go play in the field.'

I did not want to play in the field. I was hungry and Mother had locked the meat-safe before leaving. I crossed the courtyard, edging close to the well and under the shade of the coconut tree, on to our side and had barely sat down on the stairs of the veranda, legs spread apart and my cheek resting on my hand, when Sharaf mama turned up from somewhere. It was something about fetching a runaway cricket ball or the small piece used for danguti. Dressed in a black vest and a pair of white shorts, Sharaf mama was bigger than me by an entire hand's length. His brown eyes darted from the trees to the closed door behind me, to the black cat in the courtyard and the empty chair visible from the living room, before resting on me to ask, 'Where's Borobu?'[5]

'Not here,' I shook my head, my face still resting on my hand. 'Where has she gone?' he asked, as if he needed something to do with her right then. Climbing up the two flights of stairs and plopping down beside me with two thumps on my back, Sharaf mama continued, 'What are you doing sitting here alone?' 'Nothing,' I answered, hungry and forlorn. Sharaf mama repeated his earlier question about when Mother was going to be back while firmly removing my hand from my cheek. There was a momentary pause and then his voice softened as he spoke. 'Don't rest your face on your palm like that. It brings bad luck.'

I should probably have told him I was hungry, should have told him about the locked meat-safe and everything. Instead, as if about to share a grand secret, I moved closer to Sharaf mama and asked him if he could guess where Mother was. Then, inching closer ever so slightly, I pressed on, 'Promise me you won't tell anyone if I told you?'

'No, I won't tell anyone. Tell me.'

'Promise?'

'Promise.'

'You swear?'

'I swear.'

'In Allah's name?'

Getting impatient Sharaf mama snapped. 'I told you I won't tell anyone! Now tell me!'

'No, swear in Allah's name first.' I was still steadfast in my faith back then that anything sworn on Allah's name was forever and truly binding. His face growing serious, Sharaf mama relented to my demands. 'Fine, I swear in Allah's name I won't tell anyone.' 'She's gone to watch a movie,' I whispered immediately.

Sharaf mama wasn't shocked or astonished at all. All he had to say to the revelation was a simple 'Oh', as if Mother had gone out for something as banal as peeing or visiting Sulekha's house. She wasn't allowed to go to the movies. Nana had firmly warned her that such habits were sinful and if she continued to leave the house as she wished to despite being a woman, she was going to have to suffer severe consequences. I was astounded that Sharaf mama didn't find it thrilling enough that Mother was flouting such a direct order. Instead he said observationally, 'I went for a movie too, yesterday.'

'You went by yourself!' I could scarcely hide my surprise.

'Yes I did,' he replied, his eyebrows dancing.

'What if Nana finds out?'

Instead of answering my question Sharaf mama turned away with a 'Let me show you something fun!' and started walking towards the black tin fuel shed at the farthest end of the house, beyond Dada's room on the eastern corner of the courtyard. The front door of the shed was jammed shut; one could open the back door if one knew how. Usually there weren't too many people on that side of the property so there was a sort of a ghostly silence that permeated the atmosphere there. The space behind the shed itself was overgrown with wild broad beans, weed and dead leaves. We never ventured this side for fear of snakes; Chotda had once seen a rat and a snake somewhere there. Before following him into the hedge crowding the back door, I warned him about them.

'Oh, don't be scared! You really are a fool, a scaredy-cat! Come. Let me show you something fun. No one knows about this,' he finished before plunging into the overgrowth, as if totally secure in the knowledge that all serpents and such were sleeping in their holes.

'Tell me what it is first.' I was much less certain about things.

'That will spoil all the fun.'

He looped his hand inside and opened the back door from within. Seeing him going inside I crossed the hedge in one blind run and followed suit. I was so curious about whatever 'fun' thing Sharaf mama was going to show me that for a moment the other fears regarding the room receded a little. As soon as we stepped inside, we were assailed by the stench of rotting rats and the sound of scurrying little feet. Straw was stacked in one corner and the other corner was occupied by a small, old bed. Apprehensive about being

made fun of again if I admitted that I was scared I decided
to put up a brave front. Sharaf mama was very daring; he
used to roam about the city on his own and even go off to
the riverbanks time and again by himself. Amazed by such
displays of bravery and still trying desperately to quash my
own fears I asked him,

'Mama, does Foting Ting live by the river?'

'No,' he replied, his feet swinging off the edge of the bed
on which he had sat down.

'Will you take me one day?' I implored.

'You won't be scared?' he teased, poking me in the stomach.

'No,' I countered immediately, still struggling with fear.

'No, you will be afraid. I know you will,' he said this time
with a swift tap on my head.

'Believe me I won't be scared. I am big now, I am not
afraid any more.' I had crossed the hedge with the snakes. I
was not going to be afraid any more.

'No, you will be afraid,' Sharaf mama insisted, pushing
the door close with his feet.

'Believe me. I swear . . . on Allah . . . I won't be afraid,' I
insisted, touching his hand.

'This is a nice place. No one will know where we are,' he
observed instead.

Sharaf mama used to do this quite often, suddenly pull
a vanishing act. Once he had pulled me behind the kitchen
promising a new treat. He had then proceeded to light a jute
stem and smoke it like a cigarette, even offering me a few
puffs after I promised not to tell on him to anyone. He was
like that, daring and uncaring, doing exactly what he wished
whether in the open or in secret.

'What did you do with the money you got from Naseem?'
I had wanted to find out for a long time.

'I buried it,' he answered immediately, without even waiting to make me swear not to tell anyone else.

Sharaf mama was promising to take me to see the river, he was revealing the location of his buried treasure to me, only to me and away from all other prying eyes and ears, all this was nothing but emboldening to me. At that moment it didn't feel like my head was full of shit any more.

'Where did you bury it? Here?' I whispered.

'Yes! When I grow up, I will buy a ship with the money.'

'Ship! Will you take me on it?' I could hardly control my excitement. I could almost visualize it: a huge ship, sailing down the river and out into the open sea, me on the deck watching the sunlight play on the glistening surface of the water. It resembled a photo I had once seen on the pages of a pharmaceutical company calendar.

Sharaf mama's eyes were dancing again. But this time neither did he have a jute stem to smoke nor did he have magnets hidden in his pockets. I never knew what magnets were before he had shown me. He used to pretend to do magic and stick the magnets on random things—the grills on the windows, the tube well, the buckets, on the door knob— and I would be amazed at the fantastic feat. It had made me want to pick up a random piece of metal and imitate what he was doing, trying to do magic tricks of my own. He had laughed at my antics.

But in that isolated shed his eyes were dancing with a different light and there was a strange half-smile hanging from his lips, neither of which I could interpret. Suddenly, with a 'here, let me show you that fun thing', he pulled me closer and pushed me down to the bed, beginning to take off the pleated and colourful half-pant I had on. Stunned for a brief moment, I tried to pull my pants up and exclaimed,

'What fun thing did you want to show me? Why are you taking my clothes off?' Laughing my words aside, Sharaf mama pushed me down on the bed with his weight and forced my pants down entirely. Then he took off his own and pressed his penis hard against my body, the weight of him knocking the wind out of me. Trying to push him off me, I could only gasp out stray words. 'What is this Sharaf mama? What are you doing? Let me go!' Despite my best attempts, though, I could barely move him an inch off me.

'This is the fun thing I wanted to show you.'

He laughed again and bit down on my lower lips with his teeth.

'Do you know what this is called? It's called fucking. Everyone in the world fucks. My parents do, so do yours.'

As his thrusts became more urgent a feeling of terrible disgust washed over me; it was all I could do to cover my eyes in shame. A sudden sound of scurrying feet on the ground seemed to break the spell. Sharaf mama jumped off me, giving me the chance to pull up my pants in one swift motion and run out of the shed. This time I did not hesitate one bit thinking about snakes while crossing over the hedge. My heart was beating frantically, as if a hundred rats were scurrying to safety from something. All I could hear was Sharaf mama's strangely voiced warning in the background, 'Don't tell anyone. If you do, that'll be the end.'

Mother

Local boys were marching down the main road shouting slogans. '*Ladke lenge* Pakistan, *bir mujaheed naujawan, kabool moder jaan paran, ante habe* Pakistan, *ante hobe paak* Quran' ('We will fight for Pakistan, we brave young soldiers of the faith, we stake our lives and loves, to pave the way for Pakistan and for the holy Quran'). Abandoning the hop-skip-jump she was in the midst of, Mother rushed to watch them marching past. After they were gone, she raised her hands and let out a whoop of '*Ladke lenge* Pakistan', probably without even understanding what it was all about. Soon after, one morning she received news that the British had left the subcontinent and a new country had been created for Muslims: Pakistan. Local boys took out marches where they sang and danced to 'Pakistan Zindabad' while in the schools too pro-Pakistani messages gained momentum.

The birth of Pakistan, however, caused hardly a ripple in Mother's life. Miyanbhai continued to attend the Nasirabad madrasa, Sultan Ustadji continued to visit the house to teach her the Quran Sharif and Nana continued to read the namaz five times a day. No one had ever threatened these things in any way so she could not understand what all the fuss about the holy Quran had been! The only collateral

damage amidst this chaos was that her friend Amala had
to leave everything behind and move to Hindustan. The
day they left, having sold their house and property for next
to nothing, Mother stood and watched their departure in
stunned silence. She had been best friends with Amala.
Imagine how it feels when someone loses their best friend.
That's how Mother had felt and she was never able to do
anything about their leaving, about anyone's leaving for
that matter.

The schools gradually emptied out when all the Hindu
girls stopped attending. In the mostly empty classrooms,
small groups of Muslim girls were only beginning to learn
a new chapter in history, one that was telling them Pakistan
was their country and Muhammad Ali Jinnah was the Father
of the Nation. New books of poetry arrived too. Gone were
Satyendranath Dutt and Jyotindramohan Bagchi, they were
replaced by Golam Mostafa and Bande Ali Miyan. Kazi
Najrul Islam instead of Rabindranath Tagore. Mother
kept reciting the same old poems though, the ones she had
learnt from Amala's older sister. '*Hasi hasi porbo fnasi dekhbe
Bharatbasi, ekbar bidai de ma ghure ashi*' ('I will wear the
noose with a smile as my whole country will watch, bid me
farewell Mother as I set out on this journey'). Life went on
as it does, its small joys and sorrows intact. She swam in the
pond among the hyacinth just like before and ate the same
rice and fish seated on the small wooden seats in the kitchen.
The country changed, of course, but did not necessarily mean
people did too. So instead of the English, the new people she
saw on the roads were the Kabuliwalahs. They became the
new 'foreigners' for her. In her quiet life her dolls remained
her companion as usual, except for Amala's doll whom she
had married to her own and which seemed just as sad as she.

She hid a well of sorrow in her heart as things and people moved on.

Mother was married off even before she grew out of playing with her dolls. She used to often plead with her father to take her to the fair and buy her more dolls. When she had an actual doll-sized child of her own she grew out of that too. The year her oldest son was born was 1952, the same year our Urdu overlords shot and killed a number of protesters who had been marching to instate Bangla as the state language. Mother couldn't help but wonder why they had made a separate country if the end result was that Muslims were going to kill other Muslims. New processions were organized after this incident, with a roster of six primary demands. The same road that had been a witness to the pro-Pakistan and save-the-Quran processions now became grounds for 'Save Bangla, Down with Urdu' marches. While her surroundings had hardly changed (the narrow paths and the ponds full of fish remained as they were before), Mother couldn't help but be astonished as to how the nature of the processions had undergone a radical transformation.

I used to often notice a tall, lanky boy in our locality whenever I had to go to Manumiyan's shop for groceries. He lived in a tiny tin hut under the sweetest jujube tree in the neighbourhood. There was a bigger house behind the hut where his mother and other siblings used to stay. It was a custom to keep such shacks on the periphery of a property reserved for the grown-up sons of a family, just like rooms had been reserved for Dada and Chotda. One day I found out from Chotda that the boy was his close friend Khokon's older brother, Mintu. Chotda and Mintu were such friends that they even used to fall in love together, often with the same girl. To me Mintu seemed so very lonely and I would often see him walking on the street all by himself in his translucent shirt and blue lungi, or standing at his own door and whistling distractedly. The tree behind his place used to be laden with jujubes and I would tarry there a while on my way past it, contemplating whether to gather some of the fruits lying on the ground underneath. However, I was also petrified that Mintu would find out and box my ears, which forced me to control my tongue. The other boys of the locality used to at least shout out to me whenever they saw me, even if to ask me where I was going or to say something banal like be careful of cars. Mintu only watched without saying anything; perhaps he was shy. He did not come across like the other boys. It seemed to me like he was from another place, another country or city, an altogether different person who had nothing in common with other people in the neighbourhood. He used to speak to himself in the languid afternoons and sleep shirtless under the satinwood tree on moonlit nights.

It was 1969 when I was finally taken away from Rajbari School and admitted to Bidyamoyi High School. The new school was right in the middle of the city with the Gangina on its right and Notun Bazar on the left. It was farther than the previous school and the rickshaw fare for one commute was four annas. Father would leave behind exactly eight annas with Mother, which she would tie safely in the drape of her saree till ten in the morning. School started at ten thirty and every day, on my way, I would be confronted by the sight of a battered and bruised city languishing on the road. Rocks and stones and trunks of trees would be strewn about, not to forget the police vans at every crossing. Chotda would bunk school often to join the protest marches and it made me want to follow his footsteps. He usually returned home late and until he came back Father would pace up and down the courtyard with Mother sitting at the door of the living room with a lamp. Chotda was asked numerous times not to go off and join these protests but he wasn't the good and obedient boy that Dada always was. The latter could be scolded and made to sit at home but Chotda was far more difficult to control and he managed to escape at the slightest chance he got.

It was 24 January. We had been hearing the sounds of protesters from early in the morning. Soon it grew into a din, aided by a murder of crows swirling above creating a ruckus. At first, we could not fathom why the crows were so agitated or why people were running towards the sound of the protesters. Alarmed by the growing commotion Mother emerged from the kitchen and ran out of the house, her feet bare, clothes unkempt, hair untied, fingers stained with masala and smelling of onions. She ran down the lane, past the shed at the farthest end and then across the main road to Mukul's house. From Mukul's open courtyard one could see far out past the boarding house of Zilla School, past Thanda's father's jalebi shop and the hordes of people running across the rail lines. Mother, along with the mothers of Shahjahan, Mukul and Shafeeq, managed to stop some of the local boys who were headed that way. Soon enough a crowd had gathered in the courtyard, comprising sixteen- or seventeen-year-old boys like Farooq, Rafique, Chandan sporting various sorts of bullet wounds. Buckets of water, Dettol and cotton were sent out from the house while the women set themselves to tending to their wounded sons. Some were immediately put on rickshaws and sent off to the hospital.

Father returned sometime past noon. Without a word to anyone he headed straight towards Mintu's house, Mother

and I close at his heels and followed by more people from
the neighbourhood. We were met by Mintu's mother there
and Father cast a long and sad glance at her, his gaze shifting
dolefully towards Mintu's abandoned tin room outside their
house. Mintu's mother grabbed hold of his hand and burst
into tears. She had already received news that Mintu had been
at the head of the procession that had come under attack,
that he had been taken to the hospital after being shot by the
police. Father could only let out a deep sigh every so often,
unable to utter a word. We remained at the house with them
as the immensity of the news took hold. Mintu's brother
and sister were both weeping loudly as the crows circled and
cawed overhead. Scores of women from the neighbourhood
were sprinkling water and trying to revive their mother who
had fallen unconscious. From time to time, Mintu's younger
brother Manu would come up to Mother and tell her he was
going to kill the people who had murdered his brother. He
did try to go out of the house in search of them, but she
somehow managed to hold him back. How could he have
even murdered the murderers? They had the guns! How
could one wage war against men with guns with no weapons
of one's own?

The neighbours were discussing among themselves how
the procession was suddenly attacked from nowhere as it was
making its way past the veterinary hospital. As the firing had
started almost everyone had turned to run but Mintu hadn't
managed in time. The crowd at the house continued to swell
as Mintu's other brothers—Khokon, Bacchu, Humayun—
arrived. A little while later Mintu was brought back too, on
a cot covered in a white shroud.

I was standing under the jujube tree staring fixedly at
Mintu's unmoving form covered in white. The quiet and

bashful boy had been distractedly standing at the entrance of his house that very morning. He had responded to his mother calling him inside for breakfast with a, 'I'll be back soon'. His mother had kept his breakfast covered in the kitchen. When they brought in his corpse that day the food was still lying there. Underneath the tree there were so many jujubes that day, the sweetest in the entire neighbourhood. There was no one that day to box my ears but I didn't feel like picking up even a single fruit. Mother was trying to pacify Mintu's bereft mother, wiping her own tears away from time to time. The boys had sworn an oath on his blood to take vengeance for the tragedy, confident that their time was going to change. When Mintu was brought back home that day, not only his family but the entire neighbourhood broke down in grief. I had never known before that day that so many people had been so fond of the lanky, young boy. Chotda was sitting there, silent and unmoving. He had been right beside Mintu in the procession, the bullet had grazed his right arm and hit Mintu in the chest. It could have as easily pierced Chotda's heart and my brother could have just as easily died that fateful day.

Mintu was buried in the Akua cemetery. Never before had I seen my neighbourhood so united in grief and mourning. The kids did not go to the field that afternoon to play; the adults huddled in groups beside the road and spoke in furtive whispers. It was as if the whole neighbourhood had collectively sworn off their daily routines. A few days later, Sheikh Mujib himself came to visit Mintu's family. What a crowd descended there that day, everyone hoping to get a glance of the man! I remember Chotda telling us that if he had died instead of Mintu, Sheikh Mujib would have come to visit us instead. As if he would have been happier if, indeed, he had died that day at the procession instead of Mintu! Never have I met another person who regrets not dying as much as Chotda did that day.

Like the others I too went to see Sheikh Mujib. Among a crowd of a thousand people that was no small feat. Standing with my heels raised didn't work, so a stack of bricks had to be arranged. Finally, after a small wall proved ineffective, I had to overcome my fear of toppling over into death and perch atop a bigger wall to catch a glimpse of Sheikh Mujib. The bespectacled tall man in the black coat looked a lot like Sahabuddin from our locality and I remember wondering why such a crowd never gathered for the latter! As if Sheikh Mujib had descended from heaven itself and was not a mere mortal like us. He consoled Mintu's mother, gently patting her on the head. The area around the jujube tree was yet again littered with a lot of fruit; I still didn't feel like picking up any.

It is perhaps human law that one cannot dwell on sorrow for far too long. Within a month everyone returned to their usual lives. The children started playing in the field again, the men began to be seen with their shopping bags again heading towards the market and the women went back into the kitchens. In the evenings I too returned to the old kerosene lamp and swaying to the rhythms of '*Amader chhoto nodi*'. Only whenever I passed by the graveyard, I would clasp my hands and walk silently as Mother had asked me to. But there was something she hadn't told me to do that I did nevertheless. Whenever I found a tree in full bloom in the neighbourhood, irrespective of whose tree it was, I used to take a palmful of flowers and place them on Mintu's grave. I firmly believed he could smell them.

Mother was convinced that the collapse of a fragile state such as Pakistan was inevitable. It didn't escape her that

the tide of opinions had turned; people were so disgruntled
that they didn't hesitate before abusing Ayub Khan and
his entire dynasty, that too in public. Besides, young
revolutionaries were taking out protest marches regularly,
demanding independence for East Pakistan. The Pakistani
government was responding to all this with frequent curfews,
barring people from leaving their houses. Blackouts were
announced, homes had to be completely dark and people
had stay inside. To Mother it seemed all rulers were virtually
indistinguishable. It was not as if the Pakistanis were any
less oppressive than the English had been. Wealth from
the east was being siphoned off to West Pakistan just like
the English had loaded ships with wealth from India and
taken it home. Not that Mother was especially interested in
Pakistan. In fact, she hardly cared if the country was divided
further or indeed if it went to the dogs. All she wanted was
to ensure her sons did not die at a protest. Her children were
all she had and the fact that she had them was enough for
her to find solid ground beneath her feet. If she had been
educated, she could have worked, found any job that would
have allowed her to let go of her disinterested husband, or at
least find a path towards freedom herself. Once she had even
taken Chotda and caught a train to Dhaka to find some sort
of employment there; she had heard somewhere that there
were many jobs to be found in the city quite easily. She did
end up applying for the position of a nurse in a hospital but
was turned away by the authorities who informed her that
she needed to have better degrees as well as a Nursing School
certificate. On returning home, Father had snidely remarked
that happiness clearly didn't suit her.

Mother was petrified of letting Chotda out of sight,
afraid as she was that he too was going to be shot dead one

day like Mintu. As a child he had had to be weaned off her milk with neem leaves; now she couldn't bear to separate him from her. Chotda had continued to breastfeed till he was almost five or six. As per Nani's advice, Mother used to rub neem paste on her breasts to make him stop seeking her milk. He had even started speaking much later than usual; at two he used to have difficulty saying 'Baba'. When he was to be admitted to school in class six the headmaster had asked him to spell 'puraskar'. He had struggled over 'poos' and 'pus' for a length of time before giving up in defeat; he had been taken in only because the headmaster and Father had been on very good terms. Father had bought him a wristwatch and a geometry box and promised him a bike if he did well in his studies. He had lost the watch in three days and the compass from the box became the go-to utensil for helping family members floss after eating meat. Following Dada's example, Chotda had tried his hands at teaching me as well. He would open a book and beckon me towards him, asking me to read as he read. Often, he read it wrong himself and Dada would gape at him in wonder trying to fathom what on earth he was trying to teach me with such intent.

To our mother, Chotda remained a child even after he no longer was one. She was convinced for a long time that he was the one who was going to grow up somewhat simple. Instead, it was Dada who turned out to be the quiet one, the one who hardly reacted to even the worst offences. Chotda, on the other hand, turned out altogether different. Complaints often arrived from his school about his lack of discipline.

'What is this? I heard you have no discipline!' Father inquired, dragging him into the room by the ear and looking him in the eye.

'I do!' he exhaled in exasperation.

'So are your teachers lying then?'

'Yes, they are.'

A tight slap followed that answer and Father continued. 'Why did you break the school radio?'

'I was listening to it and this boy came and tried to take it away. So I broke it.' Chotda was still fuming.

'Such excellent logic! Such a wonderfully logical boy I have, I should dance with him on my head! Here I am, working day and night to raise my children. So that they get a good education and get ahead in life. If they are such imbeciles, why should I care so much?' Father concluded, pushing him to his study table by the scruff of his neck. 'It's all his mother's fault that he is like this.'

The thing about our house was that if anyone ever got beaten up, they could expect gifts very soon. The very next day Chotda received a new cricket bat and a ball from Mother. She had bought them from the money she had borrowed from Father, notwithstanding the fact that rather than using it on the ball Chotda preferred using the bat primarily on the household furniture. So as soon as she heard he was going to the protest meetings, Mother became convinced that if she were to buy him a guitar, he was going to become preoccupied with music and forget all about the agitations. Father gave her money for a Hawaiian guitar and Mother even made a yellow cover for the new instrument herself. Invariably, all the attention being showered on Chotda did not escape Dada's attention and he tried to coax Mother to make her ask Father to buy him a violin too.

'You ask! Can't you speak?' Mother replied a tad impatiently instead.

Of course, that took care of all of Dada's bravado. He did not have the courage to ask anything of Father. He usually stayed inside, tapping on the table and making music for his own songs. There was only one song he knew, the one he had learnt from his mother when he was four, '*Ekbar bidai de ma*'. Chotda, on the other hand, picked up the basic chords of Sa Re Ga Ma Pa on his guitar and soon graduated to playing movie songs. Every month Mother would ask Father for money for the guitar teacher and every month before handing over the fees Father would invariably ask, 'Have you kept track of his studies? Or is music going to take care of his future? He has three private tutors, for maths, science and English. Do you even know if he goes to them regularly? Till when does he study at night? Sulekha's brothers study till almost ten.' Every month Father usually threw the guitar teacher's fees at Mother's direction: on the table, the bed or even the floor. The three private tutors he usually visited personally to clear their dues.

Try as she might Mother could not understand Father. She was convinced there was no one this complicated in any other family. Sometimes it seemed like all his efforts were for his family alone, that he was willing to give up anything and everything for the sake of his children. Otherwise, it appeared as if he barely cared about anything, that he had a family so people did not talk while all his devotion was singularly meant for Razia Begum. Then there were specific occasions, like when he brought Amanudaulah from Madarinagar to our house, when Mother couldn't help but feel that all his efforts were ultimately for his people back in his village. That day he returned home early from the chamber with nearly double the amount of mutton he would generally get and instructed Mother to cook mutton bhuna with lots of onions.

Plus bottle-gourd greens with broad beans and special thick dal instead of the plain version we had every day. At night he called my brothers and spoke to them.

'How are your studies going? Do you attend your tuitions regularly?'

Head bowed, his toe rubbing the ground beneath his feet, Dada was the first in the line.

'Yes, I do.'

'Studies or playing, which one do you do more?'

'Studies.' Dada knew what he wanted to hear.

'What happens to those who study?'

'They ride cars.'[1] Dada's head was still bowed.

'And you?' repeated Father, his gaze shifting to Chotda.

'They ride cars,' Chotda replied.

I wanted to ask how that could be possible. Father was educated too but he travelled by rickshaws usually. But as was my habit I couldn't voice the question and gulped it down instead.

'Hmm. There's someone new in the house today. Amanudaulah. He's your uncle. Who's he?'

Leaning against one of the pillars Chotda replied, 'He's our uncle.'

'Yes, exactly.'

Pulling Chotda towards him, Father continued, 'This is how you should stand. Straight.' Then he turned towards me.

'And you, come here. Have you seen my brother? Your uncle?'

I nodded a yes.

'Fine, all of you go study now. You can come for dinner when it's ready. Eat with your uncle. He's family. Do you understand?'

Ever the good student, Dada nodded immediately. 'Yes, we understand.'

The storage shed for fuel wood was cleaned up and set up with a bed, a table and a chair for Aman kaka. Father also got him admitted to a college in the city and informed everyone that he was going to be living with us henceforth and that Father was going to be taking care of his expenses.

'We have our own children. How will you manage so many expenses?'

'I will have to. Especially since he's my own brother. I can't very well cast aside my own brother. Besides, his staying here will help you too. You can make him run your errands and get the groceries.'

'The boys are old enough to do those things.' Mother's voice was cold as she replied.

The next day Father came home with a printed cotton saree for her. That night, having put extra khoyer in her paan, Mother put on the new saree and edged close to him in bed. 'The saree is good quality.'

Instead of going into how she was looking in it and so on, Father anxiously inquired, 'Did you give Aman his dinner?'

In a flash it seemed as if something had pierced her heart. Was all his attention only so she would take better care of Aman? Like the way people often gave gifts to their domestic help to ensure they keep serving and stay loyal? Mother couldn't help but feel like a maid working in the house. Father barely cared about what made her happy and what didn't.

Seven days after Aman kaka's arrival Mother informed Father they had been invited to Sulekha's wedding and that she wished to attend. Father's first unequivocal response was a no. Eventually, giving in to her entreaties, he somewhat grudgingly relented and gave her money to buy a gift and go by herself. Mother always put up with all of his oddities of course. Everyone knew she was the doctor's wife, that her cup was full to the brim with joy. Only she knew how the smell of another woman wafting off him had managed to sweep aside all her happiness. Only she knew how despite shamelessly offering herself up to him again and again Father usually kept his distance from her in bed, leaving her alone to wrestle with her demons one sleepless night after another.

So she took Chotda and went to Sulekha's wedding feast, even though she felt nothing but utterly alone there in the midst of a room full of people. That night Father returned late, his tongue red from paan and a merry tune on his lips. He came home and declared he did not wish to have dinner.

'Which woman fed you tonight that you don't want to eat this food?'

'There was an invitation at a patient's house,' Father replied with a laugh.

'A man or a woman?' Mother was curled up like a foetus on the bed.

'A patient is a patient. What man or woman?' Father snapped.

'I know all your tricks. Razia Begum was a patient too, wasn't she? Didn't I drag you back from her bed? You do whatever you want to because I'm so naive,' Mother said through a sigh.

Lying down beside her Father replied, 'I wish I could do whatever I wanted to! Where do I get the chance?'

In the morning Father woke up with a start at the sound of Chotda's guitar and the song he was singing.

Have you ever witnessed
How Life is defeated?
In the fires of despair
And tears of distress
How it wears away bit by bit?
Matching his voice to the tune Father began singing too—
So much news appears in the papers,
Day in and day out,
While so much about Life
Remains entirely unheard.

Entering the room with a plate of rotis and poached eggs, Mother heard him singing and stopped dead in her tracks. Adding to her astonishment Father turned to her and said, 'Kamal plays quite well. He's been singing exactly what I feel. Did you hear it?' Later that morning, before leaving for the hospital, Father called Chotda. 'Where do you learn the guitar? It's almost the end of the month. Don't you need to pay your teacher? How much do you need?' Taking out his wallet he gave some money to Chotda, much to the latter's delight, before continuing. 'Just making music without studying will not do! Music will not feed you. The brain is at its clearest in the morning. From now on study early in the morning. Make a routine if you will. Eat on time, study on time and make music too.'

Father was from a farmer's family of a remote village and had overcome all odds to become a doctor. Mother could not fathom why such a sorrowful song of defeat and loss should affect him so much, given how successful he was. Nothing about him made sense to her. One moment it seemed he was made of stone, the very next he appeared as pliant as earth. That night after Father came back home Mother put on a neatly pleated saree, reddened her lips with paan and, as he sat eating his dinner while she fanned him, asked me to go sleep at Nani's for the night. Usually the prospect of spending the night with Nani was something that never failed to excite me and Mother was well aware of that. So she was quite surprised when I immediately didn't jump at the offer.

'Go sleep with your Nani tonight.'

'No.'

'What? You don't want to go?'

'No,' I replied again, the reply a little more definitive the second time.

'What's the matter? Has someone hurt you? Tutu, Sharaf, or Felu?'

'No,' I repeated again while digging out the putty with my nails from between planks of the railing of the bed.

'No? Then why not?' she insisted, pushing me towards the door.

I stood my ground, clutching the door tightly, the vast dark courtyard stretching out beyond the room.

'I don't know what to do with this girl! Does she even listen to me? I tell her to stay indoors and she wants to go play outside. Just playing, the whole day. Then she gets beat up and starts crying and whining. Look at her, all bones! She eats like a bird! When she was young at least three of us had to hold her down to feed her some milk. No to milk, no to eggs, every passing day she's becoming unrulier. I'm telling you, go sleep in your Nani's room and she doesn't want to go. On other days you would have rushed out by now!'

I remained where I was, not having moved an inch. Mother came closer and softly rubbed my back as her voice softened. 'Go, your uncles will tell you stories. Take the ribbon with you, Jhunu will tie your hair.' Seeing how I was still not moving Father intervened. 'Let it be, if she doesn't want to.' 'Too undisciplined,' Mother countered.

To Mother I was clearly getting weirder by the day. Whenever someone came to the house I would usually run and hide behind her. She could not understand where all my fears, my reticence and my hesitations were coming from. I barely talked, let alone tell stories, although when it came to listening there was none more attentive than me. I listened to myriad stories of myriad people but could never neatly arrange and tell a story on my own. It was the same when it came to reading. *The Frog Prince*, *Thakurmar Jhuli*, the tales of the magical gold and silver sticks that could control demons, when it came to fairy tales, I had read them all. I did not read, I consumed. I was always shy, never knowing how to express my feelings. So I had no way of explaining to her why I wasn't excited by the prospect of spending the night with Nani while listening to stories from my uncles. Faced with her ire all I could do was stare dumbfounded. All the cuffs and beatings and boxed ears that I received through the day, none of it managed to cure me of my reticence. Besides, I was never one for tears anyway. I was born on the twelfth day of Rabiul Awwal. I had not had a morsel of food at Sharmila's apparently because they were Hindus. Neither did I like wearing bindis like Hindu girls did. Perhaps all of these had been signs that I could have been a different person, someone more pious. Unfortunately, I could never even feign any interest in learning Arabic. When it came to sitting with the Qaeda Sipara, all I wished to do was read a fairy tale, draw something, run to railway tracks or play in the fields. I was told time and again not to draw human figures because it was a sin, that I should draw such things only if I had the ability to bring them to life; it did very little to cure me of my fascination with the human form.

One day Mother went to Fajli khala's in-laws' house and brought back a paper with Allah's *ayat* written on a picture of the Prophet's shoes drawn in red; she called it the Na'al Sharif. The paper was put inside a little amulet and hung around my neck to drive away my irrational fears once and for all.

Serpent

I knew it was a sin. What I could not understand was my fascination for drawing people. Whenever Mother would catch me drawing, she would ask me to draw trees and plants, flowers, all of which were safe. If I could not give them life, I could not draw them. Only Allah had the power to give life. 'You ask me to draw trees; trees have life too you know,' I let slip one day. 'Do as I say! Behave yourself!' Mother snapped through gritted teeth, in the midst of tying her hair.

I had to do whatever she told me to, obviously. I had to obey her no matter what. What astounded me was the demand that I had to be able to give life to draw life! I was not *making* life, I was simply drawing a picture. Mother never managed to figure out the difference between the two; she made illogical demands instead, just because she could. And also, because, as we have just established, she was Mother. Despite her repeated warnings when I did draw a human figure again, it was not because I had really wanted to draw it. I had drawn a boat. No one had a problem with how lifeless that was, but they did not fail to point out the boatman I had put in it. As if the boat was supposed to row by itself! Unable to stand it I had been forced to draw a tiny boatman at the stern. Humaira was on a visit to Nani's place; she saw the photo and could not hold back her disapproval. In the evening, after she had left, Mother came and confiscated my crayons and drawing paper. 'That's enough with the drawing; settle down with your studies now.'

As I have already said, I was never the crying kind; I went into a drowsy stupor instead. Mother was lying by the open window. She had unhooked her blouse and was in the process of popping sweat rashes on her chest with her left hand while fanning herself with the right. To her, taking away my colours and stuff was as inconsequential as taking out the trash from the courtyard and throwing it in the dump.

'Read louder. I can't hear you read.' I came to my senses with a start.

And yet, that very night when she drew me close lovingly and cooed to me to join her in reading the namaz, all my anger and indictments were swept aside in an instant. That was how Mother was; she would be scolding or thrashing us one instant and drawing us into her arms the next. Once she had beaten Dada black and blue with a cane and had then massaged his wounds with mustard oil herself.

'If you read the namaz, Allah will love you. He will give you whatever you want.'

Now could there be any greater promise than that! Mimicking Mother's actions as she bent down in prayer, I raised my arms towards Allah and wished for what was in my heart, in my head of course since He would hear my thoughts too: Allah, please give me to two chomchoms from Porabari. However, opening my eyes after the prayers I was crestfallen to discover no sweets had appeared magically in front of me. I looked hither and thither, even under the prayer mat, and then ran to Mother in tearful complaint. 'Allah didn't give me what I asked for.'

'You must not have asked with all your heart.'

After that incident, night after night, I stood beside Mother in namaz and asked for numerous things—a wind-up car, sweets from Muktagachha, a big jar of marbles, a balloon whistle—none of which I got. I did not know how much more heart one had to put in for Allah to hear you. I slowly came to be convinced that I must have committed some great sin. Was it the fact that Sharaf mama had taken me to an empty room and taken my clothes off? Was that why Allah hated me? I was convinced that must have been what it was and the thought made me even more miserable. So that night when Mother asked me to go sleep with Nani in the latter's room, I refused her request because I was afraid of sleeping in the same room as my uncles. Mother had no idea why I was afraid. After that fateful incident, a couple of days later Sharaf mama had called me by the pond to play with magnets. I had not gone and as a result Sharaf mama had smacked me on the head on his way out. On most evenings Tutu mama used to be in his room rehearsing lines as Sirajudaulah. The children too would sit in the room watching him perform and applaud uproariously. Whenever I took a peek inside I found the room dark and I made no further attempts to go in and join the others, gradually growing averse to entering dark rooms altogether. When on moonlit nights Kana mama would be regaling us with stories of Amir Hamza, Sohrab-Rustom, or how he had lost his eye while hunting deer, with the people of the house strewn about around him listening in rapt attention, I sidled really close to Mother. So close, in fact, that she would say, 'Move away a bit. It's too hot.' I would not listen and Mother had to move away a little instead. Immediately I would be afraid; what if someone pulled at my half-pants again.

When Mother went to the movies, I begged her to not go because I was too afraid to be alone. 'There's a house full of people. Why are you afraid?' Mother would snap in retort. She would leave me with Nani and go anyway. Nani cooked the entire day. Seeing me sitting at the entrance of the kitchen and sulking, Nani would come at me like a stray mutt on the road, telling me to go away and not bother her while she worked. Mother would be back usually once the sun had swept past the last steps leading down to the yard. I would stare at the sun and will it to move faster. I cannot begin to tell you how slow the sun usually was!

Stray dogs would roam around the yard, black cats too, as well as crows cawing in the trees. An assortment of vendors and salespersons turned up at the gate throughout the day, people selling mortars and pestles, or the ones who would sell us munchies made of gram flour in exchange for old garments and shoes. Salesmen carrying wooden boxes with glass tops, full of bangles and ribbons, would come and call out. Jhunu khala sat with them under the neem tree and bought bangles, bits of ribbon, or sometimes earrings. Women came too, carrying baskets of bangles on their heads, and the cotton-candy sellers came by with their fluffy pink clouds that melted as soon as you put them in your mouth. Bear wranglers and monkey trainers came by with their dancing bears and monkeys, alongside men in long pointed hats, dressed in red, selling warm chanachur, shaking his stick fitted with ghungroos and calling out to the people of the neighbourhood from time to time in singsong refrain. My aunts would hear the familiar song and run out to him to buy chanachur. Just like him people came by selling nuts and masala puffed rice and every evening my uncles and aunts would get busy sampling and buying their wares. Sharaf

mama would buy nuts, Felu mama would come back inside
with ice cream and I would stand by the well helpless, staring
at all the tasty food with longing.

One day a snake charmer came to the house; my uncles
wanted to see snakes. She set down her basket in the courtyard,
the children standing around her in a wide circle and Nani at
the door of the kitchen. Within moments she had emptied
her basket and snakes slithered out on to the yard: red and
yellow ones, dark cobras and even a huge python. The latter
proceeded to glide across every inch of the yard, a terrifying
and dreadful sight that I had never seen before. I ran in
terror to Phoolbahari, our maid, who was sitting outside the
kitchen smoking a beedi. 'Phoolbahari, I'm scared.' Her dark
face splitting into a smile that revealed stunning white teeth,
Phoolbahari cajoled me. 'What's there to be afraid of? Those
snakes are not venomous. The charmers have removed their
fangs.'

I was still afraid and even long after the snake charmer
had left my fear refused to abandon my side. I was afraid
of walking in the yard, or even the field, afraid that I was
going to step on a snake that would immediately spread its
hood and charge at me. At night in bed I felt as if there
was a snake coiled under the bed, slowly making its way up,
slithering under the pillow and all over my body. If I did
manage to sleep, I dreamt of being surrounded by hundreds
of snakes with their hoods spread and not another soul in
sight, somewhere near the railway tracks or the main road,
or by a pond under the shade of a tree or somewhere in a
locked room. I could hear no other sound except that of
snakes hissing. In such nightmares I cried out for my mother
but there would be no sign of her in the land of serpents I
was trapped in. I would try to roll up into a ball as much as

I could, withdraw into myself and, in the process, I would wake up and hear my heart thundering in my chest. I was already afraid of snakes as well as human beings, and at such times Mother would ask me to go sleep in my uncles' rooms! I had never managed to tell Mother what Sharaf mama had tried to do to me. Some invisible force seemingly had me in its grips, refusing to let the secret out.

Notwithstanding the Na'al Sharif amulet around my neck, fear was my constant companion. After taking new rooms on rent from Nani over about eighteen hundred square feet of land, our daily lifestyle underwent many transformations. A table and chairs found their way into the kitchen where we all sat down to eat thrice a day. Father liked such western etiquettes and it was quite clear that the person we had known before, usually found in pyjamas and loose kurtas on a Hercules bicycle, was no longer who he was. He wore shoes, tucked in his shirt, wore ties around his neck and, at times, even put on a coat over his shirt. Why was such a person going to sit on the floor and eat any more? Likewise, a cane sofa was purchased for the living room. Our house was slowly being made over, while in comparison Nani's house remained in the same rundown state it had previously been in. They could have been eating the same meals as us, but they were still sitting on the floor on a mat and eating it. New furniture was brought in for our studies too but the ritual of sitting with my uncles under the light of the lamp, swaying and doing our lessons, did not seem to be in risk of falling out of favour anytime soon.

I was lying on the bed one day, staring out the window by myself, when I heard a sudden melee. Running to Nani's yard I ran into Felu mama who informed me that a pair of Jhunu khala's earrings were missing. The culprit was yet to be traced. While everyone sized each other up silently, khala dragged me to her room and whispered, 'If you've taken it just give it back to me; I won't tell anyone you did it.' Despite shaking my head vigorously, I could not help but feel a frisson of doubt cloud my mind: Was *I* the one who had taken it? Perhaps I had stolen it and hidden it somewhere, perhaps underground? Even after khala had left me alone I could not shake off a tremor in my heart every time anyone at Nani's house glanced my way. We were informed that *chaal-pora* was going to be administered. The thief was going to eat it and soon begin to vomit blood, thus revealing their identity. Imam Khatibuddin of the Akua Masjid was called to perform the ritual. Chaal-pora involved taking a bowl of uncooked rice and whispering some incantations into it. Then a handful of the charm-infused rice was given to everyone to eat. We each chewed our share silently, glancing at each other from time to time trying to ascertain who was going to be revealed as the thief by the tell-tale sign of blood in their vomit. I was still shaking inside, half expecting to start hurling my guts out any moment; everyone was then going to kneel in front of me and find specks of blood splattered across. They were going to drag me to the muddy yard and tear down all the branches from all the trees in the house to beat me with. I was certain they were also going to find the missing earrings somewhere; perhaps I had hidden it under the coconut tree, or near the stairs of the fuel room or the toilet near the outhouse. Every time I looked at Jhunu khala I felt she was right, that I was indeed the thief. I could see myself only as she saw me; I did not exist any more.

Three people did not participate in the chaal-pora episode: Nana, Sharaf mama and Phoolbahari. The first two were not at home; the latter squared her dark jaw, tucked her saree to her hip and declared that she had not stolen the earrings so she did not feel the need to eat uncooked rice.

'That guy, the one who's giving the chaal-pora, I know him very well. He's a giant scoundrel. I have worked in that maulvi's house, I know his character very well. He'll give me something and I am supposed to eat it? Never!'

She spat as she finished, having had her final say in the matter. 'How dare you call the maulvi a scoundrel, Phoolbahari? It's blasphemy!' Mother shot back with a rebuke.

Phoolbahari was lean and dark, like a fine shoot of bamboo slick with oil. Her face was marked with scars of pox, her lips were black from smoking beedis. She kept beedis tucked away behind her ear as she ground spices, did the dishes, cleaned and dusted the house; only then would she lean back against the kitchen wall and light one up.

Phoolbahari's defiance in the face of the maulvi's chaal-pora was all the proof everyone needed to be convinced that she was truly the thief. Runu khala suggested, since the culprit was not willing to eat the rice, that we try *baati-chalan* instead. Zubeda Khatun, Kana mama's wife, was summoned at once. A brass bowl coated with firm mud had to be placed in the centre of the courtyard. Once touched by a Virgo, the bowl was going to move on its own and stop only once it reached the thief. As ordained, guided by Zubeda Khatun, the miracle bowl roamed the nooks and crannies of the house and then entered the kitchen to finally come to rest near Phoolbahari's feet. She was in the middle of grinding spices when everyone following the bowl barged into the kitchen all at once. Hasem mama's voice rang out,

'Phoolbahari, return the earrings.'

Hissing like a black cobra, her own cheap gold-coloured earrings glistening, Phoolbahari replied, 'I didn't take it. You're calling me a thief because I'm poor. Being poor doesn't make someone a thief. If I wanted to steal I would've done that and not come to work. Your bowl is wrong.'

'She who speaks too brashly and lumbers like a lout, she who's of the road born and dies thereabout,' Runu khala opined, poking her. No one was willing to accept that the brass bowl could have been fallible. Nani intervened. 'Phoolbahari, return the earrings. Tell us where they are and we will go get them.'

With her turmeric-stained hands raised in the air, Phoolbahari bit out through her paper-dry, smoke-blackened lips, 'One of you must have taken them. I haven't.' Hardly had she finished the retort when Mother lunged at her, grabbing her by the hair and dragging her to the mango tree on the courtyard in front of the kitchen, while Phoolbahari struggled in vain to hold on to solid ground, what with her head being pulled in the other direction. Tutu mama grabbed a half-burnt piece of wood from the hearth and began hitting her with it. The beedi tucked away behind her ear fell and was crushed underneath her as she rolled around in the yard in pain, screaming her lungs out. 'Phoolbahari isn't a thief.'

Phoolbahari was dismissed that very day. As she was limping away from the house, I felt even more certain that she had been telling the truth, that the bowl had been wrong.

The very next day a middle-aged woman from the slums nearby was employed as her replacement. Toitoi, alias Noorjahan. Noorjahan had a few ducks and every evening she used to call them home with cries that sounded sort of like *toi . . . toi*. The ducks would hear her, waddle up from the pond and follow her home quacking. This daily ritual, shattering the lazy dusk settling in gradually around us, inspired Tutu mama to name her Toitoi; the name stuck for everyone except Nani. A short woman with paan-stained teeth, Toitoi alias Noorjahan alias Khalek's mother became our new part-time maid. Besides the usual roster of grinding spices, doing the dishes and cleaning, she was also the cook for our separate family of six, all for a monthly salary of five taka and the promise of a meal once a day.

It was not difficult those days to get maids to work at your house part-time or full-time. The slums were only a few steps away and willing women were in no short supply. If one went away there was always another waiting to take her place. Phoolbahari was accused of theft and dismissed. Toitoi was accused of being insincere about her work and let go. What was the evidence behind such a pronouncement? That she usually went back home as soon as it was evening, probably because of her two young sons and a dozen ducks.

'Toitoi has no interest in working. I have to do all the cooking for the night by myself. I can't do without a full-time maid.' Mother declared to Nani one day. 'Why don't you wait and see a few more days? Noorjahan seems decent. Doesn't seem like a thief,' Nani advised instead, but nothing she had to say could convince Mother otherwise. Handing Toitoi two and a half taka for the half month she had been employed at our place Mother informed her that her services would no longer be required and a new person was soon going to replace her.

No one was particularly perturbed by Toitoi's departure. As I may have mentioned, there were no dearth of women in the slums.

In Toitoi's absence Mother had no choice but to do the chores in the kitchen all by herself: starting the fire, cutting the vegetables, cleaning and cooking the fish and the meat. Looking around for a matchbox to get the fire going she failed to locate one in the vicinity. This job had been Phoolbahari's or Toitoi's, they were the ones who knew where the matchboxes were generally kept.

'Go get a matchbox from Amanudaulah,' she said to me, the very day Toitoi was dismissed. Mother knew Aman kaka would have one; she had seen him smoke. Kaka had been given the woodshed to stay in, the same dilapidated room Sharaf mama had taken me to on that fateful afternoon. Pushing the door open my eyes fell on Aman kaka lying on the bed. He resembled Father in many ways: fair, curly hair, a strong aquiline nose, big eyes and thick, dark eyebrows. If Father could be flattened with a brick and shortened a bit, that would have been Aman kaka. I looked around and found the room had undergone a complete transformation. There was no stack of wood or any rats to be seen. There was a photo hanging on the tin wall, of kaka himself in a pair of pumps and combed wavy hair. On its right was hanging a calendar with a woman's photo on it. A small mirror and a comb were tucked into the tin wall and unfolded clothes were piled on the clothes rack.

'Kaka, Ma is looking for a match,' I was staring at the calendar as I spoke. He got off the bed, his fingers scratching the hair on his chest and asked, 'Why does your mother need a matchbox?'

'To light the fire. To cook.'

'I don't have a match.'

I was already turning to leave when he grabbed my hand and pulled me back inside. 'Wait, I have matches. Take them, I have them,' he said through a toothy smile.

Almost as if by magic a match box appeared in front of my eyes. When I tried to take it from him, he snatched it away suddenly; for the next couple of minutes he kept doing it every time I made a move to take it from him. Now I could see it, now I could not, and this went on as if it was some sort of a game. As I stepped closer to him for leverage, he suddenly took hold of me and pulled me closer to him. Instead of handing over the matchbox he began to tickle me, on my stomach and under my arms, using it as a distraction to pull me to the bed. I curled up like a snail and my uncle picked up my scrunched-up body and tossed it up in the air as if I was no more than a plaything. His hands crept down my body to my half-pants, pushing them down my feet. Trying to roll over I could feel myself slipping off the bed till my feet were on the ground and my back was still on the bed. My pants were bunched near my knees which were hanging in the air, the Na'al Sharif amulet still hanging around my neck. Kaka pulled up his lungi and my eyes fell on a giant snake below his belly, its hood spread wide and poised to strike. The more I shrank in fear the more the snake tried to scare me, beginning to strike me between my thighs. One strike . . . two . . . three . . .

My body was frozen in fear. Staring at my startled eyes kaka suddenly asked, 'Do you want candy? I will buy you candy. Here, take the matchbox. And listen sweetheart, don't tell anyone that you saw my peepee and I have seen your coochie. These are bad things; we mustn't talk about them with anyone.'

I left the room silently with the matchbox in my hand. I could feel a pain between my legs; I wanted to pee but then I noticed I had already peed my pants. I did not know what these naked games were called. I could not understand why Sharaf mama or Amam kaka wanted to climb on top of me. Kaka had told me not to tell anyone anything. I was convinced that he was right. Even at seven years of age something inside me had taken hold that kept telling me that these were shameful things that one should never tell anyone about, that these were dirty secrets.

I still haven't figured out why I never told anyone in the house about these two incidents. Perhaps because I did not want anyone to say anything bad about either of my uncles. Had anyone tasked me with preserving their dignity in the family? Not really, it was simply a reaction to all the lessons I was taught as a child about respecting my elders, come what may. Since I had been told they were good men, that meant the most above all else. Whatever happened, the truth was not the truth at all; it was a lie or a bad dream, or a ruse perpetrated by someone who resembled these two men. Had anyone robbed me of my voice or asked me to suffer in silence? Yet again, not really. It was just that I was afraid everyone in the house was going to say I was possessed by a djinn, or I was crazy, a liar or a sneaky rascal. I was afraid no one was going to take me in their arms and love me any more, that they were going to beat me up instead. Or was it because there was no one to call my own who I could have spoken to, who I could have shown my wounds or shared my grief and tears with? If I could not even trust Mother, who was my world, a tree spread out above me under whose shade I found succour, a glassy pond whose waters sustained me, then was there anyone else I could have had faith in?

Two contrasting personalities were jostling for space inside me back then. The first one that never tired from playing *opentee* bioscope, gollachut and a host of other games with her friends. And the other that of a girl who often found herself sitting alone and miserable, by the pond, by the railway tracks or even on the stairs of our home, lonely amidst a hundred people. Gradually this girl came to grow so far apart from everyone else around her that even when she tried, she could not reach across the chasm and touch anyone, not even her mother. Every time she spread out her hands, she came away with fists filled with emptiness.

Pirbari 1

Our stint at Akua came to an end around the final months of 1969. We left the home we had known so far—the tiny pond full of fish beside the dirt track that led to Nani's house, bordered by neem, date, betel-nut and karoi trees, the courtyard and the well, a row of coconut trees and another yard further ahead, the bedroom on the southern end with a toilet alongside the stairs leading up to it, the dining room to the west with another small yard past it, the small red shack between Dada's room and the fuel shed where fuel used to be stocked after Amal kaka came to live with us—and moved to a huge house in Amlapara. In this new house there were switches to control the lights and fans and the rooms were huge with tall pillars holding them up. It was almost like a king's palace; the king and his people had abandoned it and we had found it and moved in instead. The huge glass windows—red, blue, yellow and purple-hued—were all taller than me. A flight of thirty-eight steps led from the rooms to the wide courtyard while the walls had a row of tiny alcoves like the ones they have in temples. Father later had all the alcoves filled up and also had the stairs replaced with a long wide veranda. He had seen alcove-less walls and long porches in the house of one of our neighbours, M.A. Kahhar, an influential man. I can now hazard a guess that he must have wanted to turn our house into something similar. Father always kind of wilted when in the presence of someone rich or influential, as if everything to do with them was a great thing, even their awkwardly huge terraces. Regardless, it was not always easy to predict what Father was going to do next. For instance, one day a truck would suddenly arrive at our doorstep laden with sand, cement and bricks. Seeing it we could usually guess some construction was imminent but there never was any way of knowing what was going to happen until it was done. None of us had any idea about what went on in our father's head! Our house was the tallest among all the houses in the neighbourhood, the I-could-touch-the-blue-sky-from-the-roof kind of tall. Chotda and I spent a night there alone, the day before we were supposed to move in with furniture. Chotda had his guitar with him, which he played till late in the night, with me lying on the yellow jacket of the guitar and listening. Every word uttered in the empty house seemed to echo back to us seven times, as if seven princes of the erstwhile king were hiding behind seven secret walls of the house and repeating every word back at us, mocking us. The house was surrounded by coconut and betel-nut trees while the courtyard had nearly thirty species of fruits and flowers. For quite some time I could not believe that such a huge mansion belonged to us.

Right after we shifted to Amlapara three things happened in quick succession. A burglar broke into the house by breaking the grills on one of the windows and made away with money and jewellery. Mother saw Father on a rickshaw with Razia Begum, passing by the Alaka Hall one day. And Dada and his friends started a journal called *Pata* ('Pages'), containing short stories, poems, riddles and a myriad other things. Therein, he wrote a poem called 'Ramdhanu' ('The Rainbow') and had it printed in my name: Nasrin Jahan Taslima, even though Jhunu khala had shortened my name to Taslima Nasrin while getting me admitted into Bidyamoyi School. Dada said to me one day—

'I'm getting another poem published under your name in the next issue.'

I could scarcely contain my joy. 'Then I will write it myself!'

'Right! As if you can write poetry!' Dada laughed.

Joy transformed into gloom within a matter of seconds. Gathering up a handful of jamuns in the folds of my skirt I ran up to the roof, uncaring of the juices staining my clothes purple. All I could think of was poetry. That day onwards, whenever Dada would not be at home, I used to raid the drawers of his study table, take out his book of poetry and almost devour the poems in it, all the while wishing I could write like him!

Not long after moving in, Father purchased a music-recording machine, weighing almost a tonne and a half, from an acquaintance who had just returned from Germany. Dada brought his friends over to show the new machine off, not forgetting to drop the 'Made in Germany' tag in the middle of the conversation. Forever an admirer of Hitler, Dada's adoration for the machine that had been imported from the Fuehrer's country knew no bounds. The friends could barely hide their amazement either. Hitherto they had only heard and seen the HMV (His Master's Voice) record players. This new machine had large round disks with tape wound around it, the tape of one disk rolling on to the other. It was not long before many of the friends returned, this time to get their voices recorded on the tape: Narayan

Sanyal with his one-man show, Pintu and his guitar, Mahbub with his open-voiced renditions of Nazrulgeeti. I was relegated to watching all this from behind the curtains of the door, having been forbidden to go anywhere near the recorder. Dada recorded Rabindranath and Nazrul's poems recited in his deep, baritone. The records, once released to public, made him a fairly well-known name in the city in no time. Songs of Hemanta Mukherjee, Satinath Mukherjee or Manna Dey would be playing while Dada and Chotda hunched over the machine all day long. All I longed to do was touch it just once, but Dada would shoo me away with a warning.

'Don't touch anything! Stand there and watch.'

So whenever Dada would be away from home I used go and fiddle with the machine. If Yasmin were to come up behind me with like I used to, I would shoo her away echoing Dada's warnings to me.

'Stand there and watch. Don't touch anything!'

She did as I asked. A few buttons pressed and music would start playing on its own. I would lie down, one foot over another, and listen to the music. I wanted to be Dada so bad!

Because of the burglary in the house a new rule had been implemented that all doors and windows had to be kept shut at all times. That meant even if we were about to boil to death, we were not allowed to open the windows to let some cool air in. Father had the broken window repaired and the rest fortified with three extra bars, like a cell in a prison, long and uneven. The rooms were consigned to perpetual darkness; even during the day the lights had to be kept on for us to study or eat. We were like rats, foraging about in a dark, dank house.

Ever since she had seen Father with Razia Begum, Mother had taken to her bed and cast aside everything, from cooking and housework to taking showers and eating regular meals. She even moved rooms, shifting her things from Father's room to another. One look at her and anyone would have suspected she was ailing from some serious disease: hair unkempt, uncombed, her body dotted with heat rash, the sweat-stained saree sticking to her frame. She remained like that throughout the day, waiting for Father to come back home at night when she would begin wailing in a high-pitched voice, railing about her misfortunes.

'There he is! He's come back after being with her the whole day. Is that why you bought such a huge house? So you can marry her and bring her here?'

Father never responded to anything she said. It was as if he never heard anything or did not realize someone was saying something to him. As if the only sounds in the room were that of cats meowing or dry wood sputtering in the oven. He would pretend not to notice her standing in front of him screaming ceaselessly, walking around instead asking after the children, the pets or the help. A new maid, Moni, had been hired from the slums behind Nani's house and he would summon her to serve him dinner. He would finish eating, comb his hair, sleek with mustard oil, in front of the mirror and walk out. Mother remained in the vicinity, cursing his forefathers to damnation.

'My father gave you the money to study and become a doctor. Or else what would you've been today? A farmer's son would have been a farmer. You had married me for the money. And now that you have money of your own, you want to leave me and fool around with someone else's wife? Allah will destroy you, your streak will not last and we'll see what happens to that pride of yours! I curse you, if you truly owe my father a debt, then Allah will teach you a lesson for the pain you are causing me. Your entire line and those to come will die as lepers!'

For Mother it was a foregone conclusion that it was only a matter of days before Father married Razia Begum and brought her home. As a result, whenever she was so incensed few dared to get in her way. One day, during one such bout of angry yelling, I let slip all of a sudden, 'Why do you scream so much? This is not Akuapara any more you know!' Mother lunged at me like a crashing storm and pulled me by the hair so hard that the chair I was sitting on toppled over behind me, keeling me over awkwardly against the wall. She pulled me around like a top, slapped me across both cheeks and let out a coarse scream. 'What did you say, you bastard? Has your father even looked at you ever? And now you're siding with him? But then of course you will. You carry the same blood, right? That scoundrel's blood! You have been troubling me since birth, you spawn of evil. My luck ran out after you were born. Why didn't I put salt down your throat and end you in the nursery itself?'

There she was, my own mother wondering why she had not killed me in the nursery itself. I was crying but she scarcely was in the mood to notice any of that.

With time Mother's abuses began to grow coarser. Her heat rash was back in full force and there were dark and heavy bags under her eyes. Not just Father, her anger was directed at everyone in the house. Her children were her mortal enemies, as were the domestic help. Whenever Moni served her food, she would pick up the plate and fling it outside, convinced that someone was plotting to poison her. When my aunts came to visit from Nani's house, she would sit them down and describe to them how she had seen Father and Razia Begun clinging to each other on the rickshaw. She would cry pitifully and lament how she had once dreamt of starting over with a new life in a new house.

In time all of us got used to this cycle of abuse in our lives in some way or the other. That our mother was going to hurl whatever abuses she could think of at our father who rarely made a sound in retort. When it happened all of us would generally be at our study table, trying to very hard to unsee and unhear things. I usually chose that time to do the most complex mathematical problems; the one good thing about maths was that you were allowed to scribble on the margins. People saw me hard at work and usually thought I was facing a particularly tricky sum, while in reality I would be far away from them watching seagulls by the water somewhere on the edge of a vast and desolate plain under an overcast sky. I would dream about the place, make doodles on the margins and quickly scribble over them whenever anyone came by. No one knew, not even my parents.

It was one such evening. Father had just returned. Having barely loosened the knot of his tie, he was yet to freshen up and change when Mother began.

'There, he's back! He's had his fill of that other woman finally. Bloody letch. Characterless!'

All of a sudden Father bellowed and lunged towards the direction of Mother's room.

'What do you think you're about, woman? You live under my roof; you eat my food and yet how dare you abuse me?'

His roar had stopped me in my tracks, fingers holding the pen over the doodles on the margins trembling slightly, the rest of the hand shaking too. The spell broke with a start at the sound of Mother's screams coming from within. I ran to her room and barely had I reached the door when I was met with a terrifying scene. I had never seen a tiger leap to attack its prey but that day I could swear it was probably how my father lunged at my mother, pulled her by the hair, threw her to the ground and started kicking her. He was wearing thick BATA boots, the tie hanging a little loose around his neck than a while before. Mother was trying to shield herself from the blows by receding under the bed but somehow not managing it. I stood by the door watching, Dada, Chotda and Yasmin standing behind me silently, a tiny swarm of silent rats standing and watching their mother bleeding from the nose and the mouth and screaming for help.

'Help me! Please help me! He's going to kill me.'

None of us dared go even a step further. Mother was groaning on the floor, urine beginning to pool around her.

'Will you ever call me names again? I'll kill you today,' he screamed through laboured pants.

'I won't, I beg of you let me go,' she pleaded, her hands joined in request sitting half-naked on the wet floor.

The boots turned around, scattering the rats here and there. Father walked off in the direction of his room. Mother spent the rest of the night on the floor, crying silently. I was desperate to crawl next to her, rub her back and tell her not to cry, assure her that I was going to avenge this humiliation, but I was too afraid to do any of those things. I spent half the night hunched over my maths copy and then went to bed without dinner, only to dream that I was leaving the house and going far away somewhere, to another unblemished life elsewhere.

Soon after this incident Hasem mama ambushed Father on the road one day and beat him half to death. Then he dragged Father home like a sack of sand and left him with a

warning that if he ever touched Mother again, he was going
to be fed to the dogs. The iron-clad man that my father was,
even he had to spend close to a week lying in bed trying to
recover from the beating. Through those seven days, Moni
dutifully served him food. He called me to him every day
and asked me to concentrate on my studies so I could grow
up to be someone. On the last day, the day he was to finally
get out and about again, it was a holiday too, he called me
to him in the afternoon and said, 'Learn up all your books,
just like a parrot. You must rank first in your class. The ones
who get the top marks in your class, don't they eat the same
food that you do? Then why won't it be the same with you?
Are you any less smart than they are? Tell me!' Standing
near his head, all I could do was shake my head in denial.
Although I always suspected that I *was* a tad less smart than
other people, it was hardly something I could tell my father.
With him it was best I said what he wished to hear.

'Will you comb through my hair with your fingers?' His
voice was soft and tender. I edged closer to the railings of the
bed and did as he asked, my fingers working through his hair
like an automaton while my yearning gaze remained locked
outside; out in the yard, the sunlight was dancing on the
silvery surface of the water in the tank where we washed our
hands and feet. I wanted to jump in, throw my limbs around
and swim. Alas, there was no place I could actually swim
to in a tiny square tank. All my imaginary ramblings had
to eventually find their way back to the tank, the same old
yard and the guava tree, and this house where everyone could
order me around. Like a rat wounded in a skirmish with a
cat, my fingers combed through Father's hair.

When he called me time and again, I had to answer with
a *ji*. When elders called you, you had to answer with a ji,

that was what I had been taught by Mother. A simple yes or something on similar lines was considered a serious breach of etiquettes. As it was, Mother used to worry incessantly that I did not know the rules of social behaviour too well. On Eid morning children were expected to touch the feet of their elders and seek their blessings. I could never do it willingly and Mother used to push me to touch Father's feet. Nevertheless, I would stand unmoving at the threshold, unwilling to touch anyone's feet whatsoever.

'Pull my hair a bit harder,' his voice was imploring.

Father had a full head of thick, black, curly hair. As I tried pulling harder my hands came away from the roots caked in drying blood, like course black sand. For an instant I was assailed by the fear that Father was going to die. What if he turned over and died on the bed itself? I was going to be pulling his hair when I would suddenly realize he was no longer breathing. I would remain standing there, night and day, but Father was no longer going to tell me to let it be and go do my studies. So I could grow up and become someone.

By the time I heard Father's soft rhythmic snores, the sunlight had passed over the tank and was grazing the crown of the guava tree. He was finally asleep and it did not matter if I stopped massaging his hair. Having come to that decision I turned towards the door to make a stealthy escape only to come face to face with Mother standing outside holding a glass of lemonade. Out of everyone's earshot she whispered to me, 'Go give this to your father.'

'He's asleep,' I whispered back.

'Doesn't matter. He'll have it once he wakes up. Lemonade is your father's favourite!'

Ever the obedient daughter I did as I was told and left the glass of cold lemonade on the little table beside

Father's bed. Her hair tied in a bun, head covered with the simple printed saree she had on, Mother was standing at the door watching Father's sleeping form with a tender look in her eyes. Presently she slipped in, walked up to the bed and lovingly began to stroke Father's hair.

That was all the sign I needed to know my part was done. Soon enough I found myself on the roof, eating guavas and watching girls from the neighbourhood playing gollachut on the courtyard of Prafulla's house. It was not possible to play in our yard, especially with Father staying home at a stretch. Everyone had to be within his reach when he was home. I was about to finish off the guava with one final bite when I heard Father calling me from downstairs. I ran down the stairs straight to his room to see what my next chore was going to be.

'Who left this here?' His roar left no doubt that he meant the lemonade.

'Mother,' I replied softly, my eyes downcast.

'Why did she? Did I ask for it?' he barked, in an annoyed and irritated voice that left little doubt that he wanted to soundly thrash me for my transgression. His anger was met with absolute silence at my end.

'Throw it out into the yard,' he ordered dispassionately.

Yet again I did as I was asked, pouring the lemonade over the roots of the guava tree.

'Tell everyone to stay out of my room. Tell them I don't want to see anyone's face. Nor do I want any food. I know there's a plot to poison me. I don't want my enemies living in this house.'

The silence stretched out further at my end.

The next day Fajli khala dropped by. She consoled Mother profusely and, tears threatening to spill over from her eyes, gave her urgent advice. 'Let go of the affairs of the world, Borobu. Stop watching films, stop doing things that are wrong. Free yourself of the ties of the family, your husband, even your children; give yourself up to the service of Allah. That is where peace lies.'

Since that day, whenever she needed to search for peace, Mother turned firmly away from the cinemas and turned towards Allah instead. The path towards Allah went via Naumahal, via the house of Fajli khala's in-laws. Her father-in-law Amirullah, a non-Bengali Muslim, was a teacher in a madrasa. He had left his birthplace in Medinipur, in present-day West Bengal, during the Partition and moved to East Bengal. He had had the jungles of Hajibari in Naumahal cleared and built a single-storeyed house where he had moved in permanently with his family. During his early days in East Bengal he had even worked as a peon in the municipal offices, leaving his job later and taking to teaching the Quran and the hadith to the people in the neighbourhood. Soon his new disciples had begun to present him with *hadiya*— anyone passing on the words of the Lord and His Prophet to the people had to be given alms because it pleased Allah and ensured entry into Paradise—as was the custom. Fajli khala's entry into Amirullah's house had happened with the abruptness of a shooting star. Their matchmaker, out searching for a suitable bride for Amirullah's son Musa, had found his way to Nani's ramshackle palace by the pond and it was in that house, seated on one of the iron chairs, that he had decided that his quest was about to come to an end. Hearing descriptions of the potential bride's beauty from the matchmaker, Amirullah had turned up at Nani's place with his son and a giant pot of rosogollahs the very next day in order to meet Fajilatunnesa. Fajli khala had been in school but the others in the house had wasted no time in plastering themselves against the holes on the tin walls to observe the two strange men in white robes speaking in three different languages. After Fajli khala had returned from school she had been met with the sight of two strangers in her living room ogling at her unabashedly. She had run inside but Amirullah had seen all that he had needed to. He had scarcely seen anyone better and he had held Nana's hand for permission to have the nikah ceremony immediately, and let the social formalities follow in due time.

Nani had heard from within and wanted to intervene. She had signalled to her husband from beyond the curtains but he had perhaps known what her stand was going to be and studiously ignored her calls. In fact, Nani was not an irrational person nor was she the sort that did things out of fancy. She had been in no mind to suddenly force her daughter, who had just come back from school without any knowledge of what was happening at home, into taking vows of marriage. But Nana had paid no heed to her disapproval and promptly agreed to Amanullah's demands, eager to forge a union with the holy man.

Fajli khala had been found from somewhere in the neighbourhood, wrapped in a red saree and brought to her wedding. Boromama had been so upset that he had refused to participate, gone and sought refuge under the big tree in the courtyard that Mother used to say was haunted but which, nonetheless, bore the sweetest fruits. Boromama used to be Fajli khala's tutor and within three years she could have passed her matriculation exam and gone to college. Instead, Nana had decreed that women did not need to study so much and more or less forced the marriage. The tea and biscuits served to them had been left untouched as an overjoyed Amirullah had immediately set about initiating the nikah ceremony for both the bride and groom in separate rooms, against a *kabin* (marriage contract) worth six hundred taka. Unable to do anything Nani had pleaded with him to at least increase the sum of money but Nana had shut her up saying it was not right to haggle with men of faith.

The formal wedding feast was held a few days later and soon after the weeping bride was put in a palanquin and sent off to her new home with her husband. How Boromama had cried that day! Then later, three years after Fajli khala's rushed wedding, when Boromama too was married off just suddenly—Nana had told him they were going on a trip and then sprung the news on him later—to the extremely fair, large and slightly provincial Halima, Nani had cried just the same. Boromama was the most educated among everyone in the house and Nani had dreamt her eldest becoming someone great like a judge or a barrister after further studies. After the wedding Nana had chopped off the haunted tree in the yard so that djinns would not be able to harm his fair daughter-in-law. Not that I saw any of this; all this was years before I was born.

Fajli khala had been a fairly social person, she used to be out and about the neighbourhood the whole day, sharing and gathering titbits of information. Amirullah had married her off to his son and set about to turn her into a good wife, *tasbih* in hand and head covered, to begin with. Walls surrounded the house so no stranger could catch a glimpse of the new woman in the house and Amirullah himself had taught her scriptural dictums regarding seeking happiness and fulfilment through serving one's husband and in-laws. In turn, his daughter-in-law had learnt everything and made sure to let it be known that she was perfectly fine with compliance under his roof.

And it was the roof of God! It was a place where Allah himself descended from time to time to converse with His beloved devotee. The trees in the garden were infested with djinns who had begun possessing Fajli khala quite frequently after she moved in. At times the invading entity stayed a couple of days, at times it stayed a week. When Amirullah himself exorcised her, it would finally give up and she would fall on the floor with a thud, a sure sign of a djinn leaving someone's body.

When thus possessed Fajli khala stopped covering her head and frequently went out of the house on her own without a burqa, she would chat up random strangers on the road and speak gibberish with them. Once she had apparently run into her husband near Naumahal and asked him, 'Musabhai, where are you off to? Do you want some nuts?'

Getting rid of the djinn was quite the affair too! They usually had to drag her back home and lock her in the darkest room of the house. Then Amirullah would enter with a stick.

'Why do you bother us so?'

'I don't like anything. All I want to do is roam around the city. I want to have nuts, and some chomchom from Porabari. Hee hee hee!

It was not Fajli khala speaking of course, it was a djinn named Sharafat. It was Sharafat possessing her and it was he who was making her do and say things: uncovering her head, baring her breasts, dancing provocatively and saying whatever she felt like. Fajli khala could not have been so wilfully shameless, so brazen, by herself.

Amirullah softened his voice to try and persuade the uninvited visitor.

'We have never harmed you. Why are you bent on causing us so much trouble? Let my daughter-in-law go. She is so very pious. They don't make them like her any more. Don't torment her further, release her.'

In response Falji khala sprang up on the bed and began dancing, singing as she swayed. '*Ai tobo sohochori, haathe haathe dhori dhori*'.[1]

Amirullah lowered his head rather than witness his daughter-in-law dancing. 'I know how to get rid of the likes of you,' his voice hardened. Fajli khala jumped off the bed, pulled up her saree till her ankles and began twirling, balanced on her heels. 'What can you even do to me?' she twinkled with mirth. The muscles on Amirullah's cheeks hardened.

'You're crossing all limits.'

'Yes, I will. I will do whatever I want to. If you try and stop me, I will kill all of you. I will hack you all with a bnoti. You don't know me yet,' she screamed and thrashed her limbs around.

Amirullah grasped the stick he was holding tighter and as she thrashed about, he raised it and began swinging, hitting her blindly on the head, the neck, her back. Fajli khala had never been beaten up. Nana had struck her on the back once for sleeping with her head on a book she was meant to be reading. The very next day he had taken her to Porabari and fed her as many chomchoms as she could eat. Feeling her bones break, Fajli began to plead.

'I won't do it again. Let me go please!'

'Tell me you will leave her,' Amirullah was panting from his efforts.

'Yes, I will. I promise I will.' Fajli khala bent over flat on the floor at his feet.

'What is your name?'

'Sharafat.'

'Where do you live?'

'On the neem tree.'

No sooner did the words escape her lips than Fajli khala felt the world reel as she lost consciousness. She lay there like that for a long time, unmoving. Then just as suddenly she sat up straight, shook her head and, seeing her father-in-law nearby, pulled her saree over her head. 'What is it, Abbaji? Why is the room so dark?' Without waiting for an answer, she got up and headed straight to wash up. 'I haven't yet set out the water for Abbaji to perform wudu and it's so late already!' As she went about her chores everyone in the family who had gathered in the courtyard heaved a sigh of relief as the djinn-possessed woman turned back into the good housewife right in front of their eyes.

The djinn named Sharafat used to return to torment Fajli khala time and again. Otherwise, she was a pious and dutiful housewife who did not laugh out aloud and the covering on her head never slipped. Sometimes the exorcism left dark marks on her back. Black welts on smooth-white skin, like blemishes on the surface of the moon.

Fajli khala stopped stroking Mother's hair, wiped the tears from her own eye and resumed the advice she had been imparting.

'That is where peace lies, Borobu. Come to Abbaji's gatherings, listen to the stories of Allah and the Prophet. That is what will serve you in the end. Worldly affairs will be gone in the blink of an eye.'

That is all Mother wanted, to get rid of all ties to worldly affairs. So that no matter what Father did, it would not matter to her, so she could immerse herself in thoughts of Allah and forget everything else.

'Borobu, if Abbaji can leave a word about you in front of Allah, He will surely save you from the confines of the grave. Crossing the bridge of Siraat will be a breeze then. During Judgement on the field of Hashr don't you want the balance to be heavier in your favour? If you don't free yourself of these ties what will you take with yourself to the afterlife?'

Mother nodded. She could not agree more. She had nothing for herself for the Day of Judgement. She had begun faltering on the daily five-prayer schedule and the Quran was on the shelf gathering dust as well. She was suddenly overtaken by an unsettling fear: her worldly life was already in a shambles, what is something similar happened in the afterlife too!

Fajli khala finished her advice, had lunch with rice and a big fat piece of fish, put on her burqa and went back home to her in-laws, to the house built on the erstwhile jungles of Hajibari in Naumahal. From the very next day, no sooner did she finish breakfast than Mother would be seen putting on her burqa to go out. Where to? Naumahal, that's where. Weeks passed, then months, until it became firmly ensconced in her daily routine. No one had anything to say. The four of us would sit at the dining table or the sofa or in the veranda and watch Mother gradually fade into the distance. When Naumahal beckoned there was hardly anything that could get in her way. It was like an addiction, an addiction for Allah and it was much stronger than opium.

Around a month later, triggered no doubt by something, Mother—wearing an unkempt saree under the burqa, her hair all over the place—grabbed me just as I had stepped out to play and said, 'Come with me.' I was always delighted to go out of the house; there was hardly anything at home that could match up to the joy of a rickshaw ride in the balmy breeze. I was still of the age when I was allowed to wear half-pants, which meant I had no pyjamas of my own except the ones that were part of the school uniform. That was paired with a long shirt. The white scarf of the uniform that usually had to be folded and tucked into the belt was spread out and used as a headscarf and to cover my chest, although there was nothing really to cover there yet, to be honest. Having finished dressing me appropriately we hailed a rickshaw and set off. I could not help but feel discomfited but there was no way I was going to upset Mother and disrupt our plans of going out. Passing by film posters, signboards of shops and myriad kinds of people on the road when we finally reached Naumahal, it was not where I had been expecting to reach. I had been hoping the rickshaw was going to take us further, far away somewhere.

Pir Amirullah's house had over the years grown and spread to become some sort of a small city. There were a large number of small rooms spread over a large area; the tallest one, raised above the others and whitewashed, belonged to the Pir. Ever since becoming his disciple Mother had stopped calling him by familial monikers, instead choosing to refer to him as 'huzur' because the Pir was supposedly beyond all human ties. Her first task once she entered the house was to go and touch his feet irrespective of what state he was in, asleep, eating or in the midst of his ablutions. This was the rule not just for my mother but for everyone else in that house, whether one had to go start the fires in the kitchen or read the namaz or even go answer nature's call, it had to be done after touching his feet for permission. This was primarily because he was favoured by Allah so much; not just favoured, he was a messenger of Allah and it was a well-known fact that Allah often came down to earth to meet His messengers. Consequently, everyone knew that Amirullah often met with Allah, but no one knew exactly where and when the meetings happened. Mother suspected it happened deep in the middle of the night and that the conversation usually happened in Arabic. To her Arabic was the language of Allah Himself and she was convinced that if she were to learn the language then she too would be able to converse with Him regarding her afterlife. Such was her keenness to learn the language that she would stare hungrily at anyone who knew how to speak Arabic, her greed for Paradise wafting off her in waves. Her eyes would automatically close in reverence whenever it dawned on her that Amirullah was often visited by none other than Allah in the depths of the night. Pleasing Amirullah meant the latter could ensure that Allah forgave her for her many sins. And how she needed to be forgiven, especially for how often she used to run to the cinema or the *jatra*! Could Allah ever forgive such a sinner! Having sought the Pir's blessings Mother sat down on the floor of his room and let loose the tears she had been holding back. They flowed unchecked, moistening her cheeks, rolling down her neck and soaking her clothes. Fajli, her fat, pink lips dry and peeling like paper, put her hand on Mother's shoulder and began to placate her in a perfectly cold voice. 'Why won't Allah forgive you? Seek refuge with him. He is graceful and kind and great and I'm sure He will forgive you. Allah doesn't turn away when hands are raised towards Him in prayer.'

Mother was not the only one so preoccupied with how to please Amirullah. There was a horde of young women as eager to carry out his wishes. Each day, post afternoon tea and snacks, there began a tussle among these women, my mother included, as to who was going to massage which part of the wise man's body as he attempted to rest. Mother was usually keen about the legs; whenever she got them her face would light up with joy and a smile would appear on her lips. Feet were dirty and as per her if she was willing to massage something like that then it clearly showed that even the great man's dirt was holy to her. This siesta generally lasted a couple of hours during which time the young women kept bringing him orange juice, lemonade, rice pudding, etc. Afterwards, his food arrived on silver plates to match the man's greatness, a variety of dishes like fish in yogurt gravy, chicken curry, fine Basmati rice and so on. He would eat, burp and then have a paan, something he was quite partial too, made by his daughter-in-law. He would put a paan in his mouth, chew on it six or seven times and then spit it out noisily into a pot, some of it scattering and spraying on the girls. While some would lick off the accidental stains from their own bodies, most of the others usually got into a fight over who would get the chewed paan bits and juices in the pot left by the wise man. At times the violence of the contest reminded me of similar fights that used to break out in front of Alaka Cinema Hall among women, over tickets. I had seen Mother do it and I had also witnessed these women emerge from the melee with their clothes caked in sweat, blouses torn, hair all over the place like a crazy person, but with a triumphant jubilant smile plastered on their lips as they clutched their hard-won tickets in their fists. This other fight, the one over the chewed paan bits and juices, seemed to me like a fight over who got to go to Paradise. At least to my mother that's what it was; it was not just anything she was fighting over but leftovers from the same mouth that spoke to Allah frequently in the dead of the night after everyone had fallen asleep, the same mouth that could recite ad nauseam tales of Allah, His greatness and all His instructions for His believers. Leftovers from such a great person must surely have been the best way to reach Paradise and, on his part, Amirullah too left no doubt in the minds of his believers that it was truly so, albeit always in code. Just how adults say cryptic things to confuse children while playing hide-and-seek, Amirullah would declare, 'Are you searching for a ticket to Paradise? Keep your eyes and ears open, know and understand what will please Allah. He has given you enough intelligence to do that.'

As Mother scraped up a bit of chewed paan from the pot, I remained seated at the back, alone, scared and embarrassed. I was convinced that I too could get to Paradise by simply following Mother as she went on her way. Fajli khala was sitting apart from this fracas too, watching the fight dispassionately but not making any moves to claim some of the paan from the pot. Not that she needed to. At least Mother believed firmly that absolution was preordained for Fajli khala. She had never run to films and theatres at the drop of a hat, was not a sinner like the others and as such only needed to bide her time on this earth until her turn came. As the tussle went on in the foreground Fajli khala leaned in and whispered to Mother. 'Why only chewed paan, even the spit and mucus of Allah's messenger can guarantee *sawab* [rewards].'

The softly uttered words stayed with Mother.

Before venturing into this new direction, she tucked me away with a hundred-bead tasbih on the floor of one of the rooms with a prayer written on a piece of paper that I was supposed to repeat five hundred times for sawab.

These spiritual rewards were Mother's preoccupation but she wanted me to earn them as well, which explained why she had snatched me away from my games and brought me there. Granted, a rickshaw ride was more fun than playing outside. However, if that involved spending time in a strange house where games were not allowed, no one spoke loudly and where every part of one's body from top to toe had to be kept covered at all times, then I was more than willing to spend time in a smelly toilet than stay there to sit and pray.

The great man's *majlis* or gathering started in the evening, when Mother grabbed me from the room I had been consigned to and dragged me to the assembly hall. When my headscarf slipped a little, I felt a sharp nudge of her elbow signalling me to be more careful. She had instructed me again and again to touch his feet and make sure the covering on my head did not slip. Suffice to say, neither happened as instructed. I was led to the women's section of the assembly room and Mother pulled me down to sit beside her. Women were not allowed to sit out in the public; their place was behind a purdah, away from the men. I peeked past the curtain and my gaze fell on Amirullah, sitting on a mattress and surrounded by huge tomes. He was reading out in Arabic from one book or another, eliciting 'ah's, 'ooh's and other assorted gasps of divine ecstasy from the gathered crowd. Wiping the lenses of his glasses the man went on with his sermons.

'Those who don't bring faith with them, those who don't have faith, do you know how Allah plans to burn them in the fires of *dozakh*? The heat will be as if the sun has come down very close to you, about a hand away. Millions of snakes and scorpions will sting you with their poison and you will be given only boiled water and pus to eat. Allah will pull your tongues out and nail it to your head. He will throw you into the flaming pits where your bodies will burn but you will not die; He will not let you die; He will keep you alive to punish you. Snakes will coil themselves around you and scorpions will roam all over and bite. These worldly pleasures are not for long, my friends. The Last Age is upon us. The Dajjal can be here any time, be prepared. The Apocalypse is here, Israfil is ready with his trumpet. Allah's word is to arrive soon.'

Keening cries arising from behind the curtains swept across the room. Some of the men were wiping their eyes, others were openly weeping, their shoulders shaking quietly. Who knew who had faith and who didn't?

'This material world will come to no use brothers. Prepare for the Day of Judgement. Come back to the way of Allah. If you have His forgiveness you will be saved from the dark trap of the grave and the fires of dozakh. The fires there are not of this world, they are a million times more devastating.'

I was sitting quietly behind my mother, the prayer beads still in my hand. Mother was crying, her body being wracked with tremors from time to time. I was surprised to see so many people weeping, afraid of imaginary fires. It was like scaring children, making them cry by threatening to beat them up. I felt like I should cry too since everyone else already was, but try as I might I could not summon tears. Rather, all I could recall was the description of the fires of hell and I could not help but feel how cruel Allah had to be to be able to do that to someone.

After the gruesome descriptions of one's fate in the grave and in dozakh, the great man raised his hands skywards in prayer.

'Allah, forgive them. Forgive all their sins. You are merciful and great, you are the Lord of everything. Forgive your sinful believers, I beg at your door on their behalf.'

As his voice rose, so did the sounds of his disciples crying helplessly. I curled up into myself a little more, my eyes darting here and there, behind the curtain as well as beyond it. It was a strange world indeed!

Father soon found out about Mother's daily visits to the Pir's house and that she had even taken a pledge to become the holy man's *mureed* (novice or disciple). He issued a dictum that henceforth no one in his house was allowed to consort with the Pir and if anyone continued to do so then they would have to make other arrangements. Mother heard the command and brushed it aside derisively. 'As if I care to live in an infidel's house. There is no word of Allah here. If I live here it will jeopardize my path to Paradise.'

Having pledged herself as Amirullah's disciple, Mother stopped cooking for us. One morning Moni came back from the market as usual and asked Mother what was going to be on the menu that day—bottle gourd with fish, meat with pumpkins, whether the dal was going to be thick or runny— and so on. Usually Moni used to make all the arrangements while Mother did the cooking. That day, however, Mother barely showed any interest in Moni's inquiry, telling her instead to make whatever she felt like. It had never been like this before. For a while this sudden shift in gears left Moni in quite the lurch, leaving the entire responsibility of the kitchen on her. Soon enough the keys to the store room too were handed over to her and Mother made it clear that whatever needed to be bought, stocked or cooked, it was all going to be Moni's decision. In time this sudden surge in her sphere of freedom and influence brought about certain subtle but noticeable changes in Moni, her behaviour often resembling that of the lady of the house.

After she was done with the paan, spit and mucus and the majlis and lessons learnt at Naumahal, Mother usually came back home and spent the rest of her time in prayers. If not praying she sat with her prayer beads or read from the Quran, after which she would pray again. Besides the salat or the five daily prayers, she also observed a sixth *nafl* (voluntary) namaz. She was no longer interested in the affairs of the family, nor was she too concerned whether her children were eating properly or not. She had never been a soft speaker, nor had she ever been known to be too serious. But as a novice to the Pir she would often call us and impart advice in a low and serious voice.

'The teaching of this world will make no difference, children. Make arrangements for the Day of Judgement. Observe roza, read the namaz. Don't turn into an infidel like your father. Take the name of Allah, He is merciful and He will forgive you. Read the Qaida Sipara, read the Quran Sharif. I am telling you, Allah is giving all of you a lesson through me. He is the master of the universe, He is omnipresent and omniscient. Without his will not even a leaf flutters.'

Her face dry as a parched summer leaf, Mother sighed and went on,

'You father doesn't pray. A person who doesn't pray is an infidel. I am living in an infidel's house simply because of you, my children. If I cook and serve an infidel, I'll be committing a sin. If you do not come back to the path of Allah either, I will leave for good. Go darling, perform your wudu, we must read the namaz.'

This last bit was meant for me and my blood froze at the implications. Performing my ablutions, standing next

to Mother and muttering words, touching my chest, my
knees, bowing down, touching my head to the floor, there
was nothing more tiresome than these rituals. But it was a
maternal order and had to be obeyed. Hadn't Ishwar Chandra
Vidyasagar swum the expanse of a stormy Damodar to reach
his mother?

Father came back home, saw me kneeling in prayer and
barked, 'Nasrin, come here.'

I did not need to be called twice; it was freedom after all,
in a way. Standing in front of him with my head downcast
I realized that since I had been occupied with something
serious like praying, and something frivolous like chatting or
games, I was going to be spared. But before I could understand
anything, I felt Father grab me by the neck and give a violent
push. Before I knew how, I found myself in front of my study
table and I felt Father's words, uttered through gritted teeth,
'What is all this you have started instead of studying? You've
become a big minion of your mother. Will Allah feed you
when you go hungry or do you want to learn how to do that
yourself? Go, sit down to study. If I see you leave the table
I'll crush your bones to dust.'

The words reached Mother, still in prayer, and she hissed.

'Instead of letting his daughter read the namaz, he's
trying to teach her the ways of the world. Trying to make her
an infidel too!'

The Pir had asked his newest disciple Hamima to
always keep a calm head about her. That was Mother's new
name since she began visiting the Pir's house. Edul Wara
Begum became Hamima. Whoever went to Amirullah Pir,
irrespective of their age, was given a new name by the holy
man. Renu became Nazia, Hasna changed to Mutaswema,
Ruby transformed to Madeha. As advised, Hamima tried to

calm down but even cooling down had its limitations! Father had not birthed the children, that she had done on her own. If she had absolutely no control left to exert over the children either, then there was no point of her continuing to live in the house!

Having changed out of his work clothes Father came back to stand in front of my table, firmly tying the knot of his lungi over his stomach.

'If you don't do as I say, you can leave. Why do you live here? You eat my food, wear clothes I buy for you, so you have to listen to every word I say. And if you can't do that, you can go out into the world and beg. Why don't you do that, have I stopped you? If you can't live in an infidel's house, then don't.'

It was obvious the words were directed at Mother. I had not chosen to read the namaz, neither had I chosen to get up from it. Realizing that my role in this fight between my parents was entirely inconsequential brought a measure of satisfaction. As soon as Father left the room, Mother came in.

'Yes, of course, I'll leave. Do all of you think you can tie me down? You think I have nowhere to go? I'd rather live in the jungles with wild beasts than live under the same roof with an infidel. All of you will learn a lesson the day I leave. It's not as if I'm going to inform anyone in advance, I'll leave quietly. He's turning the children evil like him. If I stay here, I'll lose whatever sawab I've earned in this life.'

Her words too were directed at him. But the entire exchange was happening where I was studying, directed at me. Since they refused to interact even with each other's shadow I was the one at the centre who had to bear the brunt of it all. Mother finished her declaration and promptly slapped me hard across the face, the kind that leaves a mark.

'Why did you get up from the namaz? Don't you fear Allah? How dare you! The Shaitan always lures people away from the path of Allah. And you heard its call and left the namaz midway? When you burn in the fires of dozakh will any father of yours be able to help you?'

My head, still reeling from the slap, could not come up with a suitable defence.

Since I was born on a holy day, Mother was not one to give up so easily. The very next day her lessons began again with renewed vigour. She bided her time till I was back home from school before catching hold of me to make me sit down with the Quran. A large group of girls used to come over to the field in the afternoon to play and no sooner had I made a move to go out along with them than I heard Mother calling for me. Unable to protest I had to forget about the field, go perform my ritual ablutions and sit with the Quran Sharif, head covered in a scarf, feet in pyjamas. While the group waited for me to join them in the field I had to sit and chant, 'Alhamdulillaahi Rabbil aalameen . . .'[2] and 'Qul huwa Alla hu ahad, Allah hu samad . . .'[3]

'What is this? I don't understand anything.' I could barely suppress the discontent in my voice.

'You don't have to understand. Reading Allah's book is enough to earn sawab,' Mother replied coldly.

I kept on reading the surahs of the Quran in the same singsong way Mother used to, my gaze straying to the window from time to time, hoping to finish the lessons at the earliest so I could go and play. Before long I glanced at the window again and realized to my dismay that dusk had fallen. By then the girls must have gone back home. A knot of disappointment lodged itself in my throat and refused to budge. Once we finished, I did as I was told and kissed the book, neatly folded it and kept it in its place on the topmost shelf of the closet. Sultan Ustadji had already been tasked with teaching me Arabic every morning but it was not enough for Mother, and hence the Quran lessons in the afternoon.

My Arabic teacher was no less a cause for anxiety. We used to sit on a balcony that had almost turned white from pigeon-shit; there he used to teach me Arabic grammar. If I were to scrunch up my nose in disgust at the smell of shit around me, he would tap me hard on the head with his knuckles and ask me why I looked like a frog while reading Allah's words. One morning when I read something wrong, he broke off a branch of the beautiful red-yellow-blue ornamental shrub and asked me to stretch out my palm. When I did so guilelessly, only because my teacher had asked me to, he beat me with the branch till my palms turned red. The afternoons were much the same, with Mother's wrath raining down on me at the slightest mistake in reading the Quran. She was convinced I had no interest in reading the holy book, because I was already too trapped within ideas of worldly knowledge, games, music, dancing, etc. To her it was clear as day that I was going to hell.

Once she was done spoiling my afternoons with Quran lessons, Mother found her next target in Dada.

'Noman, you haven't started the namaz yet?'

'Just about to do it, Ma!' Dada replied with a smile.

'If all of you don't keep your roza and read your namaz, then I'm telling you for the last time that I will no longer live here. I'll go away wherever I want to.'

Having heard the threat Dada, swinging his leg sitting on a chair in the veranda, smiled even wider.

'Believe me Ma. I swear I'll start. Don't go anywhere please!'

I came out to the veranda and took a deep breath. The field lay vast and empty in the distance. A gust of wind from the emptiness came at me with the force of a gale, going straight to my heart with a mournful howl.

In a week, Mother went after Dada again.

'You'd said you were going to start reading the namaz. What happened?'

'This Friday, Ma, for sure!' Dada replied gravely.

Come Friday, Mother caught hold of him.

'It's Friday. Go to the mosque for the Jumu'ah prayers.'

'Not feeling too well, Ma. From next Friday, come what may, I'll take Allah's name and start,' Dada replied, scratching his neck.

The promise pleased Mother. 'You remember the *kalma*s I taught you?'

'Of course, I do! What are you saying, if I don't remember them how can I call myself a true Musalman?'

That day at lunch Mother made sure to reward Dada for remembering his kalmas by dropping a big chicken drumstick on his plate.

The following Friday Dada had another excuse.

'Nothing happens, not even a leaf stirs without the word of Allah. No one has the strength to do anything without Allah's will. How do I read the namaz without His word? He is not making me do it yet! If He doesn't make me start, how can I start on my own? I have no will of my own! If I say I have will too, it will be like saying I share willpower with Him. *La sharika lahu*! Allah is One and He has no partner with Him!' He followed this up by suddenly breaking into song, a line from a *marfoti* song just to drive home the point further.

'I dance how Allah makes me, blame not the doll!'

Giving up on him Mother turned her attention back to me.

'Did you read the namaz?'

'Father asked me to do my homework,' I answered, running towards the table.

'Barely past crawling age and look at how she speaks! You're like your father after all, not an iota of belief in Allah. How can Allah make any of you do any good? You have already been taken over by the devil who doesn't let you take the name of Allah! All of you have become disciples of Iblis.'

Suddenly she began to wail. 'The devil has entered this house. Everyone here is an infidel. At least I had some faith in the children, but they too are spoilt. Allah, take me away from them!'

Allah did not listen to her, neither did he take her away from us. Mother continued to live with us in Abakash, surrounded by tall walls and a lush garden. Neither did Father's warning amount to anything because Mother's daily visits to Amirullah Pir's house behind the sweet shop in Naumahal continued unabated. On Thursday nights she continued to come back with her eyes puffy and red from the emotional upheavals experienced during the Pir's majlis, increasingly convinced that she needed to make urgent arrangements for the Day of Judgement since the Apocalypse was not far away. She also knew that Amirullah was going to make arrangements with Allah on her behalf for a single passage to Paradise. At least that's what Amirullah had indicated to her.

Unable to make any of us tow the line, one fine day Mother decided she just did not care any more. Her children were already too immersed in worldly knowledge, they were coming under the influence of the devil and giving up namaz.

Instead, Mother decided she was going to take care of her own future. Standing among the multitudes during the Day of the Judgement everyone would be chanting 'Ya Nafsi! Ya Nafsi';[4] there would be no time to look around for anyone else.

While Mother chose to walk the path of rightness by choice, as time passed the journey did not remain as inexpensive as she had first thought it was going to be. Amirullah casually explained to her one day how the path to Paradise was littered with numerous obstacles and if one had to lead someone down such an arduous terrain then there were certain expenses that had to be met, all to make the journey a little smoother. Even the Prophet had had to meet these expenses! The money spent on this cause had a special name, it was called hadiya. Arranging for these expenses was not exactly an easy task for Mother. Let alone household expenses, she had stopped receiving any money from Father even for the most basic errands. Anything that had to be bought was usually bought by him. Besides, moving to Abakash had brought not only Alaka Cinema Hall and my school to a stone's throw away from us, but Taj Pharmacy too. Father used to attend to patients there in the evening and shop from the markets of Aampatti or Durgamabri on his way back home. The only valuable thing Mother possessed was her gold chain, which she had thankfully been wearing the day the thief had broken in. One afternoon she walked to Matri Jewellers near our house and sold the chain, to donate to the Pir's house as hadiya. Besides, the ration she quietly began stowing away from Abakash to take to Amirullah's house also allowed her a measure of relief; she could assure herself that she was not going to the holy man's house to listen to the Quran and the Hadith for free.

Since Father had stopped giving her any money, she did not usually have money to pay for rickshaws. Nevertheless, that did not stop Mother's daily excursions one bit, even if she had to walk the whole way there. Nothing could deter her, not me running a temperature, Dada breaking a leg or Yasmin falling from the tree and hurting her head. Gradually, not just on Thursdays but even on Mondays and Tuesdays I would come back from school to find Mother gone. The more her presence in our every daily activity continued to decrease, the more it provoked Father's unease with the whole thing. He began to come back home twice a day to check if his home was still in place or not. The storeroom was put under lock and key and it was decreed that the main gate had to be shut sharp at nine every night. All the measures served to instigate Mother further, who felt vindicated about her belief that the devil was trying his best to lead her astray from Allah's righteous path. Her devotion deepened in reaction, as did her dedication in serving Pir Amirullah's every whim and demand. Whenever she returned to Abakash to find the big black gate firmly shut she began to return to the Pir's house to seek refuge for the night. Pretty soon we could no longer be certain if she would be home with us every night.

Finally, after she had been away for seven nights in a row, Father relented and sent Dada to Naumahal to bring her back home. After a triumphant return there underwent a veritable transformation in how Mother was treated by everyone at home. For her part, she was left in no doubt that the house had sort of fallen apart during her absence. Making sure he could hear her every word Mother declared to us one day: 'If all of you agree to read the namaz every day only then am I going to live here. Otherwise, I'll leave. That's it.'

Having understood her intention, Father leaned back further on the sofa and softly began. 'Read the namaz, read the Quran, has anyone ever stopped you? But why do you have to keep visiting that Pir? Those who don't go there, don't they go to Paradise? The children have their studies. You don't look after them, rather you spend all your time there. Does reading the namaz and keeping the roza mean abandoning one's children? Who's told you all this? You've fallen in with a charlatan.'

'Don't you dare call him that! You are calling Allah's messenger a charlatan! What audacity! Your tongue will rot and fall off! I have nothing to do with an infidel like you. You've destroyed my life. If Fajli hadn't arrived in time and shown me the path of Allah I would still have been running frantically to the cinema hall with mismatched slippers on my feet! I had been blind before but now, after walking Allah's path of righteousness, I have learnt to see. How all this love and belonging are nothing but illusions. I have begun to understand that getting into worldly affairs will only bring about my downfall. Who will come to my aid during the Judgement? No one, no husband, no children, no family. There is no one except Allah.'

Fajli khala had meticulously explained to Mother that it was not right for her to continue staying with her husband. It was sinful to live with someone who did not read the namaz. Father did not, and as such he was an infidel. Fajli khala had explained to Mother how Allah did not spare those who chose to love and live with infidels. Mother did not want to burn in the fires of dozakh, she had been burned enough by her relationships. Her frequency of prayers increased, her fingers running along the beads at lightning speed as she chanted Allah's name. In the darkness of her room the prayer beads glowed like feline eyes as she spent entire nights kneeling in supplication.

One night I woke up to the sound of her crying. Raising my head from the pillow I inquired softly, 'Why are you crying, Ma?' She did not reply and the weeping went on. 'Don't you want to sleep? Come back to bed,' I implored, but she ignored all my pleas and neither did she stop crying. When she finally came to bed after completing the Fajr prayer at dawn I asked her again. 'Why were you crying, Ma?'

Mother sighed in response. 'I was thinking about the grave. When the angels ask me questions what am I going to say? Oh, how they are going to bury me deep from both ends, so deep . . .' Unable to continue, her voice broke mid-sentence.

Just like us, it did not take Father too long to figure out that there was no way to hold Mother back. He stopped locking the front gate at night rather than take any further risks. It was better that she came home late than not come home at all! I suspect this change of heart had less to do with any love for her and more to do with his need to have someone watch over his home and children. Around the same time, we got news that Sultan Ustadji, my Arabic teacher who had taught Mother when she was a child too, had passed away. Father declared that I no longer needed to learn Arabic and that I should concentrate more on my studies in school. The announcement did not make Mother happy in the slightest bit. She knelt before Allah in prayer and cried her heart out pleading with the Almighty to make her children more pious, free them from the terror of the grave and the fires of dozakh, and grant them the way to Paradise. Allah was merciful, the Lord of the world, the Master of everything.

Fruits from the garden—coconuts, guavas, mangoes, berries, jackfruits—reached the Pir's house regularly, transferred safely tucked under Mother's burqa. She had stopped entering the kitchen but that soon changed too. Young chickens from the coop were slaughtered and Mother cooked the meat herself with plenty of oil and fragrant masalas. That too, packed in neat steel containers, reached the Pir's table, along with an old saree or two for Fajli khala to make quilts out of. In return the Pir assured Mother that when the hour of her Judgement came and the angels arrived to ask her questions, he was going to be answering on her behalf. Besides he was soon going to be earning the title of Gausul Azam, a wise man privy to all of Allah's plans and secrets. Amirullah had received the happy news in a dream. That was one of Mother's enduring dreams: to be acquainted with Allah once. But she was a sinner and it was unlikely that He was ever going to grant her wish. The thought made Mother tear up; holding on to the container of chicken curry under her burqa with one hand she would wipe her moist eyes with the other.

One night she came back from Amirullah's house grumbling. Taking her burqa off she could be heard muttering to herself. 'Humaira has got a gold locket made with "Allah Hu" on it. Plus, three pairs of bangles, almost thirty-five grams of gold in all. Does anyone give me anything? Is there anyone more destitute than I?' Done changing, she shouted out to Moni to serve dinner. It didn't go as planned.

'Why have you served me cold rice? There isn't any warm rice? What have all of you taken me to be? All of you will be happy if I just die. Do you think I don't understand that? Who gives me what in this family? Nothing! I don't have a single good saree I can wear. Who even notices?'

Mother pushed the plate of food aside and got up from the table. As Moni took the plate away to the kitchen to warm up the rice, Mother came and stood by my table, speaking loud enough for Father to hear every word.

'People keep their wives wrapped in gold! And what do I get? I have been kept in this house to work as a guard. People pay their guards salaries, don't they? And here I am, working for free.'

'You're our mother. Why do you need a salary?' I interjected softly only to be silenced by her snarl.

'And how do I go on then? I have nothing. My father had married me off to a doctor, dreaming that his son-in-law was going to educate his younger children. Did he do it? Does he even ask after them? My wrists have been bare for ages. Look at other people's wives, look at the jewellery they are wearing. You will keep me like a slave and then there are no end to your demands: take care of the children, raise them too!

When I was six years old Fajli khala had brought news from Amirullah Pir's house that the Dajjal was about to appear in the world, that he was coming with a menacing scythe with which he was going to test people's faith. The ones the fiend found lacking in faith were going to be hacked into five parts. Terrified of impending doom everyone back at Nani's place had suddenly begun reading the kalmas twice a day. The Original Fiend could come any moment, such was the level of anxiety among the family members. Back then I used to often have nightmares of the Dajjal hacking me into pieces and I would often wake up from sleep terrified. Sharaf mama had declared that Fajli khala's house was the only place safe from the coming devastation because everyone's faith was rock-solid there; Mother had vehemently concurred with this proclamation.

As days passed I would time and again ask everyone why
the Dajjal was not there yet.

'What happened? Why isn't the Dajjal here?'

'It'll be any moment now,' Mother replied, 'And it'll be
followed by the Apocalypse.'

'What will happen during the Apocalypse, Ma?'

'What else,' she sighed in resignation. 'Israfel will blow
his trumpet. The world will meet its end. Nothing of this, all
made by Allah himself, will remain.'

Her stories had formed a picture in my head, a scene
of the end of days. The sky was going to fall on the earth,
destroying houses and crushing people like ants. Huge and
tall trees were all going to be swallowed by the earth. And
even if one were to pass the test of faith posed by the Dajjal,
there was going to be no escape from the Apocalypse.'

Just before we moved to Abakash from Nani's house,
Fajli khala brought fresh news from the Pir's house that
wearing gold was haram. Having heard that all the women in
the house had immediately taken their jewellery off. Hasem
mama had just got married around that time and the new
bride used to wear a lot of jewellery as was custom; there
were neighbours visiting frequently to meet the new member
of the house.

'Parul, take those off. The end of the world is near. If you
wear jewellery now then Allah is going to be displeased.'

Fajli khala had herself made sure to take all Parul's
jewellery off, holding the offending objects as if they were
dead rodents while she threw them away. When Hasem
mama had protested saying he had heard it was inauspicious
to take jewellery off a new bride, Fajli khala had lost her
temper and shouted in her shrill voice, 'What do you know of
what is auspicious and what is not, Hasem? The night before

last, Abbaji saw the Prophet in his dreams. He informed Abbaji that those parts of the body on which there are going to be gold ornaments are going to especially burn in the fires of dozakh.'

When Nani had taken Fajli khala aside and inquired about the jewellery the latter had asked her not to be worried about it and that Humaira's father had taken it all away to sell it off. Be that as it may, Nani had nonetheless been quite bothered by the turn of events.

Barely had a year passed and gold was halal again in the Pir's house. I looked up from the book I was reading at Mother's sorrowful face and innocently asked, 'Isn't wearing gold haram? Hadn't they all stopped wearing gold jewellery in the Pir's house!' Mother had no answers to my questions. Instead, she looked at me as if I had truly been possessed by the devil and it was he who was making me say the things I was saying.

A few days later Mother came back home with a pair of thick gold bangles from Matri Jewellers. The owner used to be Father's friend. She had got them on credit with the arrangement that Father was going to pay it off in instalments.

Faith

1.

Every Friday while coming back from the mosque after the Jumu'ah prayers Nana would have batashas—small yellow disks made of date jaggery—in his pocket. It was a custom to distribute batashas after Friday prayers and we, the children of the house, usually Felu mama, Chotku, Yasmin and I, would see him near the pond by the house and run to him to raid his pockets for the sweet treats. Nana loved us but he was usually not so amenable with the adults; he would distribute batashas among us and then go home and drive everyone up the wall. This was Nani's description of him, especially when he used to bring the roof down asking for his stick and threatening to pulverize anyone who had dared to give the mosque a miss that day. At least the sons had to go; since women were not allowed in the mosques, they could offer namaz at home. It was not as if the women of the house were not allowed to go outside, the only stipulation being they could only go out in a burqa. It was an old habit of Nana's to laze around a little on Fridays. Just before settling into a post-lunch siesta he would take stock of his children, which of the boys had missed the Jumu'ah prayers, which of the girls were not home and which of them had gone out without a burqa. The questions used to drive Nani crazy. Post his siesta, however, Nana would revert to being a sweet and kind man. He would tie his lungi tightly around his waist and, swinging his arms as if steering through air, set off towards Notun Bazar, without even bothering to wonder who was home or not. The lure of being able to meet and talk to numerous kinds of people in his hotel in the evening was always too much to stay at home. None of the women of the house, except Nani, used to voluntarily wear the burqa. My two aunts usually took the burqa with them in a bag wherever they went. On their way back they would look for Chotu near the pond to inquire if Nana was at home. If he was, they waited at a neighbour's house till he left and word was sent to them that it was safe to come back; if in a hurry they would simply slip on the burqas and walk in nonchalantly.

Only Boromama was admitted to a madrasa in the family; the rest of the children were all sent to schools and colleges. Nana had strict instructions, albeit only for his sons, that education was priceless and hence there could be no toying around with it. In case of his daughters, as we have seen, he firmly believed women did not need too much education in life. Runu khala had a BA degree. When Nana chose a prospective groom for her to marry, Runu khala turned up in front of the man with her hair disheveled and dirt and grime on her face, just to ensure the man would not like her. Sulekha's mother visited Nani often. Sitting on Nani's bed chewing on plain betel leaves one day, the talk veered to Runu khala.

'Are you planning to make Runu the resident spinster of the family? Why haven't you fixed her wedding yet. See how nicely Edul and Fajli have got married!'

'Let her study a little more,' Nani interjected, folding paan. 'She will work. Marriage can wait. In today's age even women must earn. There's no point only depending on one's husband. Who knows what happens when!'

Since Jhunu khala was the fair one she got more marriage proposals, prompting Nani to issue a stern edict: 'She will study further, there's no need for a wedding so soon. Plus, her elder sister isn't married yet so how can we fix a match for the younger one?'

Boromama passed his Fazil degree from the madrasa, did his MA in Arabic from Dhaka University and got a job in the city. He used to live apart with his fair wife and they did not have any children. Consequently, there were no dearth of relatives to point out that there was no use of the wife being fair if she was infertile. They would get her amulets, etc., to tie around her waist, presumably to help with her fertility issues. As soon as they left Boromama would take all of that and consign it to the depths of the well. During vacations he came home to visit his family, sometimes with his wife and sometimes by himself. When he walked around the yard in his wooden sandals it would not seem he was back home only for a few days, it was as if he had never left.

Hasem mama would bunk school and hang out with his friends. He had failed in his matriculation exam two–three times and then dropped out. It was decided that Boromama was going to take Jhunu khala with him and get her admitted into Eden College in Dhaka. As for the rest, Fakrul mama, Tutu mama, Sharaf mama and Felu mama, their studies were in the same state of shambles as their namaz and prayers. The more friends they made the more they stayed out, often till late in the night, and Tutu mama even took up smoking at the behest of some of his cohorts. Nana would often tie the boys up to the pillars and thrash them soundly, sort of like trying to beat the goodness back inside them. None of it mattered though, and their exam results only deteriorated with every passing day. Nani consulted with Boromama and it was decided the boys too were going to be sent to Dhaka to attend school, at least to give them a fighting chance at becoming decent human beings.

Around the time when Nani was seemingly turning grey from worrying that all her sons were going to become vagabonds, Nana declared one fine day that he was going to Hajj. Where was the money going to come from? Much to Nani's annoyance, he brushed aside the question with the cryptic answer that Allah Himself was going to provide everything that was necessary. In the end it was not Allah who gave him the money; Father lent it to him with the promise that Nana was going to pay it back after his return. The year my Nana set sail on a ship bound for Hajj, having packed his clothes and snacks in a big tin suitcase with his name written on it in white—Mohammed Maniruddin Ahmed, Akua Madrasa Headquarters, Mymensingh—was the same year that Neil Armstrong made his journey to the moon.

The moon was an emotionally charged entity in the lives of my family members. There were the usual things: distracting children by taking them to the roof to show them the moon, making nursery rhymes involving the moon and so on. Besides, the moon was most conducive to gossip, especially the kind of sure-fire gossip that Kama mama used to regale us with. Runu khala would often sit in the yard under the moon and sing Tagore's 'Aj jyotsna raate . . .' while before Eid the moon would take on its most venerable position in our lives with people gathering together to catch a glimpse of it and Nani throwing up a prayer to Allah as soon as she did.

That year too there had been no change in the routine, except for my visiting Boromama who suddenly asked Nani a question.

'Ma, Neil Armstrong peed on the moon. Why do you still worship something that a Christian has peed on?'

Fajli khala usually got permission from her Abbaji to visit her parents only at certain times. For instance, if she had to be exorcised or she was feeling particularly ill or under the weather, like an upset stomach, a fever or a bad headache. That year she had been visiting because of a chronic headache. She immediately exclaimed, 'Abbaji has said that in reality no one has been to the moon. Allah is the creator of the sun and the moon, He makes them rise and set. The moon is holy; Muslims observe Eid and roza as per the moon. This walking on the moon business is all nothing but Christian propaganda.'

'Fajli, didn't I teach you science when you were a child? Didn't I teach you how the world came to be created? Have you forgotten everything?' Boromama inquired with a laugh.

Fajli khala was in the middle of drawing water from the well for wudu and shot back at him. 'Do scientists know more than Allah? What are you trying to say Miyanbhai? Whatever Allah has said is the only truth, the rest is all a lie.' Lifting the bucket and putting it down in the yard she continued, 'Stop joking around with Allah. Think about the afterlife a little.'

'It's not the djinns that torment you, it's your father-in-law,' Boromama replied gravely.

I did not know who to believe, him or her. Both of them were special in the house. Whenever Boromama turned up, pulao and mutton used to be cooked for him.

Similarly, even if it did not happen when she came alone, at least whenever someone from her in-laws' place came over, grand arrangements used to be made for them as well. Just like Boromama seemed like a distant relative to me, so did Fajli khala, her in-laws even more so. Whenever either party came over, someone like me, a sunburnt girl with a forever-runny nose, had to stay beyond the line of the well between the houses, safely out of sight. Even if I strayed a little bit Nani would tell me to beat it and come back once the guests were gone. So I would stand and watch them from afar, the nice mat being laid out for the guests, the one that used to be kept rolled up during the day, complete with a new blanket on which Fajli khala's father-in-law and husband would be eating. Nani would be supplying warm bowls full of food from the kitchen which Fajli khala, her head firmly covered, served them. Afterwards they would laze around on the bed chewing on paan while the women sat down to eat: Fajli khala, her mother-in-law and sister-in-law, the latter's daughters Humaira, Sufaira, Mubaswera. Nani would be the last person in the house to eat, after the guests had left and the family members were done too. That would also be my cue that my curfew was off and I was allowed to cross over from our side to Nani's again.

Pacing up and down the yard, his wooden slippers making a distinct clapping sound, Boromama spoke again. 'Fine, if Allah's words are the only truth, then live your life according to what He says. Your husband can live with your housemaid, because according to Allah's decree it's all right to have relations with one's slave.'

The bucket for wudu remained where it was as Fajli khala stomped off to the room, grabbed her burqa off the rack and burst into tears. In moments her cheeks had turned red as ripe mangoes. She still looked beautiful though, like an image drawn of a Kalighat pat painting.

'Ma, I'm leaving. It's impossible to stay under this roof a moment longer. I can't stand such an insult!' Fajli khala screamed.

Nani ran to the room and snatched the burqa away from her. 'Why are you crying? Siddique has no filter; he keeps speaking rubbish. For that you want to leave, that too so late in the night? What will they say? You want to go that's fine, but at least stay for Eid.'

Paying her no heed, Fajli khala snatched the burqa back from her and began to frantically put it on.

'Not a moment longer. As if I come here because I fancy it! My head aches in the other house from so many people there. But if I come here and get insulted by my own brothers then why bother! I had thought I was going to spend Eid at my parents', but that is not to be. Miyanbhai has insulted Humaira's father. There is hardly a man more pious than him in this world!'

Despite her best efforts Nani failed to stop Fajli khala that night and in the end Hasem mama had to accompany my aunt back to her husband and in-laws late in the night. Sitting all by myself in the tense house, I could not help but be astonished as to how it was possible for anyone to land on the moon, such a tiny thing as it was! Mother used to tell us about the woman on the moon, the one who lived there and worked her spinning wheel. Boromama would tell us there was no one on the moon, no old woman, no trees, not even any water. The shapes of the old woman on the moon were nothing but shadows of the craters on its surface. Regardless of what was true, I developed a secret relationship with the moon in no time. Wherever I went it followed me, wherever

I walked or paused, beside a gorge or a pond, it too walked or stopped. If I rested, perhaps on Nani's yard, so did the moon. It even followed me back home from Sharmila's house one day, crossing Nani's yard to our side and then beyond, into the bamboo grove.

On Eid, early in the morning, everyone had gathered by the well to scrub themselves with red Cosco soap and bathe in cold water. I was dressed in new clothes and shoes, my hair tied in a new red ribbon. *Ittr* was dabbed on me, tiny cotton balls dipped in the fragrance were put in my ear. The men of the house were dressed in white, their head covered in caps, cotton balls of ittr in their ears as well. The fragrance permeated across the house, making the air heady as the men, me in tow, set off towards the field where we used to read the namaz on such occasions. Oh, such a vast place that was! And there used to be a sea of people there, spreading bed-sheets and standing in prayer. My father, brothers, all my uncles, everyone except Boromama. When the namaz began and everyone knelt down I watched in utter fascination, the scene reminding me of our PT classes back in school when we were made to bend over to touch our toes. Once the namaz was over Father and everyone else embraced their friends and acquaintances in greeting. This ritual greeting, a commonplace thing during Eid celebrations, was restricted only for men. When I returned home and asked Mother if we could embrace her, she shook her head and firmly refused. Women were not allowed to embrace; it was against the rules. Why was it not allowed? The question kept gnawing at me as I went about my way. Preparations had begun in the field for the sacrifices. The black buffalo that had been bought for the purpose was tied outside to the haunted tree with the sweet fruits. Its big black eyes were wet with tears and the sight was making my soul cry out in pain. It was a real animal sitting there all by itself and feeding on chum and soon it was going to be nothing but buckets full of meat. The imam of the mosque was sitting under the haunted tree sharpening his knives. Hasem mama brought in bamboo as Father laid out mats on the yard where the meat was going to be cut. Once the weapons were sharp enough the imam called out to the men. Instantly Father, my uncles and some other men of the neighbourhood grabbed hold of the buffalo, tied it to the bamboo with ropes and proceeded to trip it to make it stumble and kneel, with the giant animal bellowing in fright throughout the ordeal. Mother and my aunts were standing by the windows watching the sacrifice, their eyes dancing in excitement. Only my Boromama, no ittr on his body and wearing only a lungi, was standing apart in one corner watching the scene unfold.

'They are slaughtering a dumb animal so mercilessly and here people are enjoying it. Apparently, this pleases Allah! There is not a shred of kindness or humanity left anywhere.'

He sighed and turned away, leaving me standing there watching the bellowing animal fighting tooth and nail for its life against seven giant men trying to hold it down. It shook them off once and stood up, only to be tripped and made to fall again. In a flash the imam, letting out a cry of 'Alla hu Akbar', stabbed the animal in the neck with the knife. Blood streaked across the air, the animal continued to scream and struggle despite having half its neck sliced open. A sharp pain spiked my heart and I stood there unable to move. Mother had said it was my duty to watch the sacrifice, just as she used to every Eid morning. Long after, when the imam was skinning the animal, I could still see pools of tears in the dead buffalo's eyes. Sharaf mama and Felu mama was transfixed by the scene and refused to stir. I left the house and walked to Manumiyan's shop to buy balloon whistles.

Cleaned and portioned, the meat was divided into seven parts: three for nani, three for us and one for the neighbours as well as the homeless and the destitute. Eid itself was a fun occasion as this was the one day when Father always spoke sweetly, never asked me to go study and never ever gave me a thrashing. The whole day was about eating mawa, zarda, pulao and beef, running around and having fun, nearly everything was given a pass on Eid. Cutting and preparing the meat took a better part of the day. Giant makeshift clay ovens with giant utensils were deployed for cooking the ceremonial beef. The cook continued till the afternoon and afterwards Mother and Nani bathed and put on new sarees. Runu khala and Jhunu khala were already dressed by then, waiting and looking for an opportunity to go out and visit their friends. As guests began arriving Boromama, who had gone out in his lungi and an old shirt, came back and informed us that the entire neighbourhood was awash with sacrificial blood.

'It's everywhere! Who knows how many poor animals were slaughtered today. Instead, if these had been given away to the farmers they could have been employed in the fields for tilling. So many farmers don't have cattle of their own. I don't understand why human beings are such vicious monsters. A family will slaughter an entire cow to eat meat while there are countless who don't even get rice regularly.'

It was no use asking Boromama to take a shower and wear new clothes for Eid. Unwilling to push the matter further Nani interjected, 'As it is you didn't observe Eid. Do you plan to not eat too? Come eat with us.'

'Why shouldn't I eat? I will, give me food. But something
other than beef,' Boromama replied with a sigh.

Nani could barely hold back her tears. How could a
Mother bear that her oldest child was not going to eat the
holy sacrificial meat of Eid. Wiping her eyes Nani made a
firm resolution that she was not going to eat the meat either.
How could a Mother eat something her son was not willing
to even touch!

The news of Boromama not eating the beef spread
through the house in no time and a sense of unease descended
upon the adults. The sentiments were voiced aloud by none
other than Mother as she served us food. 'Miyanbhai will
return to Dhaka without eating the Eid meat. He doesn't
condone the sacrifices. The beef that is bought from the
market, does that happen without killing cows?'

The end of Eid meant returning to my usual timetable. It
also meant encountering Sharaf mama poking and grinning
at me, teasing me about a missing tooth.

'Toothless git,

Eats three pots of shit!'

After losing that one tooth Mother had taken the tiny
thing and dropped it in a rat-hole praying to the rat spirits to
take my rotten tooth in exchange for one of their sharp ones.
Till that was happening I had to tolerate Sharaf mama. Runu
khala's views on the matter echoed Sharaf mama's rhyme. 'If
you don't eat shit your teeth won't grow back.'

Shit made me queasy. While squatting down I could
barely avoid looking down, the splatter beneath never failing
to make me sick to my stomach. I usually dealt with it by
refusing to breathe as much as possible. Dada, on the other
hand, usually spent at least two hours in the shitter, and I
could never ever begin to comprehend what made him

endure the place for so long. Whenever the sewage cleaner came to the house I would scrunch up my nose and mouth and remain like that, spitting out in disgust from time to time. The cleaner usually came once a week to clean out the makeshift latrine and Nani never failed to confidently haggle with him when it came to his fees. So everything about Runu khala's words made me angry. I remember shooting back, 'You have teeth, don't you? Did you eat shit too?'

'Of course I did. When I was young.'

Sharaf mama was worse than me when it came to scatological humour. While eating if he ever managed to catch a glimpse of a chicken shitting in the yard or someone even mentioning the word shit, he used to push aside his plate in a fit of anger. Once when I innocently asked him if what Runu khala had said about eating shit was true, he swatted me on the back and threw away his plate of rice as if he was kicking aside a piece of rock. But whenever he teased me with his nasty rhyme, I could not do anything to him in return. He was older than me and one was never supposed to raise one's hand on someone older. I was also not supposed to tell anyone if that same older person was finding opportunities to take off my clothes and repeatedly telling me to keep quiet about it. Adults were never going to believe it that another one of them had taken advantage of me in a rundown room one bleak afternoon. Instead they were going to beat me for telling lies. One was also not supposed to stand up to elders, instead one was supposed to unquestioningly take what was dealt out by them, whether it was affection or punishment. Adults always had our best interests in their minds, or so I had been taught by them.

After Tutu mama and Sharaf mama were circumcised, for quite a few days they remained wearing their lungis.

Whenever they had to walk, they would lift their lungis a little and walk in this strange manner with their legs spread apart so that there was no painful friction with their sore parts. It was hilarious and it never failed to make me laugh. Whenever I laughed the two of them would rush to me and give me a sound thrashing. I was not allowed to laugh, neither was I allowed to look at what they were wearing or how they were walking. The grown-ups could fix the boundaries of what I was allowed or not just as they wished.

That Eid Boromama stayed with us for quite a while. Almost the entire time he spent either in his room on his bed reading books, or in the afternoons, taking strolls in the yard wearing his wooden sandals. Sometimes, at night, he would come over to our side to chat with Father. He was a soft speaker, never shouted, and whenever he heard someone else shout, he would make a shushing sound of disapproval with his tongue. Hasem mama, on the other hand, was a frequent shouter. Out of the blue he would scream that he had fallen down and everyone would rush outside to see him hanging inside the well holding the ledge. Nani would keep telling him to stop his dangerous games lest something real happened one day. Seeing Hasem mama climbing out of the well grinning, Boromama would be at a loss for words. He did not get the point of such games and he would wonder aloud if Hasem mama was going mad. The other thing the latter would usually do was to grab either me or Felu mama, turn us over the well and threaten to throw us in. Ma's earth-shattering scream would again draw people out, including a yet-again dumbfounded Boromama.

One day, knowing well that Boromama had not yet returned to Dhaka, Fajli khala came for a visit. As soon as she arrived, without even a word of greeting or a hello to anyone else, she walked up to Boromama.

'I have something to speak to you about.'

Boromama smiled and placed a hand on khala's shoulder. 'Why are you so angry all the time? You were not like this before. Sit, take off that burqa, rest, then we'll talk.'

Shrugging his hand off, Fajli khala replied, 'No, I have not come to this house to sit. I will say what I have to and then go.'

Just taking off the headscarf of the burqa she sat on the bed, her feet dangling off the edge, and launched into the piece she had prepared.

'That day you said Allah has decreed that men can have relations with their servants. In which ayat did you find this? No, it's wrong! Wrong! Allah was not talking about servants. The Quran explicitly mentions slaves, not servants. Relations are allowed with slaves. But now there are no slaves! It's not as if we have all bought our servants with money!' khala finished with a triumphant smile.

Boromama, sitting cross-legged on the bed with his hands resting on the pillow in his lap, replied in surprise, 'Oh, is that it? How is this so important that you cannot sit and rest first? That you will leave immediately after finishing? So now tell me, why do you think slavery does not exist any more? Can you tell me why! Who abolished slavery? Did your Allah do it or did the Prophet? It was human beings who abolished slavery, do you get it? If they hadn't, can you imagine what state we would have been in? And think about it. Be it a servant or a slave, what kind of God condones—'

Before he could finish Fajli khala's voice rose over his.

'That was then! Back then women had no security. Slaves had nowhere else to seek refuge. So Allah—'

This time before she could finish her argument Boromama cut her off—

'If you truly believe that the Quran was only written for those times then that's a good thing. Then leave the book to the age it belongs to! Why make such a fuss about it now? And why did Allah only speak about those days? That's a question that needs to be asked too! If He is omnipresent and omniscient then how did He fail to see that there would be no slavery now, in the future? He could have also predicted the invention of electricity, cars, planes, rockets, and that human beings would one day travel to the moon in them! Why waste energy on things that do not belong to our age? All of you are too scared.'

Wordlessly Fajli khala stood up, her face overcast. Grabbing hold of the headscarf of her burqa she turned to Boromama again. 'It's shameful the depths to which you have stooped. It's a sin for me to even look upon your face.' She walked out of Nani's house over to ours and told Mother she had a headache and was going to sleep in our room for a while. Leaving her to rest Mother turned towards the kitchen to make some food for her: fine rice with roasted pigeon was on the menu.

Most of Boromama's conversations with Father were about land. He would time and again advise Father to invest in land in Dhaka while the rates were still low and Father too always nodded and said he was considering it. All I wanted to do was hear Boromama tell stories of Dhaka, what it looked it, what all one could find there. But I noticed he never paid me much attention, perhaps because his princess, all dusty and muddy, was no longer quite princess-like as she had been as a child. That year the only conversation I managed to have with him was the day before he was finally set to return to Dhaka. On my way to the latrine I had come across a piece of paper on the ground with something scribbled on it in Arabic. Since learning Arabic alphabets, I had been taught by Mother that if I were to ever find something like that lying around, since Arabic was holy script, I was not supposed to throw it in the dirt or step on it. Instead, it was to be thrown into the water, which is usually what I always did. I used to kiss such papers if I were to find any and set it afloat on the water like a boat. That day I had picked up the piece of paper and brought it to Mother to show her what a good girl I had been for listening to her and not disrespecting the holy script. Mother was in the yard putting up clothes on the line to dry and she asked me to hand the chit over to Boromama who took it from my hand and read out aloud what was scribbled on it. Hearing him recite the lines in Arabic, Mother turned to him with admiration shining in her gaze. Knowing Arabic was a sure sign of being a person of faith and, in this case, it did not matter that Boromama never went to the mosque to pray, not even on Eid.

'What will you do with this?' he asked me. Clutching Mother's saree a little tighter, more for emotional support than anything else, I answered that I was going to kiss it and throw it in the pond. Throwing the piece of paper away he bit out, 'You're going to kiss this? Do you know what was written on that? "I will fuck your mother, you bastard"!'

Mother's face reddened in an instant, the wet saree on her shoulder that she was about to hang out to dry all but forgotten. Phoolbahari, on her way inside with a pitcher of water against her hip, stopped dead in her tracks. A crash rang out as the watering can that Nani had been watering the chilli pepper trees with slipped from her grasp, the water spilling out all over the yard. Amidst the hush I stepped a little closer to Boromama and inquired in an awestruck voice, 'Boromama, isn't Arabic the language of Allah? You can abuse in it too!'

'Why not?' Boromama replied, his wooden sandal slicking as he walked, 'Arabic is the language of the Arab people. The Arabs drink alcohol, do terrible things, kill people. They abuse too. And the men marry numerous women, some as many as hundred!'

'Siddique, stop it!' Nani warned. Her oldest child, raised with much love and care, a madrasa-educated scholar of Arabic, did as he was asked and did not elaborate further.

I remember Mother staring at him with the deepest suspicion in her gaze that day. She could not believe that she had grown up with the same man in the very same house, played in that very yard under the haunted tree with the sweet fruit. Every day, after coming back from school, the two of them used to race through their lunch so that they could run to the ponds of the Nasirabad madrasa afterwards. After swimming the entire evening when they used to remerge from the pond both their eyes would be red. Returning home like that meant inviting Nani's wrath so the two would sit by the pond and rub yam leaves, made potent with gibberish chants and spells cast on them, over their eyes to get rid of the incriminating red glow. Only then they would return home like meek and docile children. Back then there would only be a few horse-drawn carriages about at that hour and every day Mother used to come and stand for a while at the head of the lane that led to the house. There was a house there where a foreign woman used to stay, a memsahib, and Mother used to stand there to watch her. Every evening the woman used to sit in the balcony and have tea, her occasional laughter cascading off her smooth, fair white skin and legs.

Boromama used to drag Mother home by the skirt, telling her, 'They are Christians. If you stare at them so much Allah will punish you.'

Tables and chairs were bought for Boromama to study on; nothing was done for Mother. Nana used to buy grapes and oranges in secret for Boromama; they would be kept in the drawers of his study table and not once did they ever offer even a single grape to Mother. Instead she was put in charge of tidying her selfish brother's books and clothes and at the slightest infraction, a stray ink stain somewhere on one corner of the table perhaps, she would invariably be soundly thrashed. And just like that, one day they were both grown up, but while Boromama could aim for the skies Mother remained moored to the ground like she had always been.

Yes, Mother was envious of Boromama. But was she envious of the man he was gradually becoming? She could not help but feel that this man, the person she called Miyanbhai, was not the person that she once used to know.

2.

Mother resumed her visits to Amirullah Pir's house after the 1971 Liberation War. Not that the Pir had had to flee anywhere during the troubled times; he had managed to lead a rather comfortable life in the interim, even striking up a rapport with a couple of Biharis during the period. Besides, his reasoning was he had fled India to come and live in a Muslim country. Now if Pakistan was to no longer exist in the scene then what was the point of staying there any more? He had thus impressed upon a few zealots to attack and set fire to around ten Bengali houses in Naumahal, convincing the fanatics that there was nothing wrong in what they were doing; that it was all for the cause of jihad meant to save Islam from enemies. Despite not having a particularly clear idea about jihad, since she was the Pir's *murid* (disciple)—and a disciple was not supposed to entertain doubts or questions about the master's words or deeds—Mother usually avoided any queries that could possible hurt the holy man or cause him any sort of anxiety. Soon she began preparations for the fatwas that came in the wake of jihad, buying yardage of plain white material to be tailored into plain salwar-kameez sets. The holy Pir Amirullah had recently directed all his female disciples to dress like the Prophet's wives, in such white salwar-kameez instead of sarees. Neither were they allowed to grow their hair any more, having been instructed to wear it short like boys.

A few swishes of the scissor and gone was the buttock-length hair that, despite not boasting much volume, Mother always attempted to buff up by using tassels. With her new shoulder-length hair and loose salwar-kameez wrapped snugly around the head and chest, I could barely recognize her. Sad and disapproving, I prodded her.

'Why are you wearing these, Ma?'

'They won't wear sarees any more. Hindus wear sarees, it's the garment of kafirs. It'll bring sin.'

No matter what fatwa was issued from the Pir's house, Mother followed everything without any doubts or misgivings. In the process she had no trouble forgetting about her childhood friend Amala, memories of visiting the Rathyatra fair with friends to buy popped rice, toys or dolls, going over to Saraswati's house for sweets during Lakshmi Puja or strolling through Durga Puja pandals of the locality with her girlfriends. She also forgot how, when I had cut off my own hair on a lark, she had soundly thrashed me and told me I was looking like a ghost for butchering the hair she had so carefully nourished.

She was changing, becoming a different person, and it was happening right in front of us. We would all sit at the table to eat but Mother would take her food elsewhere, on the floor, on the bed or even just holding the plate in one hand. She did not want to use chairs and tables because it was haram and because, according to her, 'the faithless Jews use tables and chairs to eat'. In our entire neighbourhood there were probably only two-three Muslim households, the rest were all Hindus. There was usually a series of pujas and religious rituals that were held in the locality throughout the year. Earlier, boys and girls from these houses would always come over to pluck flowers or bel leaves, things they used in their rituals. Often, they would also pluck fruits in the guise of taking leaves and I would let them; I hated the fruits and never liked it when Mother made smoothies with them for me to drink. Mother too used to strike up conversations with many of these boys and girls, asking them their names, about their families and loved ones and suchlike. But once she began visiting the Pir, new rules were implemented in the house. Anyone who came over for flowers or bel leaves from our garden began to be snapped at and turned away and Mother told me strictly to never give anything to any Hindu boy or girl for their pujas; they were all apostates and helping their faith meant inviting sin for ourselves.

Dejected, I asked her one day, 'Why do you call them kafir? I know them, they are all good people.'

Muttering as she prayed, her beads in her hand, Mother answered, 'Anyone who is not a Muslim is a kafir. Be it Hindus, Buddhists or Christians.'

Keeping myself well out of her reach I carried on. 'Imagine a child is born today, its parents either Hindus or Christians. The child had no hand in choosing where to be born, it could easily have been born in the family of the imam of the mosque. The child has no fault, it learns what is taught by its parents, to perform pujas, sing kirtans or go to the church. Will such a child go to heaven or hell?'

I could see her lips move as she prayed but no answer to my question was forthcoming. Emboldened I went ahead a couple of steps and asked again, 'Tell me Ma, heaven or hell?'

'If the child becomes a Musalman, if it becomes faithful, then it will go to heaven. Or else, hell.'

'Hell? Why? What is the child's fault?'

'It was born in an apostate household,' Mother bit out through gritted teeth, 'and that is fault enough!'

Finding my moment to shine, my reply shot out of my lips like an arrow. 'You always say nothing happens without Allah's consent. If Allah chooses to have the child be born in a non-Muslim household then isn't the fault His? Why blame the child instead?'

Before I knew it, the hand with the beads shot out and grabbed me, pulled me closer and began shaking me by my hair. 'You are speaking against Allah! How dare you? Who has taught you all this? If I hear you speaking ill about Allah or the Prophet ever again, I am going to choke the life out of you. If I have given birth to you then I also have the right to get rid of evil like you. In fact, killing such a sinner will bring me more sawab.'

I could not fathom what bad thing I had uttered against Allah or the Prophet! All I had been trying to do was to explain to her that a child had no role in choosing where to be born or which faith to grow up believing in. Since Allah was the one who purportedly made these decisions, the responsibility too had to be His. Mother did not like leaving any complex decisions or responsibilities up to Allah. In fact, the extent of the things she disliked was such that soon enough anything I did began to be perceived as potentially sinful.

For instance, I would be drinking water and Mother would ask me why I was standing and drinking. Apparently standing and drinking water was akin to drinking the devil's piss. Or, for instance, when she began checking my hands and feet every time I came back from the bathroom to see if they were wet. If they were not then that meant I had not washed my hands after peeing. Mother would say it was something the Hindus did, not washing their hands and feet, and that the ultimate fate of such apostates was hell. There used to be a hasnuhana tree on the east side of our house. The flowers would bloom through the night and their fragrance would float into the room and spread to every corner. Whenever she found me lying on my bed with my head near the window, she would snap at me for sleeping with my feet pointed towards the west. The Kabah was in the west and to avoid sin I would invariably have to turn around and face the other direction. By then I had developed a sense of direction and I knew fully well that there was a temple on the west side of the house. But saying anything of that nature to her meant inviting her wrath and perhaps a beating or two. So I usually shut up and did as I was told and turned my feet away from the direction of the Kabah Sharif of Mecca, despite my feet and the holy shrine being a thousand miles apart with immense stretches of land and sea, as well as millions of toilets, temples and churches lying in between.

My mother's faith in religion was completely irrational to me. The few stray answers I got from asking questions provided me with only basic information: Allah had made humans from earth and djinns from fire and during Judgement both of these races were going to be tested. The djinns usually inhabited the air and were thus mostly invisible. And where was Allah? Allah was the light; He was invisible too and He lived up there, somewhere in the sky. Wherever He lived, He was omniscient and omnipresent.

On the night of Shab-e-Baraat she would cook rotis and vermicelli and make arrangements for night-long prayers. On one such night she told me, 'Tonight Allah will come down from the seventh heaven to observe more carefully what His devotees are doing.'

I could not hold back what was churning in my mind. 'Ma, can Allah not see things very clearly from above the seven heavens? Is that why He has to come down?'

Gritting her teeth Mother snapped at me, 'Don't ask so many questions. Have blind faith in Allah, he is the Almighty! There is no one else to worship other than Him, He is forgiving and merciful, He is the one and only!'

I had heard Pir Amirullah say more or less the exact same things, so when Mother said them, she seemed like a pet mynah repeating rote lines. We used to have a mynah like that in Nani's house. Runu khala had taught it to alert everyone about guests and to offer them food. Consequently, the starling had forgotten its own sounds and used to keep repeating what it had been taught. My mother repeated verbatim whatever she was taught at the Pir's house, and all that she learnt was generally applied on me relentlessly as experiments. She was determined to infect me with faith too, although time and again she would tell us to find our own path and that she was only trying to direct us towards the right way of things.

'On the Day of Judgement when Allah will ask of you if anyone had told you about Him, would you be able to deny that I had? In fact, all that I tell you about Him is nothing but what He already wants me to tell you. I am merely a pretext.'

Often, we would sit inside the house or on the veranda and Mother would test me on how much I remembered of the kalmas that Sultan Ustadji had taught me before his demise. In the garb of being a pretext to Allah's sage advice and with her voice soft and mellow, 'Recite to me the Kalma Tayyab, love.'

'*lā ilāha illā-llāh, muhammadur rasūlu-llāh*—'[1]

'And the Kalma Shaadat?' would be her next request, even before I could finish the first.

'*Ašhadu an lā ilāha illā-llāh wahdahu lā šarīka lahu, wa ašhadu anna muhammadan 'abduhu wa rasūluhu.*'[2]

I would recite all this perfectly dispassionately, as if I was reciting rhymes about flowers blooming and leaves trembling. Hardly did I know flowers, let alone leaves!

My efforts usually elicited a smile of content from Mother, a smile that did not take long to curl into distaste the day I decided to probe further.

'You say it has made everyone on earth.'

'He, not it!' she corrected me promptly.

'He. He has made everyone from earth. But where is the earth in our bodies? It's all skin on flesh and bones underneath!'

Her dark lips curling further in disapproval, the soft edge of her voice now harsh and pungent, she snapped back. 'Do you think Allah's earth is just any kind of earth? That it's something that belongs to this world?'

Sharaf mama would often rake his nails over his skin, point at the white streaks and claim that was the earth Allah had made us with. Mother's terse reply managed to curb my curiosity a bit. Perhaps it was indeed what she was saying, that Allah's earth was no ordinary thing. Perhaps it was some unique object that could be found somewhere above the seventh heaven! Seeing how deeply preoccupied I was with these questions she sought to drive home the point further.

'There are no limits to His miracles. Submit yourself to Him. Take those green coconuts, for instance—' She stopped abruptly, raised her glazed and pious eyes at the coconut tree in the yard and continued. 'Such sweet water Allah has put inside them. Do human beings have such power? Or take sugarcane, for instance. It's like syrup in a stick!' Her adoring gaze moved past the coconut tree and swept over the other trees in our yard. 'Then take jackfruits! Such sweet arils He has built up in stacks within each fruit! Can a human being create something like a jackfruit? Submit yourself to Him. He has made such wondrous things for his people to eat!' Done with the jackfruits she moved on to the pomegranates. 'Or take those, for example! He's put tiny crystals of sugar inside those juicy clusters of seeds! No one but Him can do such a thing.'

Mother's descriptions usually managed to sway me. Swaying me to her opinions always calmed Mother down and never failed to spark tenderness in her eyes.

One day I caught hold of Mother just as she was about to step outside on her way to the Pir's house, a black burqa covering her from head to toe.

'Ma, why do women have to wear burqas?'

Turning her surma-lined eyes towards me, Mother took a step back and replied, 'To save one's honour. Allah has decreed that no stranger must ever see a woman's body. If they do so it's a sin.'

We were talking on the stairs, Mother standing right on the last step and me a few steps above her. Climbing down a couple of steps to get closer to her I asked again. 'Why hasn't Allah asked the boys to wear burqas too? What if strangers see their bodies too?'

Lacerating me with her burning grey eyes Mother exclaimed, 'You have to do what Allah has commanded. He hasn't ordered the boys, He has only ordered the girls. You have to do as He wishes without a peep. Asking questions is a sin.'

Sin. The word was enough for me recede three steps. Everything was sinful, asking questions as well, and being sinful meant being cast into hell by Allah. There were snakes and scorpions in hell and I was deathly afraid of both. Ironically, in school our mathematics teacher used to write a problem on the blackboard and immediately ask us if we had questions. He would tell us it was not possible to learn maths without asking the right questions.

Asking anything meant Allah was going to punish the errant person and make them eat the fruits of the yakkum tree. It was a formidable thing, capable of making someone regurgitate their guts. I had first heard about the fruit and the tree from Nana who had shivered and described them to me, full of thorns, thorns upon more thorns. The description used to always remind me of a cactus pear and I was convinced Nana had tasted the fruit at least once in his life to be able to vouch for how detestable it was.

Ever since returning from the Hajj, Nana was no longer interested in descriptions of the burning pits of hell. He was more interested in describing the menu that one could expect in heaven. He would close his eyes as if the spread was already laid out in front of him, a soft smile hovering over his lips, and he would describe what exquisite culinary delights one could expect in heaven, food so grand that even the burps after the meal would be fragrant. To me it seemed as if his five-time namaz schedule was primarily meant to ensure that he could have such a grand meal in the afterlife, as well as for the fragrant burps promised afterwards. The day he returned everyone gathered around him in the living room. As if he had returned from meeting Allah Himself! Nana was sometimes crying and sometimes laughing as he described his experiences of Hajj: how he had gone around the Kabah, kissed the Hajr-e-Aswad, the Black Stone that absorbed sins and became black, how he had thrown shoes at the Devil, how he had shaved his head and donned unstitched white garments and how he had completed a pilgrimage of Hazrat Muhammad's tomb.

Neighbours too had gathered to hear him and from within the congregation Sulekha's mother was the first to express her admiration for his feat. 'Going to the Hajj means one is absolved of all sin. You are indeed a lucky man.'

Feeling the need to make myself heard in the adult conversation, I quipped from where I was lolling about on the floor. 'Those who do bad things, who kill people, like the police who shot and killed Mintu, Allah forgives all of them?'

'Yes, all their sins,' Nana replied.

Mother used to say there were many kinds of sins. Of these the Gunah-e-Kabira, the twenty-one cardinal sins, were the worst and thus completely unforgivable.

'Even the Gunah-e-Kabira are forgiven?'

Nana had no further answers to my questions. Instead, a visibly unhappy Mother grabbed hold of me and led me to the tube well.

'It's been a while that Phoolbahari has kept water out for you. Go take a bath.'

I did as I was told and began to pour the cold water on myself with a mug by the well. All the adult males and the children of the house took their baths in the open by the well. Nani and her grown-up daughters had to make do with the bathroom that also served as a toilet: open on top, walled on three sides with a half wall and a curtain in the front. There was a similar bathroom-toilet in the corner of the yard on our side as well, with its floors stained yellow from urine. Since the tube well was in Nani's yard we usually took our bath there, although Father always used the yellow-stained one on our side. Usually it was Phoolbahari's task to draw water in a bucket and keep it in that bathroom for his use later in the day. The tube well on Nani's yard was not that old either; earlier all our water for washing, bathing and even drinking used to be drawn from the deep well. Later when the government built taps by the road for public use, servants would be sent there with pitchers for drinking water. When Mother was young, they used to drink the water from the pond; back then washing clothes or bathing in it was prohibited. I could not help but think about how different it used to be back when Mother was young and how much things had changed for us.

Even though I was in the middle of scrubbing myself thoroughly with soap, it was not the soap whose smell was occupying my senses. Jackfruits had ripened in the trees on Nani's yard and the smell was causing an odd sensation in my throat, like I had suddenly swallowed something slippery. The first time I had tried eating jackfruits, a ripe aril had got stuck in my throat, forcing me to throw up to get it out. From then on Mother used to squeeze the juices out of the arils and mix it with milk and muri. Although that ensured I did not choke on anything, I still could not stand the smell. Mother used to tell me to pinch my nose with one hand and sip on the bowl of jackfruit-infused milk and muri with the other. I used to find that even more strange! It reminded me of shitting in our latrines and pinching my nose hard with one hand to avoid the smell.

Still scrubbing the soap, I spoke to the dog sitting and panting in the yard. 'Oye, doggo, shit and jackfruits smell the same, don't they?'

The errant canine, red tongue hanging out, gave no response. This dog had quite the reputation in the neighbourhood. It would often invade kitchens and run away with meat, its tail firmly between its legs. The neighbourhood boys used to chuck rocks at it at every glance. Pouring water on myself again to wash off the soap I spoke to it again.

'You want to go on Hajj? All your sins will be forgiven, even the Gunah-e-Kabira.'

Water falling off me splashed on the dog but it made no fuss; it simply got up, shook itself off and walked away. Within the house Nana was pouring drops of holy water brought back from the Well of Zamzam in Mecca on the outstretched palms of the people who had gathered around him. Nani was in the kitchen cooking chitoi pitha, a sweet dish that was Nana's favourite.

The same month Nana returned from his Hajj pilgrimage, Boromama went abroad; he took a flight and flew off to Karachi. He sent us photos from Karachi, pictures of him

riding a horse, wearing a suit and a hat. Nani had the photo
framed and hung it in her room beside the bamboo bank;
soon neighbours began to visit to see the photo of the son who
lived abroad. One such visitor was Sulekha's mother. Taking
out a paan from Nani's box and popping it in her mouth,
followed by a pinch of lime, she spat into the yard, looked this
way and that, pulled her headscarf firmly over her head with
the four fingers that were not yet stained white and whispered
to Mother, ' I heard Siddique has become a communist. The
job abroad has to do with communists as well.'

Before Pir Amirullah happened Mother never used to
go on about snakes and scorpions and such things. Even
the namaz she used to finish fairly quickly, often getting
distracted by Father or my brothers returning home, or even
a dish clattering in the kitchen, and choosing to forgo the
sunnat component of the namaz in favour of only the *farz* or
the compulsory prayer. However, post the entry of the Pir in
her life she would refuse to get up from prayer even if a storm
was about to rip through the house. Despite the sunnat being
optional she insisted on reading that too and she would
remain bent in prayer till she felt sure that she had done her
best and not until she could be certain that Allah was not
going to consign her to the venomous creepy-crawlies of
hell. This thing about the snakes and scorpions and eternal
damnation was something that refused to leave my head.
Hell to me was ostensibly a giant fiery pit within which men
were consigned to be eternally tormented by snakes and
scorpions and what not, with Allah standing by the mouth
of the pit, a white-faced figure with a white beard, dressed in
white kurta and pyjamas, a white cap on His head and a stick
in His hand, observing the scene below and often letting out
a gleeful laughter. He was much like the villains I had seen

in movies. By that time I had watched a number of films such as *Kuchbaran Kanya, Behula, Rupaban*, some of them with Mother. In schools the films *Darshan* and *Kabuliwalah* had been screened. I was fully aware how bad guys in movies found it pleasurable to cause someone misery or trouble. I did not have the guts to tell Mother that I did not think too highly of Allah what with all His incessant talk of punishing and tormenting people! All I could do was snap my fingers and make smart quips. 'What if snake charmers are sent to hell? They can control all the snakes there. Haven't you seen the charmers showing their tricks, how the snakes listen to every word they say!'

By then I was already the girl who was reading English, Bengali and science, getting a lot of marks in exams and smoothly sailing through school, regularly stealing grown-up books from under my brothers' pillows and devouring them. Whenever Mother ordered me to read the namaz I would do my ritual ablutions, cover my head and go through all the motions of prayer, right down to mumbling the Arabic verses whose meanings I did not know. This was despite the fact that in school my teachers used to tell me time and again to never go for rote learning. It was something the stupid girls did, while the smart girls attempted to understand things first and wrote on their own, instead of trying to learn everything by heart. My queries for my mother were rather basic. Why could one not read the namaz in Bengali, for instance. Did Allah not know Bengali?

'Don't talk so much,' avoiding my question, Mother snarled in response. 'And stop bothering me so much. I had so many hopes with you, you were born on such an auspicious day. My daughter was going to read the namaz and keep her roza! That you were going to be a loyal believer.'

This was around the time when Mother had begun to perform the zikr every day, sitting in a dark room all by herself repeatedly chanting 'Allah Hu' and shaking her head from side to side. A zikr, a ritual prayer or litany, had to come forth from the soul and not merely one's vocal cord and usually hours passed with Mother continuing to pray and shaking her head. Allah Hu! Allah Hu! The room would reverberate with the sound, making the cat seek refuge on top of the fence in fear and prompting the pet dog to bark in terror. No matter what happened it scarcely made any difference to Mother because it was well known that anyone performing zikr sprouted metaphorical wings with which they could transcend earthly boundaries and find their way to Allah above the seventh heaven; it was a way to achieve oneness with Him. It was also believed that once one reached that state Allah held them by the chin and kissed them deeply on the lips, prompting the devotee to lose their consciousness in divine adoration. Allah often resembled Pir Amirullah or Jaigir Master from my childhood, or even Sultan Ustadji in his long flowy robes. That was not how it was supposed to be though and Mother would shake her head vehemently. Allah could not resemble the Pir of Naumahal or my mathematics tutor or my deceased Arabic teacher! Allah was supposed to be formless and infinite! The more concrete Allah appeared to her the more she would shake her head to get rid of the spectral images. The cat remained curled up safely atop the fence throughout.

One afternoon, having come back home early quite unexpectedly, Father heard the loud chants and, looking around for the source of the commotion, chanced upon Mother in her engrossed state. This was the same man who used to come to my room and chant Sanskrit shlokas before launching into whatever he had to say to me. One hand in his pant pocket, another on his waist, he said, 'What is your mother up to? Has she gone mad!'

'She's doing the zikr,' I replied, trying to adjust the copy of Tagore's *Daakghar* (The Post Office) that I had nicely fit inside the jacket of my geography book.

'She's lost her senses in her search for Paradise. Who says it pleases Allah if you renounce family and society and only chant His name? Haven't poets said there is no heaven or hell somewhere in the distant cosmos, that whatever exists, paradise or perdition, exists right here in the midst of humanity!'

He came a few steps closer to my table; I clutched the book tightly in my hand, desperately trying to ensure he did not catch a glimpse of the book hidden within the one he could see.

'Concentrate on your studies. This is the biggest asset you will ever have in your life. It's not something you can give away to me, it belongs solely to you. I had to face many hardships for my education. I used to tend to the cattle after coming back from school and study at night in the light of a tiny lamp. That is how I used to rank first in class. I have ensured you don't have to face such adversities. Study hard, so you too can stand first in class. Make sure you know your books from cover to cover!'

I had no response to Father's advice except silence.

Done with her zikr Mother re-emerged from darkness into light, her swollen eyes, stubby nose, dark lips and bony cheeks awash with a smile of content. Sensing Father's departure I brought out the book I had been actually reading. Previously I would have got a scolding from her as well for reading something other than what was in my curriculum, but that day she did not glance twice at what I was busy with.

To her any and every aspect of earthly knowledge was already futile. She walked to the rose bush in our yard, still smiling but not quite in her senses, and began to stroke the red blooms, paying scant attention to the thorns. It did not matter if she got hurt; a few thorns were not going to deter her! As she stroked the flowers her smile stretched wider and reached her ears and tiny dimples appeared on her face, like two tiny betel nuts on her bony cheeks. Every time I glanced up from the book my eyes strayed to the door right in front of me and the yard beyond, with numerous flowering trees all around it, the fence, the cat and my smiling mother. Her strangely satisfied smile, like a deer flitting through the foliage in a dense forest, drew me out into the yard.

'Why are you stroking the flowers, Ma?'

'Look what pretty colours Allah has given these flowers,' she began even before I could finish my question, 'and such soft and delicate petals! The petals are arranged in layers, all of the same size, not an iota of difference among them. And such fragrance! Do human beings have the power to make flowers? There are no limits to Allah's gifts!'

She remained captivated by the flowers as if she had never seen or smelled one before, as if she had just realized how everything in heaven and earth was Allah's creation.

'Each flower is different from the other, each one's fragrance is different too. There are so many kinds of leaves on so many kinds of trees, and so many different varieties of fruits! Allah's power is truly immeasurable.' She turned towards me; it was not my face she saw but another instance of Allah's creative influence. Her eyes then strayed to the heavens, yet another manifestation of Allah's abilities, the sweet smile on her face making it evident that her mind was no longer in this world any more.

Evening was setting in. It was time for Mother to get back inside, chant the Ayat al-Kursi[3] and bless the house to ward away misfortunes and troubles. But troubles and misfortunes were not that easily driven away. Dark clouds were churning in the sky, rumbling and clashing, signalling a gathering storm. A hurricane was going to crash without warning, making the leaves of the tall coconut trees blow in the wind like the hair of a little girl running. The broken branches of our fruit trees, black plums, guavas, mangoes, were all going to be mixed up together, especially the mangoes whose seedlings would all be scattered across the yard. Someone's tin roof was going to fly off and come crash on our jackfruit tree and the gale was going to uproot the custard-apple and ilang-ilang shrubs. Mother was going to scream at Allah to come and protect us all, to stop the terrible storm. Her screams—fuelled by her zikr, five daily prayers, roza, the holy Quran, the short-cropped hair and the clothes that resembled that of the Prophet's wives—were going to perhaps reach till the second heaven, the third or the fourth at the most, before crashing along with the tempest. Barring ourselves indoors, surrounded by the sounds of breaking branches, creaking roofs and crashing pillars, terrified, Moni, Yasmin and I were going to cling to Mother and hope that she was going to intercede with Allah and do something. Mother was going to be praying aloud and then just as suddenly, to our utter surprise, she was going to ask, 'Who knows where your Father is? Where are your brothers?' Right at that moment Mother was going to resemble the woman we used to know once, worried about her husband and children, the storm having brought her back with a jolt to her long-forgotten worldly affairs. She was going to bend over on the floor, as if begging in front of the goddess Kali, and pray to Allah to save my father and brothers wherever they were. The storm was, however, only going to lessen much later and something in my heart was going to tell me that it had nothing to do with Mother or her Allah. But right then I was not going to be able to fathom why that was so; I was going to try and reach out to the answer only to come away with shadows. But long after the Nor'wester, long after the passing of Baishakh, Jaistha and the next nine months, in the month of Chaitra nearly a year later, I was suddenly going to come across a copy of a Bengali translation of the Quran in my mother's wardrobe. And I was going to read the book, primarily because I had always wished to know the meaning of the verses I was made to recite: surah Fatiha, surah Nisa, Lahab, Ikhlas, and so on. The Bengali hidden beneath the Arabic, the true face beneath a mask.

The sun was beating down relentlessly outside. The neighbourhood was drowsy and quiet, like someone taking a siesta with their head resting on their knees. Rocket, our pet Alsatian, was sleeping outside with its legs outstretched. The trees were dozing too, their limbs numb and unmoving. Moni was dozing on the stairs leading up to the roof, under the shadow cast by the bael tree, near a bucket full of wet clothes that were yet to be hung out to dry. I was lying with a ball of tamarind in one hand, from which I was taking the occasional lick, the translation of the Quran in the other. As I kept reading my blood began to run cold. The moon had its own light! The earth was a stationary entity, which was prevented from tilting on its axis by the mountains, which were driven into its surface like nails holding something together. I read the sentences twice, thrice, turned them around and reread them, any way that would help me make sense of what was written in the book. There was no way the earth was stationery! It had to be revolving around the sun!

So was the Quran wrong? Or was what I had read in my school books incorrect?

I was assailed by doubts. So was there no such thing as gravity? Was it truly because of the mountains that the earth was not tilting on its axis? But I had read in my science books that the earth rotated on its axis every twenty-four hours. That meant it indeed was tilting!

Which was correct? Science or the Quran?

The tamarind still in one hand I remained where I was on the floor, legs outstretched, the book lying open in my lap. The Loo blowing in from outside was playing with the curtains, ruffling my hair and pages of the open book.

My soul too had taken flight. The higher it soared the more expansive it became, my physical being simultaneously shrinking till all that was left behind was a dot, alone, helpless and immobile. I was jolted back to my senses by the cooing of a spotted dove outside, my eyes straining to focus on the pages open in front of me. They fell on their next discovery: women were made from the ribs of men. That too from a crooked rib, which meant women were always destined to be crooked and incapable of straight talk and action. Women were also like a fertile field for men to cultivate as and when they pleased. If a woman refused to listen to her man, he was allowed to first banish her from his bed and then explain to her how things ought to be. If that still failed to teach her a lesson then he was allowed to beat the lesson into her. Women were entitled to get only a third of their father's property while men were entitled to two-thirds. Men were allowed to marry as many as four women but women had no such rights. Men were allowed to break off a marriage via triple talaq but women did not have the same rights. When it came to giving testimony against some crime, the word of one man held as much weight as that of two women.

Whether the moon had its own light, whether the sun was moving or stationary, whether the earth too was mobile or not, I had seen none of these with my own eyes and so I could reserve judgement on them. But why should people be different? Why should there be a difference between men and women? Once Chotda and I had peeked into the room of a medical student who lived in our neighbourhood and seen an entire human skeleton hanging in his room. Chotda had told me that it could be a man's skeleton or a woman's, there was no way of telling for sure just by looking. The human body had 206 bones and it was something our teachers at school used to say too. Try as I might I could find no difference between my older brother's neck and mine; his was as straight as mine was. In fact, Dada had the habit of cracking his joints—his knuckles, neck vertebrae, shoulders and back—complete with the distinctive sharp cracking sound. He was usually never satisfied with just doing it to himself, he tried it with others too. He would push me up against the wall and crack the joints of my neck with the same cracking sound. Whether it was Dada, Chotda, Father, Mother or me, we all had the same number of bones in our body. It was not as if Father had one rib less, which had been used to make Mother! If a man was allowed to marry as many as four times then that meant four missing ribs from his body! I could scarcely believe any of it. The woman that Nana had suddenly married and brought to the house for fifteen days, had she been made from his ribs too?

The word of two female witnesses had the same weight as that of a single man. Was it because only men were capable

of telling the truth and not women? Was Sharaf mama
always so truthful? Had he not denied taking Jhunu khala's
earrings, the ones which had ultimately been retrieved from
the knot of his lungi? He had been sleeping and the earrings
had fallen out of the loosened knot. Nani had seen them and
kept them with herself. Sharaf mama had woken up, realized
what had happened and run away from the house, only to
be brought back later after being promised that he was not
going to be scolded or thrashed.

Why were men entitled to a bigger share of their father's
wealth, why such discrimination against women? Why was
Dada entitled to an extra share, were we both not our father's
children? The only difference was that Dada had an extended
penis while mine was flat! Mother would frequently lament
how Noman, my Dada, had absolutely zero common sense
or smarts. Yet he was entitled to more simply by dint of the
fact that he had a penis. I did not want to believe that such
discriminatory views were written in the Quran, the book we
had to kiss with reverence every time we took it off the shelf or
put it back. I may not have always wanted to read the holy book
but that did not mean I had ever imagined to find such things in
it! It simply meant Allah too did not consider women as equals
of men. In many ways that made Allah much like Gnetu's
father from our neighbourhood in Akua. Gnetu's father used
to physically abuse his wife because she did not listen to him.
Once her screams had drawn us all to their yard; I had followed
Felu mama through the bamboo grove to go join the others
from the neighbourhood who were already there. There we
were met with the sight of the shirtless man—Gnetu's father
used to sell curd and cream in front of Thanda's father's jalebi
shop—his lungi folded above his knees, barefoot and sweating
profusely, with crew-cut hair and round, stupid eyes.

'You bloody bitch, the fat has gone to your head, has it? You cook without salt and then dare to talk back?' As he was ranting, he was kicking her, beating her, hurting her with burning logs of wood from the clay oven. As her skin was burning wherever the log was touching her, she was squirming in pain like a chicken being slaughtered. The people gathered in the yard had their hands crossed over their bellies or around each other's shoulders, like a human chain encircling the scene. Some held their hands behind their heads, fingers interlinked, the head leaning on the hands or vice-versa. Some women held their hands over their lips, the other hand supporting the elbow, some had one hand swinging by the side while the other rested on their hips. Their eyes, however, betrayed the indolence their bodies were trying to portray; the eyes were voraciously consuming the scene, Gnetu's father's physical strength and his wife's beaten, bloodied face.

What the man had done afterwards had finally managed to shock them out of feigning dispassion any longer. Standing in the middle of the yard like a triumphant hero, the man had made the ultimate proclamation.

'I'm done with you, bitch! *Ek talaq, do talaq, teen talaq, baayin talaq.*'[4]

The slaughtered chicken was not moving any more, or groaning. The eyes watching her were curious and hungry. Her clothes were in tatters; her hair, like sunburnt hay, was caked with dirt and mud. Gradually the eyes had begun to turn away, feet turning as people began to thin out, like what was supposed to happen once the curtains came down in a theatre after a film's exhilarating climax. A tiny hut, bottle-gourd vines growing on its thatched roof, a sliver of a yard neatly wiped with dung-water and a defeated, divorced woman lying in a heap in the centre. The people were done, they had had their fill of entertainment, the final scene had played out and it was time to leave. Felu mama had come away from the scene and I too had swiftly followed him home.

The neighbours, on their way back, were discussing what had just transpired in front of them.

'She put so much salt, no wonder the man was so angry!'

'She was difficult too! Now she'll learn a lesson.'

'She didn't take care of him well enough, that's what it was. Don't they say, if you are a shrew, your man will fly too!'

The woman in question had stood up from the final scene, walked to the pond and sat and cried there the whole day. No one had bothered her any more. Only I had stayed plastered by my window, watching her from afar. The pond was where she used to wash clothes, where she used to take baths using detergent powder once she was done with her laundry. Afterwards she would walk by our house, the wet saree on her body making a squishing sound as she walked, the clean, wet clothes bundled in one arm. Everything remained as it was, the ponds, the fish, the neighbourhood, everything except her, sitting by the water, like a lonely hill of termites. Everything remained the same long after she was gone, except of course she was no longer there, washing her husband's undershirts and lungis or her child's pee-soaked blankets. Mother had screamed at me to move from the window and stop staring at her. 'This girl has eyes for only the *chhotolok* [lower class].'

Everyone at Nani's place used to call those living in the slums chhotolok. The people living in the big houses were the upper classes by that logic. Whenever people from this latter category came to visit, they were seated in fine chairs and given warm vermicelli pudding to eat. They ate with spoons, drank water from the tube well in nice glasses and tea in bone-china cups with glucose biscuits on the side. Whenever any member of the chhotolok came over, they had to sit on the floor; neither were they treated to warm pudding, nor were they offered tea and biscuits.

Within seven days of divorcing his wife, Gnetu's lower-class father married a girl barely past her teens and brought her home. 'That man is an outright scoundrel,' Mother had said, 'he divorced the women just like that without rhyme or reason.' Phoolbahari's son-in-law too had four wives and Mother's assessment about him was no different.

In fact, she evaluated Father on fairly similar lines, believing firmly that he was a scoundrel at heart because she was convinced he was going to marry Razia Begum out of the blue one day. What I could not fathom was why Mother maintained that she was devoted and dedicated to every one of Allah's rules and prohibitions. Was it not Allah who had decreed that men were allowed to marry when they wished to, divorce their wives at will and marry as many as three–four times? Were these men not following the path that had been set for them by Allah Himself, just as it was meant to be? Then how could Mother abuse them so! It simply meant she was not as dedicated to Allah's will as she liked to claim, not really! Perhaps my mother was not aware that she too was committing a sin by speaking against Allah's will!

The Quran was still open on my lap, its pages flying in the warm Loo just like the curtains on the windows and the wisps of hair over my face. I felt as if I had secretly found someone's hidden treasure. I had chanced upon a pot of gold that was being guarded by a venomous snake coiled around it. Common sense dictated that such an object must be full of wealth. Was that really so or was it nothing but an empty promise? Don't empty vessels make the loudest noise?

Customs

Mother rarely, if ever, ate with us. She would feed everyone at home and then, almost at the fag end of the day, sit down to eat. That too she usually ate whatever was left over after we were all done. For instance, if chicken was made at home she usually ended up with the necks, the ribs or the spine. Whatever was left after she was done was given to the servants. It was fine if nothing was left over for them, because their food was separately made: fish, meat, etc., for us and runny dal and *shutki* (fermented fish) for them. This was the rule, so it had been at Nani's house too; Nani too used to eat later, after Nana and the children and everyone else. Once the whole family was done the servants had their lunch, generally comprising paanta-bhaat mixed with salt and chillies or perhaps a bit of souring, stale dal. When we used to eat Mother never allowed any of the servants to come in front of us; she used to say they would give us the evil eye. Once when I was seven, I remember Mother telling me, after I had complained of a stomach ache, that she had noticed Phoolbahari staring when I had been eating earlier that day. Apparently, that had jinxed me. Mother had fetched betel leaves from Nani's room, smeared them with mustard oil and rubbed them on my stomach while muttering words about warding off jinxes and evil-eyes. Then she had taken the three leaves, skewered them in a small twig and burned them over a lamp.

'That's it, I've burned the jinx.'

'What's a jinx, Ma?'

'Some people look at things in a certain way, it jinxes things. There was this beggar woman who came home once. She noticed the young papaya tree in the yard and said, "Oh, so many papayas!" Barely had she stepped out of our house when the tree suddenly keeled over and fell. Its roots were intact, there was no storm or anything, but just like that it fell, right in front of our eyes. Phoolbahari must have stared at your food and become greedy at the sight.' Once the jinx was burnt the stomach ache too had gradually lessened. Of course, Father had given me medicines by then. Nevertheless Mother seemed convinced that it had happened because of her little ritual of burning the jinx.

Mother used to often talk about three women back in Akua who were similarly known to have always jinxed things. If they looked at a tree, the tree perished, if they looked at someone intently, the person would get severely ill, often to the extent of it being fatal. The people in the neighbourhood would lock their doors whenever they saw these women. When two trees in Nani's house were about to die some enchanted water given by one of these women was poured over their roots and both the trees survived. Nani's mother, my mother's grandmother, used to give medicines to women who had been bitten by dogs to prevent them from giving birth to puppies later on. No one knew what exactly the medicine was. It looked like black pepper and she used to sprinkle it inside a banana, a specific type of dessert banana called 'sabri' or 'mortoman', and feed it to the person concerned. The only instruction one had to follow was not have another banana of the same variety for three months. The mystery medicine clearly worked, since there were never any reports of any woman giving birth to a puppy. Some people from the neighbourhood would come to Nani's mother for the medicine, although most preferred to go for 'saat-pukurer-paani' instead. A mixture of seven palmfuls of water, each from seven different ponds ('saat pukur'), was known to be able to cure hydrophobia as well as ensure human women did not get pregnant with canine offspring. Although as a child when I was bitten by a dog I was not lucky enough to receive such mystical medicines; by then Nani's mother had passed away. Consequently, I had to depend on Father and his injections; during the procedure I remember Sharaf mama laughing hysterically and telling me I was going to get pregnant with puppies. So scared was I of the prospect that I used to press my belly often to check if everything was all right and there were no puppies growing inside me. If I were to swallow jujube seeds by chance, Sharaf mama would say a tree was going to grow out of my head; I would keep touching my head to see if a tree was indeed about to grow out of my skull. If we were to bang heads with someone else, we were told we were going to grow horns unless we bumped heads with the same person again. But once when I had butted heads with Fakrul mama near the tube well, I deliberately did not go in for seconds. We were never really very close; after our return from Ishwargunj, Boromama had taken him to Dhaka for his studies. After finishing his matriculation exam he had come back home to wait for Boromama to return from Karachi, after which he was supposed to get admitted into college. To me people from Dhaka were celestial bodies, things you could see but never touch. Besides, Fakrul mama had assumed it was the handle of the tube well that had struck him in the head, not me. He had been sitting beside the well soaping himself, eyes closed to avoid the suds trickling in, and I had gone with a jug to fill water. I had ended up sitting with a mirror the whole afternoon to see if a horn was indeed going to grow out of my forehead. When I told Sharaf mama about it he began teasing me, telling me the horns were going to be out any minute. Thankfully, regardless of what he said, nothing of that sort had happened.

Fakrul mama had finished his bath and changed into a clean lungi and shirt. Then he had stood in the yard, staring intently at a bunch of jute sticks Nana had gathered there. When Mother had asked him why he seemed so interested in them he had replied, 'No, I was just wondering, what if we set them on fire! I want to see how they burn!'

Mother had turned towards Nani and yelled, asking her to come and check what Fakrul mama was up to. Nani was making tea and had only smiled in response. Every afternoon she used to make tea for the grown-ups and hand out toast biscuits from a jar kept in the meat-safe. At one point that evening the bunch of jute sticks in question did catch fire. Fakrul mama, however, was nowhere to be found; he had had his tea and biscuits and gone out for a stroll. Without dwelling on who the culprit was Nani had set about pouring buckets of water from the well on the burning mass. Unfortunately, her efforts were all in vain; the fire had sputtered, the flames rose nearly as high as the coconut tree and burned the trees and vegetation around the well. After he was back home when Fakrul mama had heard about the fire he appeared genuinely dejected. 'I so wanted to see how it burns! And I was the one who missed out on the whole thing.' The entire

blame for the incident was placed on Phoolbahari, especially
after Tutu mama's testimony that he had seen her smoking
a beedi standing near the well. She must have thrown the
stub into the bunch lying there! Threatening to beat her into
a pulp Mother had issued a strict edict forbidding her from
smoking in the house ever again. Phoolbahari did eventually
resume smoking, on the veranda in front of the kitchen near
the field.

She was like a dark python, her face speckled with scars
from measles, always the scapegoat for anything that used to
happen in the house; I began feeling really bad about her at
an age when I was old enough to start wearing pyjamas. One
fine morning, standing on the inner balcony of Abakash,
brushing my teeth with coal I had just crushed into powder,
she suddenly crossed my mind. Phoolbahari used to make
bhapa pitha on winter mornings, delicious steamed sweet
dumplings, a layer of date jaggery within the white puffy
pocket; she would cover the plate with a thin cloth as steam
would rise off them. Ever since moving to Abakash, winters
passed without anyone making bhapa pitha any more. While
brushing my teeth in the cold and misty morning air all I
could think of was if someone could make me some that day.
What were winter mornings without date jaggery, bhapa
pitha and fresh shiuli flowers in my lap! Mother used to wrap
a shawl around me and tie the ends together at the nape in a
knot. Once the fog dissipated, I would go out for a stroll in
the winter sun. Once we moved to Abakash there remained
slim chances of taking strolls, what with our sudden urban
lifestyle. Winter mornings at Abakash meant wearing thick
woollen sweaters and staying indoors to eat bread and eggs.

Moni brought by some water in a flagon so I could rinse
my mouth after brushing. I had not asked her to, she did

it anyway. Phoolbahari used to do this too. I would have
hiccups and she would silently place a glass of water in front
of me. I used to trip and fall and she would come rushing,
to pick me up and pat me down. Moni did not look like
Phoolbahari but was like her in so many ways, doing things
even before she was asked to. I could not fathom how they
managed to do so much. Waking up at the crack of dawn to
sweep the yard clean. Leaving behind breakfast on the table
at just the right time and taking away the dishes to wash
near the tap after I was done. Hastening to help me wear
my shoes after I put on my school uniform. Cleaning and
tidying up all the clothes I would keep lying around here
and there, washing them when they got dirty. And then
at the end of the day sweeping my bed clean with a hard
broom and hanging the mosquito net. I would go to sleep on
my neatly tucked in bed while they went to sleep very late,
after everyone had turned in, after having cleaned our dirty
dishes and eaten our leftover food. Usually most of them
slept on the floor, tormented by mosquito bites, no nets or
beds for them; the mosquito bites on their faces would begin
to resemble measles scars. Winters were much the same,
without any bedding or quilts all they could depend on were
worn-out old blankets. Such were the rules and like everyone
I learnt to live by these unwritten codes. Like giving them a
blow or two if required. Or making them sit on the footrest
of the rickshaw if one had to take them somewhere; it was
unthinkable to have a servant sit beside you on the rickshaw,
irrespective of whether there was place. They got clothes and
shoes once a year, on Eid ul-Fitr, and Father usually went
and got the cheapest things he could find in the market. Plus
the cheapest soap and the more economical soybean oil for
their hair, instead of coconut oil like ours. While we studied

in the evening they would sit at our feet with a hand-fan to keep the mosquitos at bay. If we asked for water, they would rush to get us some. Back then none of us knew how to pour ourselves water, so used were we to being served all the time. Whatever we wanted they got us and it was their duty to fulfil all our demands. The sole purpose of their birth was to serve their masters and that was perhaps how they were destined to die. They got rebuked if they fell sick; if they died then the blame was placed on their misfortunes. They were dirty, we were clean; they remained below, while we were the upstairs folk; they were chhotolok while we were upper class.

By then I had learnt to read poems and prose in Bangla and English. I had learnt grammar, history, geography, had been introduced to mathematics and science. The world around me had already begun to teach me about upper class and lower class, about caste and creed. I was not arrogant about what an advanced student I was and neither did I hate poverty. However, the universal axiom that humanity was the highest truth above all else always ended up reaching the threshold of our home and invariably stumbling. We lived by an old system, one that was predicated upon the oppression of the impoverished at the hands of the wealthy. I was, without even realizing it, already tied up in these invisible shackles.

Once I was done rinsing my mouth Moni brought in a cup of tea. The habit of having tea in the morning went right back to our time in Nani's house. There used to be two breakfasts in the morning. First, a small breakfast at about seven in the morning when we would pour muri into our cups of tea and scoop it out with a spoon. Then a bigger breakfast at around ten, comprising thin atta rotis and leftover meat or vegetables from the night before or fried eggs.

Barely had I taken a sip of my tea when I heard a commotion from the direction of the kitchen. Mother was hitting and kicking Moni. As she pulled the girl violently the old shirt of mine that the girl was wearing ripped down the middle. Her crime: apparently stealing some meat and, after getting caught, putting the blame on the cat.

'Not the cat, you ate it,' Mother screeched, 'You're a thief! I feed you so much but you are still hungry! Do I not give you meat? How dare you touch the dish?'

Moni was refusing to admit she had stolen anything. Mother picked up a broom and began to beat her with it.

'Own up! Own up that you ate it!'

Her saree slipped off her shoulder in the struggle but she remained unmindful of her modesty as her desperation for a confession from the maid reached a feverish high. Moni was silently withstanding the torment, tears trickling down her cheeks. I butted in—

'Just say you won't do it again.'

'I won't do it again,' Moni mumbled faintly.

Mother stopped, but snapped at me to go away and mind my own business. Such scenes were daily bread for Moni though. The very next day I chanced upon them together again, Moni telling Mother about her life.

'I was so small then, was still being breastfed. Nuni and Chini too were small. Our Father left for a job as a mason in Jamalpur and never came back. Ma later found out he got married there again. He got married for a son, he had always wanted one.'

Mother was listening with only half an ear, dozing off time and again. Moni was picking lice from the roots of her hair, placing them on her left thumb and crushing them with the right.

'He was angry because he had three daughters so he left. If Ma had a son he wouldn't have. But how was that possible! Allah hadn't given her a son! Allah had not spared a thought for her. And why should I even blame Him? My father was cold-hearted, or else how could he have left us like that? Today if he had been with us I wouldn't have had to work as a servant in someone's house. He had had the means to feed us and take care of us.'

Moni let out a forlorn sigh, wiped her eyes on her right arm and continued—

'Ma went to all my uncles from both sides of the family. Every single one of them drove us away. I remember, in one house they had just put the rice on boil. The smell was so exquisite, I still remember it! Not a single person offered us any rice. When we cried from hunger, my sisters and I, Ma would gather shapla flowers and tubers from the ponds, boil them and feed them to us. There was no rice so she would go around the neighbourhood begging for starch. We were gaunt and sickly from hunger and soon Nuni got very sick. She kept asking for stinging catfish curry and rice but who was going to give that to her! Ma cried and begged in front of Allah but He was too selfish to care. Then Nuni died. Oh, how she cried when we were putting her under! After that Ma decided to look for work in people's houses. The ladies of the house were not willing to keep a mother of two as a servant so Chini and I had to take up work instead. We were destined to be slaves! The house Chini used to work in, the man had bad intentions. He would keep touching her and groping her. The wife found out and dismissed Chini. Ma looked everywhere for a job for her but the women of the houses were all wary of taking her in; they did not want a nubile young girl at home. She works in one house now

where the man stays abroad for work most of the time. The
woman lives here with her children.'

'It itches on the right. Look there, you'll find some,'
Mother interrupted her.

Dutifully working on the right side of her head Moni
said, 'Mother used to use a lice comb on us. You buy one too
and it'll all fall off in the blink of an eye.'

She was wearing a faded top with a torn pyjama. Only
two days a year she put on sandals, during both the Eids. But
she had to take them off the very next day to stow them away
safely for the next Eid. On Eid she would take a shower,
put on new clothes and her shoes and then come to us to
ask for face powder. Then she would run off to her broken
mirror and dab her face with it, almost making herself look
white. That was the extent of her annual revelry because she
soon had to touch the feet of the adults of the house to seek
their blessings and then return to the kitchen. Eid was an
especially hectic occasion and she would barely have time
to breathe. Eid went by generally in cooking meat in giant
vessels and for her the whole day passed by in keeping the
fire burning and washing dishes. By Eid evening her new
clothes would appear dog-eared, with masala stains, ash and
grime all over them.

'Everyone tried to convince her,' Moni went on as she
picked out another lice and crushed it against her nail, 'to
get married again. But she did not. What if he was the same,
what if he ran away too? Once I have saved enough of my
salary, I will take Ma and Chini and move to the village. I
will build a small house there and raise chickens. With all the
eggs and the chicks, I am sure we will be able to live well.'

Her dreams swam in her eyes like a swan streaming
through the currents. Her monthly salary was five taka.

She had never seen the money with her own eyes. It was all kept safe with Mother who had promised Moni she was going to use the saved money to buy her a pair of gold earrings and a nose ring when she got married.

'What will I do with gold? And if I get married and can't give birth to a son, what if my husband runs me out too? Rather, give me the money when I go.'

The swan in her gaze had its neck arched high. In her dream house the three of them were going to eat meat and steaming rice to their hearts' content and then go to sleep under fine blue mosquito nets, a beautiful handwoven nakshi kantha giving them warmth. Moni did not know how to dream anything more than that.

A week or two later I came back from school to an empty house—my parents were not home, no one else was about, neither had the neighbourhood girls come to play—and found Moni in the courtyard washing dishes with a coconut husk smeared in ash. It made perfect sense to me to join her and scrub the aluminium dishes sparkling white. Grabbing the utensil from her hand I began to scrub with the ash-coated husk. Her face turning blue, she gulped and tried to dissuade me.

'If khala [my mother] finds out she's going to kill me! You go from here. Let me work.'

'No one will know. Don't tell anyone. Let's finish this quickly so we can play ekka-dokka [hopscotch],' I argued instead.

I could see her eyes dance with joy. She may have played ekka-dokka once, a long time ago, but never in our house. In our house the servants were not allowed to play around.

'You want to play with me? If khala finds out she will whack me for sure.' She looked around as she spoke as if expecting to see someone. Despite knowing the house was empty her eyes glazed over with doubt.

'No one will find out. If we hear the gate opening we can stop,' I tried convincing her, addressing the hesitation in her gaze.

We set about drawing the court on the ground, us girls from two different classes. I had never seen Moni so happy before. I was no longer her master's daughter. I was her old friend, both from the same class, both poor, or perhaps both rich. At least I believe that is what she was thinking of while we were playing, as we hopped from one box of the court to another, both covered in dust and dirt, Moni taking 2 and 4 as I took 1, 3 and 5. The spell broke with the creaking of the black gate, jettisoning us in two different directions. Moni rushed towards the kitchen while I brushed the incriminating marks from my feet and ran straight for my study table. Picking up a load of glassware from the kitchen that she had been asked to clean Moni ran towards the tap. She was almost there when she tripped, the load tipping over from her hand, glasses, plates, cups crashing to the floor and shattering into a million little pieces.

Mother came in and saw the shards of her precious china on the ground. She grabbed hold of Moni by the head and banged her head against the handle of the tube well; the girl's forehead split open, blood gushed out, trickling down her face and the handle of the tube well as well. Unable to speak Moni turned towards me, her face ashen. That was Moni's last day at our house. Tying up her two tattered dresses and the sandals she had gotten for Eid, Moni wiped her eyes and turned to Mother before leaving: 'Khala, my salary?'

'How dare you ask for your salary? You buy me my dishes, the stuff you broke. I will use your accumulated salary to buy new dishes. Get out! Get out of my sight!'

Picking up her bundle Moni walked out of the house, her grand earnings after two years of service amounting to two worn-out dresses and a torn sandal with black straps. She was going to go back to her mother who was going to again look for a job for her somewhere else, perhaps again for five taka a month. Moni was again going to dream of her future. I stood by one of the pillars of the house watching her leave; she disappeared into the darkness without turning back even once. Phoolbahari too had similarly walked away, limping into the darkness without a backward glance. The evening was humming with the buzzing of insects. Mist was beginning to envelop everything, me as well, tiny droplets of dew gathering in the corners of my eyes, the fragrance of blooming shiuli from Prafulla's garden spilling on to our courtyard.

Mother was desperate to rise above worldly affairs but said affairs were not willing to let go of her just yet. So terrible was her grief over losing the glasses and china that she could barely concentrate on her Maghrib namaz. Rocket was sitting in the veranda and whining. Kneeling on her prayer mat Mother screamed in anger—

'Someone get rid of that dog! Angels don't come to a house that has dogs.'

A priest from the Christian mission had left Rocket behind with Dada before leaving the country after the end of the war. Dada used to go to a house near the mission for his guitar lesson and every day he would see the giant dog following the priest around. He was fascinated by the sight of the animal, playing fetch with the priest or lifting its paw for a handshake when asked to. The arrival of the dog at our house brought in considerable tumult in its wake. Rocket, when called, would shoot like his namesake everywhere and extend his paws at us in greeting whenever we did the same. Father was completely on board with the idea of a dog in the house, having immediately decided that having Rocket around was going to be a strong safeguard against thefts and such. He would get a special cut of meat from the butcher, with lots of bones, which was boiled and fed to Rocket. The dog had its own bad habits: getting up on the sofa at every opportunity it could find or jumping on the bed with dirty paws. Back in Nani's house too there had been dogs, nameless, homeless ones that used to roam on the road and go from door to door with a forlorn face looking for food. They used to feed happily on leftovers or scraps thrown at them and sleep under the shade of the tree. Such dogs were beaten, stoned, abused while Rocket was used to being treated with all the comforts reserved for humans usually. Any time someone petted or stroked him he would wag his tail in delight.

Mother, however, was less than amused. 'Dogs are impure, get that impure thing away from here.'

Soon enough an embargo was placed on Rocket entering the main house. Instead, arrangements were made for him to be kept tied in the veranda during the day. The chains were taken off at night when he was supposed to be guarding the house from robbers. Rocket stayed out of sight during the day; anyone hardly ever went to the veranda adjacent to the tin shed, used for storing junk and scrap, where he was kept tied. In time it so happened that his tin plate with a hole would remain empty through the day; Mother would forget to feed him. At night Rocket's whimpers would echo through the house.

Often I would come back from school and ask Mother if she had fed Rocket.

'I did.'

'When did you feed him? I think Rocket's hungry again. Give him some more food.'

'Don't meddle in this, I'm telling you! I will decide when and what the dog will eat,' Mother would snap at me, annoyed by my questions.

One look at Rocket's forlorn face was usually enough for me to be convinced that he had not been fed. I would eat only half my food and give the rest to him, making sure Mother did not find out. He would jump on the food at once, his tail wagging, and once done he would look up at me with expectant eyes for more.

Time and again Father too noticed that something was amiss. 'The dog seems to be getting thinner and thinner by the day. Don't you feed him?' His questions annoyed her just as much as mine, making her grit her teeth as she answered. 'Of course I feed it! If you overfeed a dog all its fur will fall out. If you care so much why don't you cook and feed it yourself!'

Nevertheless, Rocket continued to shrivel in size, reduced to bare skin on bone, a skeletal shadow of his older self. He had, in the meanwhile, figured out how to escape his shackles and would do so whenever he found the front gate unlocked. He would run out to the road to rummage through garbage for scraps of food and get attacked by stray dogs. A single Alsatian against a pack of strays; usually the former lost. Rocket's body was soon covered in wounds. One day Mother declared, 'The dog's sick. It throws up when it eats rice. No rice from today.' Chotda was usually busy with his guitar or could be found strolling down the street whistling some tune or the other, the sound of which drew our neighbour Dolly

Pal to her window. Besides, he had friends visiting him from time to time. He would style his hair and go out with them once they were done spending time at home. In all this he barely had time to keep track of how Rocket was doing.

Despite Mother's repeated outbursts that angels did not tread in houses that kept dogs, nothing she said managed to convince me otherwise. I pretended not to hear her, as if I did not care if the angels descended upon our house or not, forcing myself to train my ears on the sounds of insects buzzing outside. Mother often expressed her dissatisfaction and concern about how I was turning into a book-reading detached girl. It was how it was. It was this sort of detachment, nursed in secret and anointed with dewdrops, that kept alive in me the secret hope that Moni was going to find her way back to me one day.

After firing Moni from her job Mother took up the duties of the kitchen for the next couple of days. It only made her angrier, much of which she took out on Father after he returned home.

'You won't let the girls into the kitchen. Won't they ever get married? Won't they have to feed their husbands? All girls learn how to cook when they are in their parents' house. But see these two, they go about as if they are boys.'

'They study,' Father cleared his throat and continued, 'why should they have to get into a kitchen? Haven't I kept people to help you? My daughters are not to go into the kitchen. It'll be bad for their studies.'

'Oh, they are changing the world with their studies!' Mother was thoroughly exasperated. 'When their father isn't home all they do is play around. Look for someone again. I can't do all this work by myself. Whoever we keep, the moment they learn all the work they leave!'

As a result Mother stopped going into the kitchen entirely. The hearth lay unattended and no one knew who was going to gather the wood, pound the spices, do the laundry and the dishes or even who was going to cook. The idea was to show Father that our home had come to a grinding halt. So when he asked for food he was told there was none because there was no one to cook and clean. Of course, without his knowing, she fed us! She even managed to convince a beggar who had come for alms, in exchange for one meal a day, to do the dishes, cook the rice and get the spices and other ingredients in order for cooking. In the end, Father struck up a conversation with a young migrant girl in Notun Bazar whom he had chanced upon sleeping on the footpath and, after making the most basic inquiries about her background, brought her home as our new maid. He requested Mother to make do with her for the time being. Regardless, Mother was in no mood to hire anyone without a proper interview.

Mother sat on a chair in the inner veranda, the new girl standing by one of the wooden pillars. She was barely nine, with a runny nose, feet covered in calluses, hair burnt red by the sun. She wore a dirty half-pant, which had perhaps been white once but was now a dull brown with dirt. Her feet, cracked like dry earth, were caked with mud.

'What's your name?' Mother inquired in a sour voice.

'Renu,' the girl said through a snort, trying to stop her nose from running.

'What all can you do?'

Renu made no answer. Instead, her gaze strayed towards the plants on the yard and the chickens and the ducks.

'Have you worked anywhere before?' Mother asked again, scanning the girl from head to toe.

'No,' Renu answered.

'You don't have parents?' The question came out more like a reprimand.

'I have a mother, no father,' she replied without batting an eyelid, as if such a thing hardly mattered.

'More siblings,' Mother's voice softened at the question.

'No,' Renu replied, disinterest apparent in the tone.

'Will you be able to grind spices? And do the laundry?'

Renu nodded her head in response.

Pursing her nose, perhaps because of the stink coming off the girl in front of her, Mother asked again, 'Can you cook rice?'

Yet again the only reply was a tilt of the girl's head.

Nevertheless, it was deemed enough for her to pass Mother's test and be hired. That very moment itself Mother handed her a bar of soap and directed her towards the tube well to scrub the grime off herself and take a bath. Once done, she gave the girl some oil to put in her hair and one of my old dresses to wear and then fed her leftover dal and paanta-bhaat. Then she asked Renu to sweep the house and follow that up with grinding the spices and putting the rice on boil. All the while she kept an eye on the girl's work from afar.

Truly, maids in our house were easily replaceable. A Moni could be replaced with a Renu in the blink of an eye, one lower-class person for another. The city was filled with such lower-class people and one did not have to look too far and wide for them. Thus, there was nothing that could possibly inconvenience our life of luxury and indulgence. Putting the reins of the house in Renu's hands Mother resumed her visits to the Pir's house. She would go and listen to the sermons, cry her eyes out and invariably come back home uttering the choicest abuses against worldly affairs. Not that she ever missed a beat in dealing out punishment if Renu were to make mistakes, like if the rice was overcooked and squishy. Mother's temper vacillated between extremes; those who worked for us were afraid of her enough to remain as inconspicuous as possible. Just as suddenly there would be an outpouring of love from her end, like when she sat Renu down to teach her Arabic at night. Renu too complied readily. In time more of my old clothes were passed down to Renu. The affection of the rich is a strange thing, one never knows what one is going to get in return.

Before Renu could properly settle down in our house, Rocket passed away. Discovering his dead body in the veranda one day, Mother sent word to Father to call one of the sweepers to clear away the mess. Father sent over a person from his medicine shop who tied a rope around the dead Alsatian and dragged his body out on to the road, leaving a dusty trail across the yard in their wake. Unable to contain myself, I ran to the bathroom to cry, the only place in the house where I knew I could hide myself from everyone. Rocket was no more, he was not going to run to me when called nor was he going to jump and take biscuits ever again. When we used to go out, he used to go out with us, much to the astonishment of our neighbours. We would walk to the main crossing and ask him to go back home and he would always listen to us and run back like a good boy. Our good boy Rocket, starved and ill, died silently, his sad, teary eyes watching us expectantly till the very end. No one bothered to take him to the veterinary hospital even once. I was the awkward girl of the house, abused whenever I tried to make my opinions heard. As a result I learnt early to turn a blind eye and a deaf ear to anything and everything as much as possible.

After Rocket's death Mother brought home a new puppy, a local breed, from Nani's house. I wanted to call this new one Rocket but Mother declared the dog was going to be called Poppy. One of the jailors back in Pabna had a dog named Poppy and Mother wanted to call her new dog the same. She already had goats, pigeons and chickens; now there was a dog in the mix. After Poppy came home Mother never forgot to feed and take care of it. Dogs were no longer impure things and neither were there any more fears about angels giving the house a miss because of them. In time Poppy and Mother became quite inseparable. She was the dog's master and she fed it meat from her own plate. When I tried teaching it to fetch, it showed no interest in leaping for the ball. Poppy was like any average guard dog and Mother took care of it a lot, just like she took care of Renu. Renu gave her body massages at night and rubbed her scalp as well. Once she had finished with the Arabic alphabet Mother moved on to teaching her Bangla.

Despite everything, time and again, we would find Renu sitting by herself and softly weeping. She said she missed her mother.

'I have done so much for you and you still cry,' Mother would berate her. 'You're a servant and will remain a servant. You'll have to earn your keep as a servant always.'

When he found out about it Father managed to somehow locate Renu's mother and brought her to our house. He coaxed Mother into keeping her, asking her to give the heavy work to the mother and keep the errands for Renu. The next day Father brought home a simple printed cotton saree for Renu's mother to wear. Mother took the saree in her hands and felt it with her fingers to check the weave.

'The weave's good. It's expensive. Even I don't get these!'

Right from the outset Mother would lash out at Renu's mother over the slightest pretexts. When Father came back home she would complain to him about her.

'That woman, her character's not right.'

'Why? What has she done?' Father would ask curiously.

'The grocer sent over our things with his man. I saw them whispering. I gave her a blouse to wear but she won't wear it. Keeps hovering around the guy without one!'

Father usually stayed quiet during such reports. His silence only fuelled her rage further.

Months limped past with Renu and her mother managing the house. Mother had again begun visiting the Pir and was regularly coming home late at night. Like before she could again be found frequently sitting in prayer and calling for Allah. With her presence becoming next to inconsequential, quite without her knowledge most of the control of the house shifted to Renu's mother. Be it salt or oil, spices and what not, Father usually asked her about everything. In her free time she would tie her hair while humming a tune, a scene that made Mother seethe with anger. She would often snap at the woman to stop and behave like a servant and keep working silently. Renu's mother never failed to comply immediately.

One night—I had barely wept myself to sleep over Sarat Chandra Chattopadhyay's *Devdas*, which I had been reading after everyone had gone to sleep and which I had hid under my mattress before turning in—when I was awakened by a sudden loud noise. For a moment I could not quite figure out what it was I was hearing but after listening a little intently I could single out the sound of Mother shouting and loud banging noises on a door. Someone was banging on a door, trying to break it open! The first thought was we were being robbed. My limbs froze in fright, my body soaking with sweat, as I lay in bed trying not to breathe too loud, eyes closed, as if I was asleep, so that the robber would think twice before slaughtering someone so innocent. Someone was running down the veranda, someone else too, loud voices could also be heard outside. Someone was talking in a low voice; what, to whom, I could not comprehend.

Beside me Yasmin had woken up too. 'What is it, Bubu?'

'I don't know,' I whispered.

To add to the frozen limbs, my heart was threatening to burst right out of my chest, as if someone was beating a mighty hammer on a massive anvil. In a little while, once the commotion outside had died down, Mother woke up Dada and Chotda to tell them what had happened. She had not caught a thief or a robber in the house, she had caught our father. In bed with Renu's mother. At around two thirty in the middle of the night on the bed in the kitchen. Mother was a light sleeper. She had woken up suddenly and had been walking around the house checking if all the doors and windows were fastened properly, especially since theft was a regular menace in the neighbourhood. The door of Father's room that opened out into the veranda was unlatched and she had peered inside and found the room empty. She had looked everywhere for him at first. Suddenly, tipped off by a noise from the direction of the kitchen, she had gone closer and immediately heard Father's voice from within, along with creaking noises from the cot Renu's mother had been spreading her bedding on for the past week.

Father had been found in bed with Renu's mother in the depth of the night. I lay on my bed staring up at the mosquito net, Yasmin lying beside me just as lifelessly, her large, round eyes unmoving and wide awake. My world-renouncing Mother could be heard weeping through the rest of the night. The sighs of us four siblings, Dada, Chotda, Yasmin and I, stayed awake and kept her company.

Pirbari 2

Entering the pirbari always gave me the heebie-jeebies. I was convinced that all the trees of the property were infested with ghosts and djinns and I was terrified one of them was going to latch on to me while walking beneath them. I clasped Mother's fingers tighter as we walked towards the Pir's quarters. As it was I did not want to enter the place. She wanted to and I was simply being forced to tag along. Since becoming a disciple of the Pir, Mother had given up wearing sarees in favour of long tunics and pyjamas. Most of the time she did not even seem like my mother at all!

There were six–seven girls in the Pir's room, in long, loose robes that covered their feet, their heads covered with scarves. The robes clung to them in a manner so as to give the impression that they barely had a stitch of clothing on. One of the girls was wearing a saree. She had four amulets hanging around her neck and her headscarf was pulled low over her forehead. With a forlorn expression on her face she was touching the Pir's feet in entreaty—

'Huzur, my husband will give me talaq if I don't bear him a son.'

Pir Amirullah was a soft speaker; he would scratch his beard with his fingers whenever he spoke. Looking up at the ceiling, his eyes brimming with compassion, he spoke—

'Take Allah's name! There is no one who can grant a wish other than Him, I am merely a tool in His hands. Pray in the middle of the night. He is the Sustainer, the Lord of heaven and earth, cry in front of him, Aleya. If you don't, how do you expect to soften his heart! If a servant extends a hopeful hand, can Allah ever turn them away! His mercy is immense.'

Aleya, bent over his feet as if in prayer, began to cry. If it meant having a son, then she was willing to pray all through the night. Amirullah's hand slipped from his beard and came to rest on her back, his gaze shifting from the ceiling to her dark tresses from which the head scarf had slipped.

'Allah is One, the Only, formless and omnipotent. He has no beginning nor end. He has no parents or children. He is sightless yet omniscient, He possesses no ears but He still hears everything. He can do anything but He does not possess limbs such as ours. He is omnipresent. He does not sleep, nor does He require food like us. He has no discernible shape, nor can He be compared to anything corporeal. He has been forever and He will be forever too. He eradicates wants but He wants for nothing Himself. He is immortal, beyond death and destruction. He is immensely kind and generous. He is the Lord of the highest status, which He distributes among his servants. Pray to him, you will surely have a son and your social standing too will be salvaged.'

Huddling behind Mother, Allah's formlessness occupied my thoughts. It was a lot like the magician who had visited our school a while back. He had been covered in a black cloth and once the cloth was removed he was no longer there! It was as if he had disappeared into thin air. If I was formless, I could have roamed the entire city or even gone and sat beside the Brahmaputra all by myself. No one would have been able to find me to force me back home.

The Pir slowly shifted his feet from under Aleya who was still bent over in prayer. Humaira, one of the young girls in the room, came forward, picked the woman up and took her out into the courtyard. Standing under the hibiscus tree, Aleya untied a knot in the drape of her saree, took out a currency note and passed it to Humaira. An expert at this already, the latter swiftly passed the note to the Pir, the money changing hands like in a relay race. The Pir shoved the money inside a pocket of his robe that was his mobile cashbox for the moment. Finding my gaze transfixed on his hands, he stared intently into my eyes and then asked Mother—

'Hamima, who's this? Your daughter?'

'Ji huzur,' Mother replied, pulling me to stand in front of her, 'she was born on 12 Rabiul Awwal. She reads the namaz with me. Has just finished the Qaida Sipara and started on the Quran Sharif. Bless her, my lord, so she can find her faith.' Pushing me towards him she commanded, 'Go, touch huzur's feet.'

I stood my ground and refused to budge. I did not want to touch his feet. Mother nudged me from behind yet again but instead of moving forward I began to step back from him, a couple of steps at a time. He had a long white beard and he wore a robe that fell right past his heels and a cap with Allah's name written on it. His arm shot out and grabbed hold of me, as if plucking fruit from a tree; he dragged me into an abrupt embrace, my little form almost disappearing within the voluminous drapes of his robe. As I struggled to breathe I heard him mutter some words under his breath and then blow air on my face in blessing, splattering me with speckles of spit in the process.

Extricating myself from within his robes I ran to Mother, his faithful disciple, and hid behind her. Wiping my face on her sleeve I heard him ask her, 'Is your daughter studying about worldly affairs?'

'Yes, huzur,' Mother could only sigh in reply, 'I have no control over the children. Their father, that's what he's teaching them. The girl, in fact, has a lot of curiosity about Allah, wants to know things. So I thought bringing her here would make her feel better, and maybe turn her a little more towards Him.'

Making a sound of regret with his tongue, the holy man reclined on his bed and continued. 'You know where the trouble lies? Such worldly knowledge invites the shaitan to possess you and once that happens it becomes very difficult to extricate oneself and return to the path of the Lord. Take these girls for instance, Nazia, Nafisa, Munazzaba, Motia. All of them used to be in college; now all four have quit. Instead they have focused on learning the ways of Allah. They are saving up for the Judgement. It is only now they realize that they had been seeking false knowledge thus far. They were shrouded in darkness, never having been exposed to the true light of knowledge.'

Signalling me to go and make myself scarce in the courtyard, Mother picked up a palm leaf fan and began to fan the Pir. I edged out of the room. Barely had I set one foot on the steps to the yard when I was waylaid by Humaira and whisked off to a room on the northern quarters of the house. The mattresses in the room were kept rolled up during the day, with only a reed mat, called a shitol-paati, covering the bed on which Fajli khala's girls used to read the namaz. None of them were in school, having decided instead to dedicate themselves to learning the ways of Allah. Humaira was about five years older than me. She had a big, round face, almost like an elephant apple.

'You are my eldest aunt's daughter, we're cousins, do you know?' she asked, poking me in the shoulder. 'Why do you study worldly knowledge? These things make Allah angry, He will hold you as having sinned.' As she finished she dragged me to the bed and sat down beside me. 'Your father is a kafir. If you listen to him, Allah will consign you to dozakh too!'

Her eyes were closed as she spoke and she shivered as if terrified by the hell she was clearly imagining in her head. Before I could understand why she had grabbed hold of my hands in her own, a shiver crawled down my spine and it seemed to me as if I too could see what she was seeing. A giant fiery pit, numerous people floating in a lake of boiling water and screaming in pain. I was there too, I was burning and screaming just like them. By then seven other girls had appeared in front of us, there sharp gazes all but lacerating me, a strange creature tainted by knowledge of the material world. I could see a wave of pity in their gazes too, like a school of fish leaping in and out of water, as if they could already see me burning in the fires of hell from their blessed perches in heaven. As many a sigh of pity echoed across the room one tallish girl spoke: 'Humaira, does she want to find her way back to the path of Allah?'

'Yes, she does, but her father is not letting her,' Humaira replied through a sigh of her own, deeper than the others perhaps because we were cousins. She made a familiar twitching sound of regret with her tongue, the others followed suit in the same vein, as if a clutter of cats were slurping milk from a bowl all at the same time. I sat and counted them: seven, six, five, four, three, two, one. Tall, short, medium, short, short, short, medium. I wanted to make them stand in a row during morning assembly in school: short, short, short, short, medium, medium and tall. I wanted to make them stand in an assembly and sing. My train of thought was interrupted by another poke from Humaira. 'These seven girls, their fathers have led them down the path of Allah. They live here now and learn the Quran and the hadith.' Another deep sigh and she went on. 'If only we could have given uncle some sound advice, I'm sure he would have found his way back to the Lord. And helped his children do the same as well.'

I can't say for sure if Father would have found the path they were talking about, but sound advice had definitely managed to sway Munazzaba's father. Her father, a judge, had been swayed enough for him to dedicate his sixteen-year-old daughter to the service of Allah. It was Humaira who informed me that Munazzaba, the tall girl, was the daughter of a judge from Dhaka. The city Humaira mentioned in such a tone so as to leave no doubt as to what an esteemed man he was. What had been the matter? The sixteen-year-old girl, despite being good in studies, had begun to act in uncharacteristic ways after falling in love with an entirely unsuitable boy. Then some people had claimed to have found the two in a compromising position in the dark somewhere and in no time the rumours had spread all across the neighbourhood. The judge had stopped his daughter from going about her studies and confined her to the house as a result. It was at such a juncture that someone had brought the name of Amirullah Pir to his attention, the holy man who taught the Quran and the hadith to girls, taught them to be regular with their namaz and constant with their faith, where girls learnt to stay indoors at all times and live a strictly regimented life behind the veil. Hearing about such a man the judge had paid a visit to one majlis held by the Pir; the latter's behaviour had succeeded in melting his heart. In a few days he had firmly carted his wayward daughter off to the Pir's house to be brought to line. The judge's daughter Rubina was rechristened Munazzaba; Munazzaba put on large robes, covered her head and was soon trained to obey the laws of the veil. She learnt to occupy her time with the holy books, cry her heart out during the graphic descriptions of hell while the Pir delivered sermons, and often give the man massages as well. That had been the beginning of young girls being sent to this house to be tamed, girls from influential families, daughters of police officers, lawyers and bureaucrats. Hazrat Ibrahim had been ready to sacrifice his son at Allah's behest, so why would modern fathers not be able to let their daughters walk the path of Allah! That was what Humaira believed at least. In the Pir's house, girls were told to fall obsessively in love with Allah, something that they promptly did. Their love story with the formless Almighty grew in leaps and bounds as soon as they stepped into the Pir's parlour. It made the Pir heave a sigh of relief. To him these girls were not Munazzaba, Nazia or Nasima, to him they were simply like flowers in the garden of Paradise.

In his courtyard, gleaned out of a cleaned and reclaimed woodland, Pir Amirullah had built small huts for the girls, some with tin roofs and some with cement. None of the huts had any windows though and the suffocating heat made it impossible to live in them. But he had explained to the girls how, back in the day, houses in Arabia used to be similar; that the prophet used to live in one such hut himself. Living in such a hut guaranteed sawab. If the girls could go through the same struggle that the Prophet had

had to go through, then during the Day of Judgement the Prophet himself was going to stand as their witness in front of Allah. It made the girls heady with emotion, made them cry out in ecstasy. They did not need windows! If they could have, had it been known that the Prophet had foregone the use of doors too, they would have probably been ready to renounce that as well.

After a couple of years, when the fathers had come to take their faithful daughters back home, the girls had refused to return. Munazzaba's father had been grievously ill so her mother had turned up to take her back but she too refused. She had no desire to go back to the polluted world outside. She was convinced that stepping out of the house would cause angry boils to erupt on her skin from all the sin outside. Not just Munazzaba, but the other girls too, when their parents came to take them home after fixing a match with some suitable boy somewhere, refused to go back home with them outright. They informed their parents clearly that they were going to continue to serve Allah instead. It was the last age of man and marriage during such an epoch was not the right thing to do, that was what the Pir huzur had explained to them. They were no longer interested in doing things that were not right; unable to sway their steadfast minds their fathers returned home empty-handed.

I was curious as to why it was not right to get married and they had the answers raring to go. The holy Pir had apparently had a word with Allah Himself, in the depths of meditation, when the two of them had been strolling down the garden of Paradise. The very thought of such a thing made Munazzaba close her eyes and imagine herself as a bird floating over the divine gardens. Allah had reportedly told the Pir that the last age of man had commenced. It was time for Israfil to blow on his trumpet, the Apocalypse was nigh. In the last age there was no point pursuing social or familial ties. There was no time and it was advisable instead to make arrangements for the Day of Judgement. The girls were convinced that the Pir himself was going to help them across the Pul-e-Sirat; the man had promised them that he was going to hold the hands of his favourite disciples and lead them to heaven with him, otherwise he was not going to go in either. Thus, during such a cataclysmic age, the girls were not willing to let their huzur out of their sight. For his part the huzur too had promised that he was soon going to take them to Mecca with him. He wished to live out the time left before the end of days in the land of the Prophet.

'Allah will send us a steed to take us to Mecca,' Munazzaba spoke with conviction.

What steed? The seven girls and Humaira were soon in deep discussion regarding the nature of the ride. It could perhaps be a Buraq, the divine steed that transported the prophets. None of them had any clear views on what it was going to be but they were nonetheless absolutely certain that it was going to come for them someday soon. In fact, lists were ready as to who was going to join the expedition in which batch and Munazzaba had found out that her name was on the very first. The much-discussed list was supposedly stowed away safely under the holy Pir's pillow.

Terror glistened on their faces as if *qayamat* could come any moment and soon a bit of their fear seeped inside me too. Father wanted me to do well in my studies, grow up and become successful. But what if qayamat came before that, what if the world simply imploded? There was going to be judgement on the field of Hashr where Allah Himself was going to sit with a scale to weigh the lot of humankind.

The very thought made my heart race! What if when I
stepped up to Him the first thing He asked me was whether
I had dutifully read my namaz, counted my beads and recited
the holy Quran! What if He asked me if I had lived by His
word. What was I supposed to say? If I said yes, I was going
to be caught immediately. Because Allah already knew my
destiny, right? If everything was preordained then what was
the point of gathering everyone on the field and asking them
again about their deeds? For some odd undefinable reason I
came to believe that when everyone was going to be gathered
on the field of Hashr—the field whose descriptions always
reminded me of the massive meadow of Lalmatia that I had
been to while on a visit to Boromama's house in Dhaka—the
magician who had come to show his tricks in our school was
going to be able to conjure something up and cross the Pul-
e-Sirat without much ado. Just like he had vanished within a
swaddle of black cloth while performing for us.

I could almost visualize him crossing over the divine
bridge. As far as the eye could see there was a wispy thread
ahead of me stretching into the distance, a bridge so fine
that I was barely managing to not topple over. But there he
was, the magician, walking ahead swiftly, barely a tremor
wracking his body. The magician was Hindu, his name was
Samir Chanda. If a Hindu managed to cross the Pul-e-Sirat
where were they destined to be sent, to heaven or hell? If I
was to judge I would send them to heaven for having crossed
over. But it was well known that even if a Hindu was to
ever succeed in crossing the divine bridge between life and
death, no matter how pious and good they were, they were
still destined to be sent to dozakh. It was so because that
was Allah's will. I found myself deeply disapproving of this
preordained and predestined bit. If everything was already

supposed to be decided from before then why put up a sham of a trial? No matter what, the field of Hashr was going to be nothing but a theatrical performance. And all around me people were so excited to be part of the drama!

Lost in thought, I did not notice the girls leaving one by one and heading towards the Pir's room. Left alone, I had no choice but to sit and wait for Mother. There was no way of knowing when her work there was going to be done. Every time we had visited before promises of returning home by the afternoon had gotten delayed till the evening and some evenings had even rolled into fairly late in the night. And then on other occasions she had suddenly put on her burqa and told me to hurry up and get moving so we could return home. On that particular day, the fact that I was sitting in a room in the northern quarters waiting for her was the farthest from Mother's mind. She was busy mingling with people and having secretive, whispered conversations. Hushed conversations were a strange thing; no matter what they were about one wanted to know. After these furtive conversations were done she was going to fan the Pir huzur, give him a foot rub or make him a cooler, or perhaps some paan. She was going to hold the spittoon in front of him and then scrape some of the spittle into her own mouth for blessing. Only then was she going to be done for the day.

I was trying for a long time to catch a glimpse of the face of the person she was furtively whispering to, but the only thing I could see was her buttocks, large and round like the base of a heavy brass pitcher. Suddenly, out of nowhere, two young girls rushed past me, like a gust of wind brushing over my feet, towards the window. It seemed they had not noticed that there was a living being, me, sitting there already. These two had not been among the seven whom I had met previously; they appeared, at least to me, new. They were dressed like the seven though, covered from head to toe. One of the girls, I could not catch which of the two, spoke to the other—

'There he is, see! Muhammad, Fatema aapa's son.'

The other voice, again I could not tell which of the two, replied—

'And that one, the one who placed his hand on his neck. That's Hazera khala's son Muhammad.'

There was nothing in front of me except the backs of the two girls. In moments more girls appeared out of nowhere, more backs adding to the gallery by the window. Past them one could see the courtyard of the outhouse, by the pond, where the men who were going to be part of the Pir's majlis had gathered. Only a handful of men were allowed entry into the inner quarters where the women stayed, most of whom were the huzur's relatives. The men standing in the courtyard by the pond were not among those select few.

'And there's Muhammad, Nurunnabi bhai's son,' a new voice chimed in.

The girls were laughing. They were giggling, their scarves over their mouths, jostling, trying to reach over each other, pushing one's head in between two others, all in order to catch a glimpse of the boys. The girls in the front of the pile did not wish to make way for their friends behind them; the girls at the back were constantly trying to slip in undetected.

'That's it! You've had your turn! Now let me see.'

Standing right at the back, behind all of their backs, I craned my neck to peer outside and saw a bunch of men in white kurtas and pyjamas, caps on their heads, lounging about, hands on their hips or around someone's shoulder, scratching their asses, yawning, swatting away mosquitos or washing up before the majlis. I failed to understand what all the fuss was about.

More girls came and joined ranks, the newcomers part of the first seven I had met. They were all watching the numerous Muhammads in the gathering; it made me exceedingly curious as to why so many boys had the same name. I could not very well ask the question and it remained lodged in my throat like a wayward tamarind seed. The room had only one window, that too only because it was older than the other parts of the property. The new rooms did not have any windows at all, which ruled out any opportunity for the girls to ogle at their Muhammads from anywhere else.

Even Fajli khala's son, her only son, was called Muhammad. Before him there were the three sisters: Humaira, Sufayra, Mubaswera. After giving birth to three girls one after another Fajli khala's episodes with the djinns had increased in frequency. Once Muhammad was born these episodes had declined considerably. After him she had had three more girls and the djinn incidents were again on the upswing. Apparently, Humaira too had been recently possessed by a djinn that had left only after three long days and nights. That was how it was in that house, fairly frequently some girl or the other came to be possessed by djinns. When it happened the girl would be locked in a dark room, the doors and windows would be barred and the Pir would shut himself in with her to perform the necessary exorcism. I had seen Juthi's exorcism with my own eyes. Juthi used to be a class senior to me in school and was a beautiful girl. One day she was seen sitting under the school banyan tree, singing all by herself. The bell for the next period rang and the other girls returned to their classes but Juthi stayed where she was, singing. This happened again in the next period; the bell rang but Juthi did not hear it. She kept singing, her hair flying in the wind. There was a maulvi in our school, our Urdu teacher, we used to call him Urdu Sir. He heard what was going on, dragged Juthi inside and told the teachers that she was possessed by a djinn. Juthi was screaming her lungs out, begging him to let her go. Keeping a firm grip on her struggling wrist, Urdu Sir went about making the arrangements for the exorcism. Holy water, charmed with the words of the Alhamdu surah, Ayat al-Kursi and the first five verses of Djinn surah, was first sprinkled on her face. Then the maulvi held a burning piece of wood in front of her and beat her with a neem branch. He kept beating her till she lost her balance and fell forward on the floor. I had stood and watched her exorcism, along with the other girls of the school, with an entire world of disbelief clouding my eyes. I remember feeling profoundly sorry for her.

Sitting alone in the room in the northern quarters of the Pir's estate, I felt a shiver trickle down my spine. I felt uneasy. It was the house. I was afraid a djinn was going to get me as well. What if the Pir Amirullah dragged me to a dark room as well, a wicked-looking cane in his hand, to exorcise my demons!

While I sat shivering in fear, the girls had moved away from the window. Mother came by in a hurry to inform me that we were going home after the majlis. Since I had experienced a majlis before, the news was not a particularly welcome one. The majlis was usually organized in a big room, built in such a way that women from the inner chambers could easily pass into a special veiled gallery reserved for them, separate from the rest. Thin carpets were spread on the floor on which people had to kneel and sit. A raised cot up front with a mattress spread on it was where the Pir sat. The air inside was heavy with the smell of burning incense. The huzur entered the majlis hall with his right hand aloft and a grave expression on his face. Everyone stood up and spoke in unison: 'Assalamu alaikum wa rahmatullah' (May the peace and mercy of Allah be with you). As the sound reverberated across the room the Pir replied in a gravelly voice—'Wa alaikum assalaam' (And upon you be peace)— and made a gesture with his hand asking his disciples to sit. The women behind the veil smelled of fragrant powder, their eyes were lined with surma. Some were parting the veil to get a better look at the huzur, their glances straying to the men in the gathering from time to time.

The huzur passed his fingers through his long white beard.

'Do you understand, Abu Bakr, that this world is a false realm? What is the point of hankering after money in this world, when you can't take anything with you! Tell me, can you take anything with you to the grave?'

Abu Bakr, dark faced with a dark beard, a short man sitting in the front row, replied, 'No, huzur!'

'So will you give yourself up to Allah's love or to the love of wealth and prosperity?' The question, though directed at Abu Bakr, was meant for the congregation at large.

'Allah's love, huzur!' Abu Bakr replied, a bit dazed.

The women watched Abu Bakr from behind the veil, their gazes transfixed. For that day at least Abu Bakr's name was going to be on everyone's lips. The Pir huzur had spoken to Bakr, that was nothing short of a great honour for the man. Some would also whisper that Abu Bakr was indeed a lucky soul; the huzur himself was going to pray to Allah to ensure heaven for him.

The majlis went on for nearly one hour, during which time the Pir spoke at length about how poor the Prophet had been, how he had had nothing but a torn quilt to call his own. Moved by the Prophet's struggles many people gathered there were weeping piteously. In the Pir's house, the more someone could cry the more worthy they were considered. Besides, one's worth could also be adjudged by the dreams one had. Fajli khala had dreamt she was sitting beside a magnificent fountain with the Prophet for company, with beautiful white birds flying in the balmy air. She could not recall their conversation but the huzur had assured her it must have been regarding her ascent to Paradise. Fajli khala's worth among the congregation had improved considerably after the episode. Many people drew her aside to inquire about her dream, especially how the Prophet had appeared as she had seen him beside the fountain. Her face lit up whenever she was asked to recount the experience, as she described the divine light that framed the Prophet's countenance, his astounding beauty and his surprisingly delicate hands. When she spoke about it her eyes closed of their own accord, as if she was overcome with divine adoration, as if she could still sense the touch of those hands. The two of them walking towards the fountain, holding hands, washing themselves in the water, that was where she had finally woken up. After her, many other people in the house soon had their own dreams involving the Prophet, becoming as well known as Fajli khala in the process. Everyone except my mother, that is. To her profound regret Mother never managed to have one of those dreams involving the Prophet, not even after repeatedly chanting his name and occupying her mind with thoughts of him before going to bed. She could not help but feel that she had deeply sinned somehow to have never had the honour.

As soon as the majlis ended, a line of men made their way to the Pir, to touch his feet and offer him money as offerings. The hadiya or the offering could be of any amount; the huzur had decreed that it could be anything a person could afford.

With the utmost reverence Abu Bakr touched the Pir's feet and spoke.

'Huzur, I can't help but be so afraid. The last age is here, the qayamat could arrive any day. I don't pay too much attention to business any more. As it is, we have to cross over empty-handed, don't we? Who knows what fate has in store for me. My whole life I paid scant attention to such things. Have mercy, huzur, without your compassion I have no hope.' The huzur promised his clemency to Abu Bakr in response.

After the men were done, the huzur parted the curtain and approached the women. First, the women from outside were going to touch his feet and offer him hadiya. Then he was going to fling himself on the couch and the women were going to pounce on him with massages.

Pulling on her scarf, I whined, 'Ma, please let's go back home. If Father comes back and finds out I'm not home he's going to thrash me, don't you know!'

Snatching the end of the scarf from my grasp, Mother snapped at me. 'Stop it, don't bother me.'

I stood there under the hibiscus tree, in the darkness of the courtyard, all by myself. I had heard djinns attacked if they found a woman out and about with her hair untied; I pulled the scarf firmly over my head. I was not used to wearing robes and pyjamas and scarves; women wore them when they got older. At home I still used to wear frocks, etc.

But at Pir Amirullah's house, no matter how old you were you were not allowed inside the gates unless you were wearing the clothes he wanted. It was a strange, insulated little world of its own.

While returning home in a rickshaw, I asked Mother, 'Why has Allah made Israfil sit with a trumpet poised on his lips for eternity? Allah knows when Apocalypse is coming, doesn't He? Can't He ask Israfil to pick up the trumpet that very moment? Poor Israfil, he can't even go anywhere.'

'Allah is the creator of the now and the hereafter,' Mother replied from beneath her burqa. 'Israfil is but one angel. He must obey what Allah has commanded him to do. It's what all angels must do. Don't question Allah's motives. Learn to fear Him!'

'Your huzur said we must fall in love with Him. How can I fall in love with Him if I'm afraid of Him?'

I was always uncomfortable uttering that word 'love'. It made my tongue heavy and weird, as if there was some unwritten prohibition surrounding the word. The prohibition extended only to the love between a man and a woman though. I had been taught only bad people fell in love, had seen Jhunu khala falling in love in secret and Dada writing clandestine love poems to Anita. According to Dada, Jhunu khala and Rasu khalu used to have a 'thing' going between themselves. Even the girls at school never uttered the word 'love'; it was always some girl and some boy had a 'thing'. At first, it had taken me a while to understand what this 'thing' was; later, when I did understand it, I also learnt to use it in the very same way. That was just how it was, whether at home, among our relations and generally within the social circle that we were part of. Everywhere except the Pir's house. There, I don't remember ever hearing something like 'Allah and Pir saheb had a "thing"'. When it came to Allah, the word 'love' was used fairly regularly. For instance, we were not supposed to say that Humaira and her cousin Atiq were in love; instead, we had to say they had a thing and we had to say it in whispers so that not too many people heard it. It was perfectly fine, however, to proclaim that Humaira was deeply in love with Allah, loud enough for the multitudes to hear.

'You can, when it's Allah,' Mother replied.

'You are telling me Allah has kept a record of everything, each person's birth, their death, even who they are going to marry. Allah even knows if someone will go to heaven or hell. So, let's say Abu Bakr, if Allah has already decided he will go to heaven, then even if he does something bad will he still go to heaven? Or let's say it's me. If Allah has already decided I will go to hell, then what is the point of me praying to Him any more? Does Allah update His records from time to time?' I finished in one breath and abruptly went silent.

'You stay dumb in front of people all the time, it's only with me that you can't seem to shut up,' Mother shot back, annoyed.

'But Allah can do everything, right?' I asked with a world of curiosity in my voice.

'Yes, He can,' Mother replied, 'Whatever He wants, happens. He only has to say it and it happens. If He doesn't want something, no one can make it possible. Not a leaf quivers without His will.'

She was covered from head to toe in a black burqa, a thin veil dropping from her forehead over her face to give some basic visibility, at least to watch out before stepping into a hole or something. Staring at the veil, behind which Mother's eyes were surely burning, I asked again—

'Say, my hands, they're empty, can Allah make a flower appear from emptiness?'

'Yes, He can.'

'Say Allah has a hanky. Can He turn it into a dove?'

'He can,' Mother replied with confidence.

'The magician who had come to our school can do it too. Even he can disappear into thin air like Allah,' I said, pursing my lips.

'What did you say? Your piety is completely in ruins! You dare compare Allah to a magician! You naughty girl, is this how you behave! With what hopes I take you to listen to huzur's words. With every passing day you are turning into a devil. This is all your father's doing. If you speak like this ever again I will sew your mouth shut!'

Her outburst dimmed my enthusiasm at once.

Mother had once said Abdul Qadir Gilani had received Allah's command and risen from his grave. I was convinced our school magician could achieve the same feat. But I did not repeat it in front of her, not willing to withstand another onslaught of insults. But the other question buzzing inside my head I could not control, 'Why do djinns attack the people of the Pir's house so much? They don't catch me! You have said Allah himself comes down to that house. If that is so then how can a djinn dare to do make mischief in Allah's area?'

Poking me in the stomach with her elbow Mother snapped at me, 'Not one more word! Once we're back home, excuse yourself, read the namaz and beg for His forgiveness. You don't fear Allah enough, which is why these devilish thoughts appear in your head.'

My questions had no answers. Later, with the school science book open in front of me, I asked Mother again. 'Adam and Hawa, these two were made first, right?'

'He made,' Mother immediately rectified my lack of decorum.

'But see here,' I went on, pointing to images of prehistoric men in the science book, 'it says single-celled organisms evolved into multi-cellular organism, then into apes and then finally into prehistoric men. They used to live in caves, fight all the time, forage, and eat fruits as well as raw meat. Much later they learnt to strike stone against stone and create fire. Then they gradually learnt many more things, slowly becoming civilized in the process. Did Adam, the first prophet and human being, created by Allah Himself, really look like a naked monkey like this? The one Allah made from earth and then allowed to roam free in the garden of Paradise.'

Her face pinched in disgust, as if a foul odour was emanating from the open book, Mother shrieked, 'Get away, get lost! Get away from me. Whatever is written in this book is a lie. What Allah has said is the only truth, there is no truth other than that.'

There was no choice for me but to leave her alone. I could not very well ask Father any of this, every time I stood near him it made my throat turn dry. Who was right, Allah or science, there was no one to solve my quandary. Whatever I knew about Allah's views, I found scant rationale in any of them. That was a new thing I had recently learnt from Father: use reason. It was something I had heard him use often in his speeches: how I should always use reason, how I should ask my conscience before doing something and do it only if my conscience was fine with it. That every human being had a conscience. That human beings were animals after all, but rational animals at least. That without logic there would be little difference between a human being and a wild beast. It must be noted here that Father had started with the lecture only because I had almost set a pile of wood lying in the courtyard on fire while playing with matches. If the fire had spread, according to Father, the whole house could have burnt to the ground.

Science was where I found reason. Allah had suddenly dropped Aadam and Hawa on earth from Paradise, this legend seemed too fictitious to be true. They seemed sort of like fairy tales. When I said anything to Mother she usually said speaking against Allah would result in my tongue falling off. Once, just to see if that was true, I locked myself in and kept abusing Allah: Allah you are bad, Allah you are mean, etc. But nothing happened and I understood nothing of that kind ever could, that Mother had been wrong. Besides, I also had proof that Allah did not grant wishes either. I had raised my hands in prayer during namaz and asked for chomchom from Porabari, begged for the puri-boondi that Sharaf mama and all used to eat from Thanda's father's shop. Not a thing I got. I had asked for a wooden horse, like the kind I had seen in the Rajbari school and loved; even that I did not get, among the numerous other things I asked for. I had even prayed for my uncle, my father's brother, and Sharaf mama to die of leprosy. Neither of those things happened. Mother too used to pray to Allah often so that Father would get leprosy and die as well. But Father was hale and hearty; not only was he getting fitter every day, he was also not the kind to easily fall prey to illness or fever. I was the one who usually got fever and whenever that happened it was nothing sort of delightful. Fever meant no need to study, plus Father used to speak nicely to me when I had fever and he would even stroke my hair from time to time. That was one instance when paternal affection was not very hard to come by. He would bring lots of grapes and oranges and keep them by my bed; I would sit and eat them in full view of my other siblings. If they were to whine and beg I would gave them a tiny share. Mother would bring by ginger laced with salt for my taste buds. The problem arose when it was time to have the medicines. All the joys of being feverish and pampered evaporated the moment I had to swallow those huge pills. Father had an entire course of five or six medicines that he used to make me have every hour or so. I had the habit of pretending to have the pills and then tossing them out of the window. When a week would pass without the fever showing any decline, Father would get suspicious and take on the task of feeding me the medicines himself. He would make me open my mouth and pour water and the tablet or capsule inside. It would get stuck in my throat, I would retch and make a mess all over the floor and he would make me repeat it all over again. As they say, if you don't succeed once try and try again. On and on it went and Father never gave up until he had successfully made me consume the required medicine. When Father was not home, Mother would read Quranic verses over me and blow air on my chest. It was a nice sensation; besides, air was any day better than bitter pills. She would also make me drink glasses full of dirty water from the Pir's house, enchanted water she called it. After the fever went down the two of them would argue over what had worked, the dubious water with the magical properties or the medicines.

Father and I were not very close as I have mentioned before. Simply standing in front of him was as if I was in the presence of a hulking demon. Yet, whenever he said things like fevers were symptoms of diseases, how microbes entered our body and caused diseases and how medicines had anti-microbial properties that could combat microbes and cure people, his words never appeared anything but rational.

Back at Nani's, in the slums behind the property, it had been a common thing to chant words and blow on someone to cure ailments. There used to be a maulvi who would come to read surahs and blow air on the six-year-old emaciated Gnetu whenever he fell sick. He would also leave behind bottles of enchanted water that were considered equally potent. In the end, swollen and suffering, Gnetu had died. The blowing-air technique had been tried on Jhunu khala as well to cure her bouts of insanity, but completely in vain. Mother too had secretly arranged for a maulvi to come and blow air on Father, to free him from Razia Begum's clutches. Since it was literally not possible to do it to Father himself, the ritual was performed on his room. Four pieces of strings, blessed and knotted, were hidden in four corners of the room. Before departing the maulvi assured her that her husband was finally going to turn his attention towards her; I heard Mother and Nani whispering about it. The fact that it had no effect on how Father felt was something no one knew better than my mother. And yet her faith in such hocus-pocus remained unwavering.

Despite Mother's repeated claims that everything written in my school books was a lie, I had trouble believing her. Before beginning to frequent the Pir, she never used to blame school education; in fact, she used to often rue how she had not been able to pursue her own education that far. She did still regret it at times, but that had less to do with the pursuit of knowledge and more with the fact that without education she was not able to get a job, happily ditch her relationship with Father and pursue independence and self-reliance. This immense change in my mother was occurring right in front of my eyes and I could not tell if she was going down the wrong path or finally reaching her truth. It was true she spoke and acted quite unreasonably at times but it was not as if properly educated people, with BAs and MAs to their name, were known to engage in debates regarding the creation of the world and humanity. Most of them readily believed in anything accredited to Allah. Of course they did or else why did they keep roza and read the namaz? While there had been a slum behind Nani's house, there had been houses of many educated people facing the property. Since people in those houses were just as pious, could Allah be dismissed so summarily? Even my father used to fast during Ramzan every year. When I was a child I would insist on keeping the roza. I would wake up with everyone at the crack of dawn to eat rice with fish and meat, and then with milk and bananas. Around lunch, Father would come and tell me to eat something.

'But I'm fasting!'

'No, kids have to eat once now and then again in the evening during iftaari. Then it gets counted as two rozas.'

This trick with the two fasts was simply meant to make me eat something; Father did not want me to suffer the entire day without anything to eat. When the sirens rang at the end of the night I was usually not called, but the sounds of utensils clanking in the kitchen always managed to wake me up so I could join the others in their early morning meal. Not that I was keen on keeping roza because Allah had asked everyone to do so. The fact of the matter was that fasting meant extra pampering for the kids at home and that was my sole motivation. Besides the pampering, it was also sort of like a game, a game of fasting that usually ended in muri, chickpeas, pakodas made of dal or aubergines, warm jalebis and waiting for the siren to ring so we could dig into all this. There went the siren; as did we!

After an entire month of fasting, Father would celebrate Eid with a lot of pomp and show. He would buy new clothes for his children and sarees for his wife; on the occasion of Bari Eid (Eid al-Adha) he also bought cows or goats for sacrifice. That was the extent of his annual investment in religion though. Once, however, for a few days, he did employ a maulvi to come and teach him the Qaida Shifara every morning. He never spoke to anyone about what had caused such a sudden outpouring of interest, but from what I do remember, an odd incident had occurred sometime before this unexpected shift in stance. One night he had come back home and at dinner told Mother about a strange man he had met at one of his patient's houses. Long-haired, with a long beard and tattered clothes and shoes, the man had apparently written 'Allah Hu' in Arabic on a piece of paper and instantly sounds of voices chanting the words had started emerging from it. Father had taken the piece of paper in his hand and inspected it carefully, turning it this way and that to find out if there was a trick hidden within. When that had not yielded any clues, he had checked to see if the sound was emerging from a machine in the man's pockets or if the latter was making the sound himself. But try as he might he had failed to figure out how a piece of paper could demonstrate something so fantastical. Mother had heard his story and had been deeply moved but Father had simply sat there, looking a little stumped. Unable to eat he had played around with his food for a while and then excused himself and gone to bed early, like he used to whenever his blood pressure was up. Father never used to talk about his day or his patients, or even anything that might have happened in his life, at home. Never with us and not even with Mother. One morning a couple of weeks later there was a knock on

our door and we opened it to find Raatkana Maulvi—that's
what he was called, the night-blind maulvi, because he had
trouble finding his way at night—standing there holding a
new copy of Qaida. Father had sent for him.

Not that this phase of his lasted too long. Barely two days
into his newfound interest, Father began making excuses the
moment the maulvi turned up, asking the latter to have tea
and confessing he was not feeling like studying that day and
such things. The maulvi would be ushered into the living
room and served tea and snacks; he would finish them and
quietly leave with promises of resuming lessons the day after.
That tomorrow was never meant to arrive. One day rolled
into another and the teacher barely got whiff of his student
any more, until about five days later, when the maulvi's
employment was formally terminated and he was ushered
out after being paid his dues. That was the only instance of
religion managing to entangle Father in any way; that too for
only a very short while. Soon enough he was back to being
the person we knew—egotistical, upright, hardworking, hair
brushed backwards, shirt neatly tucked in, tie and coat, or an
overcoat in winter—all six seasons marked by the squeaking
of his shoes.

Every month Boromama used to send us a journal called
Udayan, the paper was usually used to cover my books and
notebooks. Only a quick glance through the photos on arrival
and soon the periodical would be turned into book covers.
This habit of covering books, etc., went right back to when
I was about to begin school; earlier Mother was the one who
used to do it for me, repurposing wrapping paper that Father
brought toast biscuits in. Later, once I had developed a sense
of aesthetics, I would do it myself using colourful pages from
calendars, mostly those of Glaxo before making the switch

to *Udayan*. The journal was published by the Department of Culture of the Soviet Consulate where Boromama was co-editor. During each one of his visits to Mymensingh, Boromama would carry loads of books with him, some of which he would always drop by at our place. Who knew why he used to bring them: maybe he believed my brothers read them, neither of whom had any interest whatsoever in even flipping through them. On lazy afternoons I was the one who usually rifled through titles like *Chhotoder Lenin* (Lenin for Children), History of the Second World War, *Samajtantra Ki O Keno* (What and Why Socialism), Maxim Gorky's *Mother, Amar Chhelebela* (My Childhood), *Prithibir Pathshala* (The Classroom of the World) and such.

Whenever Boromama visited us Mother would cook delicious food for him. Then after he left she would say with profound regret, 'I can't believe what he has become! He studied in the madrasa and see, now he's a communist! Shame!' Her shame made me curious and I would ask her, 'Mother, what is a communist?'

'What else! Doesn't believe in Allah and all!' She would reply dejectedly.

That was probably the first most profound realization of my life, that there were people in the world who did not believe in Allah. I knew Boromama could talk without hesitation about Neil Armstrong peeing on the moon or declare that Arabic was just like any other language in the world and hence it was possible to write dirty things in it, but no one had told me that he did not believe in the divine. All I wanted to know was why, why did he not believe in it? But I had no way of knowing why. Boromama lived far away in Dhaka and whenever he did visit us, I was always his little princess. He did not notice that I was growing up, that I had too many questions piling up inside me, feeling content instead to slip a candy or two into my hands as if that was enough to distract the naive little girl.

It was while flipping through the books left by him at Abakash that I came to the firm realization, even though I was still a little girl in frocks, that the world was not just a place of superstitions and witch-doctors. That there was a much bigger world out there, a world of reason. Not everyone read the namaz or kept a fast, not everyone studied the Quran and the hadith. Begging in front of clay idols was not something everyone wanted to do, neither did everyone perform numerous pujas through the year. *Milad*s and kirtans were not always the norm. Christians were not just nuns and priests in the missionary's black habit. That there were other things outside the purview of what we assumed. During such a time of personal crisis, suddenly one day we received news that Boromama was going to be visiting Abakash with a foreigner friend of his. A veritable decoration plan was set in motion at once. The house was cleaned and dusted, the floor was polished till it shone, clean sheets were brought out for the beds, as well as a cover on the dining table and new curtains for the doors and windows. We were all instructed to take showers before noon, dress in our finest and wait patiently in the living room for the guests to arrive. When Victor E. Piroico was going to arrive and extend his hand in greeting, we were supposed to extend ours in response. Alongside, we were taught to say 'How do you do?' to him. Only that much and no more since we were supposed to go inside after that and remain there. It was decided, by Dada himself, that since he could speak in English he was going to be sitting with Victor and Boromama at the table for lunch. It was all set, Victor arrived as per schedule, we shook hands too. But no matter what I tried, for my life I could not remember the 'How do you do?' that I had learnt by heart. The sentence sounded too rumbly, like hadudu.

That was one more thing back in those day, the inability to agree with things I was being taught I had to do. A lot of food had been cooked that day; they ate and then Victor was taken on a tour of the house. The shed in the courtyard where Alam used to live, he went and peed in the bushes behind that.

He was the first white man I met in my life.

And how white he was! White enough to impress even my mother who had seen her share of white Englishmen.

After Victor was gone, Dada, still in his neatly ironed shirt and pants and polished shoes, plopped down on the chair in the veranda and began to swing his leg in content, as if Victor's visit had sanctified the entire building.

The next day, though, after returning from Pir Amirullah's house, Mother seemed to have had a change of heart. 'So what if he's white? I saw him standing and peeing, not even washing up afterwards. Devils stand and pee! And he's a communist, of course he does it too. He doesn't believe in Allah or the Prophet, if I had known earlier I wouldn't have cooked for him.'

Mother was convinced that devils were gradually taking over the world.

The Favourite

Bidyamoyi School was one of the most renowned girls' schools of the city. It had been so named by a king—Suryakanta or Sashikanta, he was called—after his sister Bidyamoyi Debi. A large, red two-storeyed building on a lush green field surrounded by a wall, shaded by tall banyan and peepul trees, overlooking a lotus-covered pond on one side of the field. When I managed to get through the entrance exam, on the first day of school, Jhunu khala, since she had studied there too, took me around the place and showed me the various classrooms, the teachers' rooms and the assembly hall, before taking me to class four and finding me a seat right in the front row. She settled me in and before turning to leave leaned closer and whispered in my ear with a smirk, 'The senior girls might come and ask something of you.'

'What will they ask, Jhunu khala?'

She only glanced at my petrified face and laughed, the secret safe with her.

It did not happen on the first day, but on the second. Recess at school entailed a one-hour break. I had finished my tiffin and was standing by the main stairs all by myself, watching a group of girls playing on the field, when I noticed a girl, clearly a senior and someone I did not know, leaning against the railings and watching me with a smile on her lips. I had barely averted my gaze and taken a couple of steps towards my classroom when I heard someone, presumably her, hailing me from behind.

'Hey you, new girl, wait a moment.'

I stopped abruptly. She caught up with me and asked, 'What is your name?'

'Why do you ask?'

'Because you are very pretty, that's why!' She was tall and dark, her long hair braided into a fishtail.

She caught hold of my hand in hers, pressing lightly on my fingers. I shook off her hold and stood my ground, a bit discomfited. The unknown girl spoke again.

'Don't be scared. I won't do anything to you.'

My eyes were fixed on the ground, my heart almost about to burst out of my chest. She edged closer and spoke again, softer so that no one else could hear her.

'Will you be my favourite?'

I did not know what that meant. Unable to respond my eyes welled over; she wiped away my tears and said, 'Oh you foolish girl! Why do you cry?' Just then, seeing a group of girls making their way towards the stairs, the girl turned away in a flash and was gone.

The ceiling of the classroom was covered in long colourful fans made of cloth that the ayahs pulled from outside. Despite the cool air, I spent the rest of the class sweating in anxiety, thinking all manner of things about what sort of place the girl had been trying to lure me to.

The next day at recess I was again standing by myself near the stairs when the girl approached me and offered me a ripe guava. 'O shy girl, won't you be my favourite? Say yes and I will love you to bits.'

'No,' I bit out in a choked voice.

Nevertheless the girl smiled sweetly and took hold of my hand again, my fingers curled up into a fist within her grasp.

Some girls from my class, whose names I did not know yet, cornered me after school that day and asked, 'Who's your favourite? Is it that tall one? It is, isn't it?'

Try as I might I could not fathom what being a favourite meant! The girls were whispering about each other's favourites. No names were taken though, as if everything was a big secret.

I learnt later from Jhunu Khala what being a favourite meant. It was an age-old tradition in Bidyamoyi School where senior girls chose younger, beautiful girls as their favourite, sort of like forming a sorority. The rule was that it had to be a secret from everyone else. No one could know that the favourites met regularly, after school, during recess or even during games, underneath a tree, by the pond or behind a wall somewhere, to hold hands and talk, the older girl often bringing the younger one presents. Jhunu khala's favourite was Beauty, a girl who, true to her name, was a stunning beauty. Whenever Jhunu khala spoke about Beauty her face glowed and she smiled fondly, just like how that tall girl had smiled at me.

As time passed I came to be convinced that this tradition of 'favourites' was an exciting one. All I wanted was for someone else to approach me and ask me to be their favourite again. All they had to do was ask once and I would have jumped at the opportunity. As soon the recess bell rang, the pretty girls of the class vanished somewhere, like birds flying off in a gust of wind. One only had to listen a tad carefully and there was no dearth of information: Mamata's favourite had given her a necklace, Shahana's favourite was a girl called

Banya and so on. It spilled over into the fights as well, some claimed Shahana's favourite was not Banya, some claimed it definitely was because they had seen the two standing together quite close behind one of the banyan trees.

And there I was, stupid as ever and shy to a fault. No favourites, no friends and no one to ask me to play. Neither could I answer questions in class—staring dumbly when questions were directed at me—nor did I have any talents in singing, dancing or sports. Once in a Bengali class I was asked to name a flower. Instead of answering I had gone off on an internal debate as to which name to give, since there were many kinds of flowers and I wanted to name one that was most fragrant; finally, the master had testily asked if I could speak.

Dumb! Yes, dumb, or else I would have had to stand up and tell the master, 'May I go to the bathroom' that fateful day. That was what we had been taught to say, in English, when we wished to go to the bathroom; and the master had the right to turn down the request too. Being turned down meant sucking in your breath and sitting still in one place and risk everyone figuring out your plight eventually. Being allowed meant having to run through the crowd, or worse, having to cross one's legs and limp past them, with everyone speculating whether I was going for number one or two. Such things were difficult to suppress in public and hence I had decided not to use a request like 'May I go . . .' at all. Instead I was chose to stay dumb and use sheer strength to resist nature's call. It did work in a way, till the master left and I could somehow drag myself to the bathroom that was at the corner of the field, pretending as if I was just going there casually. But then I stood there, I just could not go in and do my business. Girls turned up after me, went in, got done and left but I could not manage to get my business done. A force in motion, wishing to bust forth, was at war with my gradually weakening and exhausted self. I kept trying to tell the force to hold back a while longer but it was all in vain. The vengeful army burst forth, staining my pyjama in mere moments. Terribly ashamed, I remained standing there, my back against the wall, eyes downcast, wondering if anyone was ever going to help me in such a state. Someone did. A girl came up to me soon and sweetly asked why I was there all alone. It was her, the one who had wiped my tears and given me a ripe guava. The earth never parted when one wanted it to, so one could find refuge within it and hide from shame. Perhaps it did part, but only for Sita and that hardly helped my case! Seeing my head hanging resolutely as if it was going to fall off any moment, the girl understood my piteous condition. She spoke to the headmistress, fetched my books and things from the class herself and had me sent home escorted by Ramratiya, the school sweeper. If only someone else had done it, it would have been easier to bear!

I tried my best to hide the incident at home but in vain. I had come back home early from school in a yellow-stained pyjama and escorted by a sweeper. At least the adults of the house had the decency not to make noise while laughing, the children were not as kind. Dada was especially happy because his reputation in this department was now no longer exclusive, I too had joined the ranks. I was the 'shit cart', or so the tuneless rhyme that he made up went.

I was called a variety names at home over the month that followed: shit basket, Ramratiya's best friend, etc. Mother tried shooing Dada away from time to time, repeating the excuse that I must have had an upset stomach. Her support gave me strength to make a face at Dada and hit back at him.

'You used to shit your pants in school too.'

'Eeee! Not when I was a grown up like you! I was small then, was only in class one!'

As a child a rickshaw from the experimental school used to come to pick him up. It had a belt attached to ensure he did not topple over en route. Quite often the rickshaw-puller would return Dada home before school got over, along with his soiled half-pants. One day, unable to contain himself any longer, the man had told Mother to make certain her son's stomach was doing fine before sending the boy back to school. Presumably Dada had been fed tinned milk once as a child and that had fundamentally upset his tummy. Although Mother could never be certain if the fault lay in his stars or in the can of milk powder.

Regardless, memories of his reputation with an upset tummy managed to provide me a measure of relief, that I was not the only one at home who had such a shameful secret. No relief was to be found at school though. I knew I had lost the chance of becoming anyone's favourite any more. Besides, after that episode whenever I saw the tall girl at a distance I turned away as soon as I could. It was beginning to seem to me that anyone looking at me knew about the unfortunate incident and the thought always left me red-faced with embarrassment.

When the schools reopened after the War we were all promoted to the higher class without having to appear for the annual exam. During school assembly, standing under the flag, we were asked to sing 'Amar Sonar Bangla', the new anthem, instead of 'Pak Sar Zamin . . .' It was as if people's heights and sizes had undergone a transformation, just as much their thoughts and language had too, becoming sharper, more energetic and full of life. As if people had grown almost a decade in a leap, as if the girls were no longer girls, they had become women. Some had had their houses burnt, their brothers or fathers had been killed, some had sisters pregnant with unwanted children, products of rape during war. We had all been through such experiences, through rows of dead bodies and the air being rendered apart by the sound of tortured screams.

The memory of when I had returned home as a girl with soiled clothes was too insignificant in the face of such things and was soon forgotten.

Opentee Bioscope
Nine-ten *teiscope*
Sultana bibiyana
Saheb babur baithakkhana

I no longer felt embarrassed to chant the rhyme, no longer hesitated in putting garlands around girls to get them in my team. Neither was I stiff any more about running to the gym during games or occupying the court during recess so only we could play on it. In fact, I participated in sports just like the others did. Come the annual games, however, I remained the absolute dud I always was. Shahana and her four sisters, Heera, Panna, Mukta and Jharna, despite being absolutely hopeless in studies, could run like rabbits, all sorts of races, long ones, short ones, ones where you had to hop like frogs or ones with biscuits. They were the ones who always ended up winning all the medals. Shahana, one of the most popular girls, was endlessly fascinating to me; it was not long before we became fast friends.

And then something happened in the middle of all this, something that made my heart beat faster again. It made my gaze drop, made the tip of my nose go red! The day I met her, my entire body trembled when her hand brushed against mine. I would wake up from dreaming about her and throughout the day her thoughts would cross my mind and make me smile. Her image would float in the forefront of my consciousness while falling asleep, her smile, the way she used to speak, her walk, the wave of her hand and the swell of curly hair fanning her back. I had never seen anyone more strangely beautiful. No one had eyes as pretty; one glance into them was enough to make me forget the world and cause an odd sensation to wash over me.

This was how it all began. I was on my way to school one day when Chotda and his friend Milu caught hold of me and handed me a letter to deliver to a girl called Runi who was staying in the hostel and studying for her matriculation exams. The letter was from Milu and I was instructed explicitly to not reveal anything about it to anyone in the family or even to any other girl in school. It was not much of a task, truth be told. I did as I was asked and delivered the letter to the girl in question, Runi. Runi did not open the letter immediately, instead pushing it inside her shirt and stowing it away somewhere. I simply stood there staring at her, at her startlingly beautiful eyes, wishing she would remain in front of me for as long as possible so I too could keep on gazing into their depths. Even after Runi had left with her letter I remained there, transfixed, leaning against the hostel wall, until the bell rang to shake me out of my daze. From that day my eyes would keep searching for her in the crowd. Sitting in the classroom my gaze would often stray towards the field outside the window, hoping to catch a glimpse of her walking past, praying we run into each other again somewhere.

A couple of days later, school had just got over, when Runi approached me from the direction of the lotus-covered pond. She came up to me and handed me a letter, a reply for Milu. Seeing me make no move except stand there with the letter in my hand she smiled and spoke to me.

'Do you want to say something to me?'

I shook my head in denial. What could I have said to her!

'You are so shy. You hardly speak. Visit me in the hostel sometime, we can chat.'

She finished, held my hand and pulled me towards her, the smell of flowers cascading off her and sweeping me away. She was like the enchanted dolonchapa, the white garland lily from the fairy tales that had been turned into a princess. My body trembled with content, heart thumping loudly inside my chest as if a hundred lotuses were blooming together in a pond somewhere within. I wanted Milu to write to her more, wanted her to reply to his letters more, all so I could get closer to her, have her hold me by the chin and talk to me in her husky voice, her hair flying askew in the wind. I wanted to rest my head on her chest and let the smell of dolonchapa wash over me.

Paying attention to my studies soon became impossible. All I could do was scribble her name over and over again in my copies. While doing maths, without even realizing it, I would draw her dark eyes on the margin. Notwithstanding the zeros I was getting in school, Runi had soon completely taken over all aspects of my existence, tiny as it was. The fields no longer attracted me. Instead I would sit by the pond and think about her, finding her dark eyes reflected in the dark water in front of me. The arm that she had held, I would brush it from time to time to replay her touch in my head again. My dolls, playing gollachut with the girls or singing '*Opentee* bioscope . . .,' everything receded into the background. I was content with being left in the company of my woe, all by myself under the kadam tree, secretly tortured by my desire to feel her close to me again.

Runi and I never managed to have one long conversation together. Whatever little and unsatisfying time I used to get with her, she usually spoke about herself, with me listening in rapt attention, on the steps of the hostel or on her bed with our feet swinging off the edge. As if the lily-princess had come out of her book of fairy tales to wander through a dense forest, singing, her wavy tresses flowing about her. All I wanted to do was love her, deeply and secretly. As if looking into her eyes was akin to telling her my entire life's story, her touch enough to bring me all the joys that life had to offer. She gave me fine glass bangles to wear and a new necklace, our proximity making the fragrance of dolonchapa even more intense and heady. I kept falling in love with her, kept getting swept away in a rising tide of bashfulness and embarrassment.

The bangles and necklace had to be taken off when I was at home. Father disliked us wearing anything other than clothes and shoes. Mother had got my ears pierced hoping to deck me up in jewellery but had been soundly reprimanded for it. He disapproved of bangles and such trinkets. Once, on my way back from school, I had come across a bangle seller and bought an armful of bangles from him. On finding out Father had smashed all the bangles to pieces, slapped me across the face and warned me that if he were to catch me doing something like that again he was going to break my bones. When he had caught me with aalta on my feet he had grabbed hold of me and asked why my feet were bleeding. Mother had laughed at his words and told him I had painted my feet with aalta on a lark.

I did not need to wear Runi's gifts, I could feel her love within me. While my deep and secret love for her was at its zenith, on one fateful night my body underwent a new kind of awakening. Some unseen force made me get up from my own pristine bed, walk silently to the bed spread on the floor a few feet away and slip under the covers with the 'chhotolok' huddled inside. Moni had been brought back to the house a while back and she had returned a full-grown woman. After catching Renu's mother with Father in the kitchen in the middle of the night Mother had gone through a number of maids acquired from the Akua slum. She had finally settled on Moni again whom she had found sitting by the pond, alone and hungry. I swept aside Moni's clothes, my hands tracing her naked form, testing and teasing the firm globes that had suddenly appeared on her chest, like two ripe guavas. No one had touched her breasts, hidden beneath her clothes, before me; I traced them with my fingers, my lips, my nose, as if playing some old forgotten game with a dear old friend. Moni was like a live puppet I had bought from the fair during rathyatra, mine and mine alone to play with. Roses were blooming in my heart and the bashful eyes of the just-awake buds, deep within the folds of the still unfolding petals, were half-closed under the light. In the darkness, my gaze left a lingering kiss on Moni's breasts. In the depths of the night, away from every prying eye, this new secret game that I had begun playing with a very dear friend went on uninterrupted.

It was like our old game, gollachut. But instead of the small mark or object, I was the one who had been flung by mistake, soaring past old dusty rooms, tiny play kitchens and wedding feasts of dolls, to land squarely in the midst of life itself; left to scramble up on my haunches and gaze upon a body with a world of amazement colouring my vision, to search for the secret body hidden within the one I could see.

Who could have predicted that the silly, little girl that I was could have made something like this happen!

This new girl did not need to give Milu's letters to Runi any more. Instead she could very well steal paper from her Dada's drawer, ornate quality ones with flora and fauna etched on it, and pick words from the garden she had nurtured in Runi's name within her heart to compose lines meant for her. When Runi answered these letters the girl could clearly smell the fragrance of lilies in them, the scent infusing her unadorned and indolent life with new vigour. No one knew at home obviously! I was living two separate lives: the outer one that was marked by my parents' verbal and physical reprimands and the inner me, the other me that had been tossed far, a diver in a sea of love.

'*Chhatranam adhyayanang tapah*! The greatest goal of a student's life is the search for knowledge. Nothing in life is more precious than knowledge, or so great men have always said. What have they said?'

I did not need to answer, that was Father's thing to reveal to me what great men before us had supposedly said or done. Great men had opined that success was the fruit of hard labour. Hence, I too had to cast everything aside, playtime, relaxation, everything, and concentrate solely on my education.

'Get educated. Become a learned and refined person. Then people around you will accord you respect and you will be able to move in society with your head held high. Don't study just to prove to me that you are doing it, do it for yourself. Even crazy people know what's good for them! And if you don't wish to do the work, if you wish to become

a dunderhead and hope that you will live off your father and
have no worries, do you know what will happen then? You
will have to beg on the streets! So study, earn knowledge,
become a true human being. Work hard and it will pay off
in the end. Farmers work hard and are rewarded with their
grains in the end. If you spend all your time in games and
lounging about and having fun with friends, you will end up
empty-handed. People work hard day and night to become
doctors, engineers, judges, etc. You must not go to bed before
ten! Does your tutor come regularly?'

This I had to answer. 'Yes, he does.'

'If your next exam results are not up to the mark,' Father
chewed out, 'I'm going to skin you alive.'

The sound of his boots signalled he was turning away
from the door. It was a regular thing for him to stand at the
door and shower me with sage words and advice. I guess
it was a challenge he had taken on, to make his children
get a proper education and become successful in life. After
bad results in his matriculation exam a terrified Dada had
not returned home for three days. Father had waited the
time out on the porch with a sharp cane and pitchers of
cold water to pour on his head to keep it from exploding
in fury. Ironically, other friends of Dada who had passed
with similar results had more accommodating fathers who
were visiting their relatives with sweets to share the news
of their sons just about making it through. After three days
Father had caught hold of Dada, dragged him home by
the ear and given him an ultimatum that if he did not do
well in his ISC examination then he was going to be shown
the door. Almost immediately three new tutors had been
appointed to help him reach the goal. Nevertheless, despite
all efforts, Dada only managed a second division in his exam.

In spite of his insistence that it was in fact a 'higher' second division, his lofty self-assessment failed to provide him any actual leverage. After two unsuccessful attempts to get into medical college, Father's blood pressure began to read higher than ever before, driving him to popping pills dime-a-dozen. For his part, having committed perhaps an unspeakable crime, Dada soon realized that his worth in the house had considerably lessened and with each passing day this realization only served to make him more wretched. This was especially reflected at the dinner table when Father would pass the juiciest and best bits of meat to Chotda, leaving Dada to dolefully toss his rice about in just some gravy and perhaps a hollow bone.

Chotda had four tutors—for mathematics, physics, chemistry and English—whose houses he would go to in the afternoon. Yasmin and I were tutored at home. Mine used to reach almost as soon as I would return home from school; as we were growing up the number of our tutors too had gradually risen. Soon Father drew up a schedule for us: Dada and Chotda were to study from evening till midnight, me till ten and Yasmin till eight. My brothers were allowed to not read loudly because they were older, but for the two of us it was obligatory that we read everything out aloud so Father could hear us from his room and be assured that we were studying and not dozing off. Unfortunately, the clock had to barely touch eight for me to start falling asleep. Father would tiptoe behind me to catch me in the act. He would then proceed to shake me awake and make me put mustard oil in my eyes to ward off sleep. Like a patient taking their eye medicine I had to pour drops of mustard oil from the bottle into my eyes. It stung like mad but it served to reassure Father that I was not going to be falling asleep after that.

Chotda would usually sit down to study in the evening and promptly fall asleep with his head on the table. The moment there was a sound of the black gate opening I would wake him up and tell him Father was home. He would wake up with a start, the book wet with drool, traces of it leaving a dry, white trail from his lips to his cheeks, eyes bloodshot and immediately start mumbling and reading. Not that he ever read anything actually, it was just a particular groaning sound he used to make that seemed to convince Father from afar that his younger son was yet again going to get star marks and salvage his honour.

As long as Father remained home everyone spoke in hushed voices, the entire house seeming like a silent grave, as if the four children of the house were busy acquiring education so they could each become philosophers or scientists. Each child had their own lecture. For Dada it usually went something like this:

'This ass is good for nothing. I wanted him to get into medical but he couldn't get in anywhere. The only thing left for you to do is to get your BSc degree and find employment as a clerk. See if you can even manage to get into a university! Your friend Jahangir is studying to become a doctor. So is Faisal. Did you have any less brains than these two? Did they eat rice and you didn't? I kept so many tutors for you but you still couldn't manage a first division. Aren't you ashamed? I would have hung myself from a yam tree if it had been me!'

In case of Chotda it was something else:

'Forget about the world, Kamal. This is the most precious time of your life. You have star marks in your matriculation exam and your entire future now rests on the results of the intermediate exam. If you don't do even better in this then you will not last among the competition. You have to study medicine. A doctor's son has to become a doctor. No more addas with friends. You must work very hard to get into medical. I had always hoped my eldest was going to become a doctor. That did not happen. Now you are my only hope. Focus on your studies, son. Study at least eighteen hours a day. For the sake of my honour you must do well. I was a farmer's son who became a doctor. You must become a bigger doctor than me!'

Every morning Father would disseminate his counsel from room to room before leaving for work. The moment he was gone, four sets of chairs would creak back: one would run to the field, one to the radio, one would perhaps begin singing loudly while another would plunge headlong into bed. In the midst of all this the black gate of Abakash was our constant saviour. It creaked and we understood immediately if Father was leaving or coming back. Besides, there was a particular sound associated with him that only happened when he opened the door. We could close our eyes and say for sure if it was him, although Father was as wily as those demons we read about in fairy tales: he would leave saying he was going to be late and return around midday, or promise to return early and come back late. We did not have too much faith in his words, so we usually stayed as vigilant as we could. He would sometimes try and open the gate silently, trying not to make any sound so he could creep up behind us and catch us red-handed. Many a times he did manage to pull it off too. Once, having found me sorting drumsticks on the porch of the kitchen instead of studying, he beat me back to my table with said drumstick. Another time he caught me playing with girls from the neighbourhood; I was beaten and sent back to study, the girls were shouted at and scared away. I cannot count the number of times when, after being punished, I fervently wished for my father to fall seriously and fatally ill, the number of times I wished he would die. As I have mentioned before, Father was always a sturdy man while I was the one who frequently got unwell. But medicines were something I was not a big fan of. Worse were injections; even the thought of them made me more sick. Whenever they would get people to give us measles vaccines in school I used to go and hide in the toilet. When they came home I would disappear, not to be found the entire day, even roaming around the streets hungry if need be till I was sure they had left. On one such occasion Father found out I had skipped the vaccination and gave me one himself. No matter who I escaped from, there was no way of escaping him.

We had three exams every year—two quarterly and one final—at the end of the year that you had to pass to be promoted to the next class. That year I had just returned home after getting a thirty-three in English on my first quarterly. Thirty-three—pass marks—the last number that was written in black. Any less than that and marks were written in red, which was catastrophe. Consequently, imagine the state of my mind on that particular day! As it was I was depressed; to top that I was so terrified that my throat seemed permanantly dry, forcing me to keep drinking water. I edged closer to Mother, hoping that she was somehow going to be my saviour. At that moment I agreed with everything she believed in, that the pursuit of worldly knowledge was something fruitless and in bad faith. There was no escape from showing the progress report to Father though; one did not need to stretch one's imagination to envision the caning that was about to follow. Mother advised that I should wear thicker clothes so it would not hurt as much. Doing as she had asked I piled on a few extra layers and sat stewing in heat waiting for Father's return. However, to my utter shock, he returned home, heard everything and, instead of beating me black and blue, gravely announced that henceforth he was going to teach me English. On any day that was a way worse outcome than I could have expected. At least if he had skinned me alive it would have been less terrible. It was like a predatory tiger stroking my back and assuring me that henceforth it was going to be preying on me in instalments every day. His word was law; judges could be moved but not laws. From that day onwards he would come back home from work at eight, change out of his clothes, tie a lungi around his waist, grab hold of the cane and sit me down with my new English lessons. With one eye on the cane and the other on the book I sat through Father teaching me. If I yawned during the lessons, the cane would swoosh through the air and land on my back causing me to spring back up straight. Past, present and future tenses, their forms and variations, each lesson was akin to Father taking my brain out of my skull, putting all the information inside and then putting it back and sewing my skull shut with the cane so I would never forget it again in my entire life. Let alone life, I usually forgot them the very next day. The same routine every day, one eye on the cane, one on the book, a ramrod stiff back because Father had said only lazy people sat hunched over things. The swishing cane and the snap against skin whenever there was a mistake, the more the snaps the more the mistakes, tears and more swings of the cane on the back. Once I told him I wanted to drink water, with tears in my eyes, but that request too was turned down. When he sat down to teach me I was not supposed to feel hunger or thirst, neither was I supposed to want to go to the bathroom. According to Father all of these were ways of shirking work.

Afterwards Mother would rub a salve on the marks left by the cane.

'Will it do any good beating her like a cow? If it has to happen it will happen, if it doesn't, it won't no matter what you do. How will she do well if she spends the whole year reading storybooks. If their father is home, all of them pretend to study. But the moment he leaves for work, the house turns into a fish market. And this one's especially sneaky. The leader of the pack. Keeps looking for ways to instigate the others. Now what? Serves you right, doesn't it, face down after a caning.'

The everyday beating soon reached such a state that I stopped studying other stuff altogether to concentrate solely on English grammar. Soon I began getting zeros in my homework. The gruff maths teacher would ask me to kneel down as punishment, or during science class I would be asked to stand up on the bench; sometimes a particular teacher would ask me to walk up to the blackboard, hold my ears and stand on one feet for everyone to see. Overnight I came to be known as the dumb girl of the school. On the other hand, father's bellows back home ensured that I did not remember the English grammar I was spending so much time and energy on either; the caning too went on as before. After the second quarterly exam my English marks further reduced to twelve. When I got my results Mother smirked and said—

'When I was in class seven the class teacher had asked us if any of the girls knew what the English for cow-dung was. None of the girls knew, except me. So I stood up and said it aloud for everyone to hear: cow dung! If I had been allowed to continue my studies I could have been an English teacher today.'

The second quarterly English marks increased Father's blood pressure to such an extent that he had to be admitted to the hospital. In his absence the house reverted to being a fish market again. As the revelries shot up, the study tables gradually started to gather dust. With Father absent none of us even thought twice about venturing in that direction. While the days were spent in chatting, fooling around or music, in the afternoon the forbidden rooftop was not so out of bounds any more. At night I no longer had to hide my storybooks; I could put my feet up and read them out in the open. I got the books from a girl called Mamata who was in my school. Mamata was a bookworm and we had suddenly struck up a friendship. She used to sit on the last bench in class and read books, hiding them from the teachers. One day she had been doing just that, after school, all by herself in the class, when the peon had come by and barred the door, locking her in the entire night. I was the first to discover this because I had reached the classroom before anyone else next morning. I had walked in and seen her sleeping on the bench. She had tried going out the night before only to find the door locked from the outside; she had yelled for someone to come help her but the school had been empty and no one had come. So she had gone back to her book and slept late only after finishing it. She had shown me the book, Nihar Ranjan Gupta's *Kiriti Omnibus*. Without sparing a thought as to what her mother may have been undergoing in her absence, let alone anyone else, she had confessed to being very hungry and turned around and walked off, leaving the book behind. Her mother did not allow her to return to school for the next two days, during which time I had managed to finish reading it. The day I had returned the book to her she had been overjoyed, having assumed she had lost it. Since then whichever book she used to read she would let me borrow it too, just me.

Anyway, to go back to where we were, Father was admitted to the hospital. Every afternoon Mother would pack food in tiffin containers and visit him. One such afternoon he sent back word with her that he wished to see his two daughters. After whining and mumbling about why and how for a while, I tried making up an excuse about being out of sorts; besides, my tutor was scheduled to visit too, as I was quick to point out. I suggested she take Yasmin along with her instead, but try as I might Mother had made up her mind and there was no changing it. It was not long after that I found myself in the hospital, in the cabin where my father lay recovering awash with the smell of Dettol. He had a beard, I noticed. It was not how we had ever seen him before; it made him seem older all of a sudden. Drawing me real close, he whispered a little sadly. 'Now you all must be overjoyed. The Yama is gone, all of you are free!'

He knew the name I had given him: Yama! It had been years since I had addressed him as Father out aloud; even calling him so out of his earshot had stopped ever since he had become my teacher. To me he was just one thing: Yama incarnate! Even Chotda had agreed as to how perfect the name was the day Father had turned down his request for some money to buy a new pair of shoes. I was half afraid he was going to leap out of the hospital bed, lunge at me and crush me to dust as punishment for having given him such a name. But to my utter disbelief he asked—

'What did you have for lunch?'

'Eggs,' I replied, reassured by his gentle tone.

'As soon as I return home I'm going to buy nice fresh rohu fish for you. And chicken too. Nice mangoes have come in the market as well; I will get you a basket of those.'

I nodded my head in acceptance. The best recourse was to say and do exactly what was expected of me so I could get back home as soon as possible. But to my further astonishment Father drew my head to rest on his chest and began stroking my hair as he spoke.

'Why don't you oil your hair? Oil it, comb it and then tie it up with a nice piece of ribbon. You'll see how beautiful it'll make you!'

I remained motionless, barely breathing. Rubbing his rough cheeks against mine he went on, 'I know you are talented, sweetheart. I got that while teaching you. Tell me darling, what tense is 'My father has been crying for two hours.'

'Present perfect continuous,' I mewled.

'There she is, that's my girl! She can do anything!'

His hand, still stroking my back, touched a scar left behind by a previous caning. Immediately pain shot through me like an arrow, like gridlines spreading all over me, but I remained motionless where I was with my head on his chest. All of a sudden I could not help but feel terribly sorry for Father.

Father's return from the hospital meant the familiar cold, nocturnal silence again descending upon the house. It settled down on my life as well. I was informed I would have to change schools. Bidyamoyi was a good school, that even Father agreed on. But a new school had opened—Residential Model School—where I was to be transferred. By then I had quite a few friends in Bidyamoyi and my secret interactions with Runi too had come into their own. And without even a warning or an intimation it was decided that I was just going to be uprooted from there to somewhere else. Like an evacuee trying desperately to hold on to their beloved land I launched a protest—

'I don't want to study anywhere other than Bidyamoyi.'

'Who asked you?' Father snarled. 'I want to get you into Model.'

'Bidyamoyi is a good school,' I huffed.

'Model is even better,' he replied at once with a cough.

Mustering all the strength I had in my body, squeezing my eyes shut and gritting my teeth I tried one final time to put my foot down.

'I won't go to another school.'

'Of course you will,' Father replied from in front of the mirror where he was in the process of knotting his tie. 'You will do exactly what I tell you to do.'

In the entrance examination of the new school, among other things, they asked us to write an essay: My Aim in Life. That was the only thing I did for the duration of the exam; I wrote an essay all over the answer-script. And it was while writing this essay that I realized how convenient the English language was for saying something harsh or to abuse someone, or to express anger in general. Since the Bengali language inspired a storm of emotions, strong enough for suppressed bouts of kindness to burst forth from one's heart, I carefully made sure to avoid the language altogether as I went about providing details of my aim in life. Studying in that school was not one of them, something I made sure to mention fairly clearly in the essay. The Model School was like a haunted house. Besides, I was already in one school, which was very good and that was where I wished to remain. It did not sit well with me that Father was bent on making me do something I did not wish to do. That was like saying if he wished to set me afloat on the Brahmaputra, he could do so easily, simply because it was his wish. Whether I wished to float at all was something he did not even consider.

Whose life was it? Mine or his? The essay went on to implore that if the life was mine, which it was, then I definitely did not want to be admitted into their school. My essay also expressed hope that the people of the Model School were not going to deliberately destroy my life.

I did not even bother to look at any of the other questions, pleased as I was at having managed to teach Father a lesson. I sat with the paper till the last minute, even though it was not required, and when I emerged from the classroom it was to find Father waiting for me outside in the corridor. He almost flew towards me and asked at once—

'How was your exam?'

'Fine,' I answered, my face dry.

'Did you answer all the questions?' he continued with a smile.

'Yes,' I said at once like a good girl.

'It's a fierce fight. About two hundred sat for the exam, they're going to take about thirty.' His forehead, beaded with perspiration, betrayed his tension.

I was not used to lying; in fact, I had shut my eyes and practised that lie for a length of time just so I could deliver it once somehow.

From the exam hall Father took me straight to his dispensary in Notun Bazar; there was a tiny cabin within where he used to attend to patients. He no longer needed to work out of someone else's pharmacy. After the War he had bought the shop not too far from Nana's and named in Arogya Bitan. Helping me on to his cushioned chair and feeding me chomchom bought from Porabari, he opined, 'Be more mindful with your studies. You must stand first in every class, set about it from right now!' Even though he did not know how his dreams were all going to wither away in a few days, I knew it very well. It was my little secret, as clandestine as taking Moni's clothes off at night.

A couple of days later Father came home with the good news that I had passed the entrance examination. To me it was like my whole world had begun spinning. How was it possible! Clearly whatever Father wanted became possible, if not for everything, then at least when it came to me. Shifting me to that quiet and desolate building in the middle of a vast desert-like landscape, my new school, was perhaps Father's way of saying he did not want me to be swept away by the Brahmaputra.

'You are my daughter. You were born of me. No one wants good things for you more than me. If you happen to be drowning in the Brahmaputra, if there is anyone who will leap in to rescue you, it will be me.'

There were only a handful of girls in the whole school and only five or six teachers. Wiping the tears off my eyes I found my way to my classroom on the first day; my friends back in Bidyamoyi, war-witnesses and battle-hardened, were busy protesting.

Try as I might I could not manage to feel at home in the new school. Similarly, Yasmin was having a difficult time adjusting in Rajbari School where she had had to be shifted since Miriam School run by Christian missionaries had closed after the War. 'Twinkle Twinkle Little Star' or 'Humty-Dumpty' had been replaced with '*Taal Gaach Ak Paye Dariye*'. Perhaps because the nuns in her old school used to take her in their arms and coddle her, used to shower her with affection, or simply because a long association with a place engenders a sense of connection and fondness, Yasmin would often, at the slightest opportunity, walk to Miriam School in the afternoon, five minutes from Abakash, and stand outside the locked iron gate of the abandoned building. She would stare at the young banyan saplings emerging through cracks in the school building and sigh. She was deeply connected to the building, forsaken and dilapidated as it was. Such was the depth of her despair over the school, the trees encircling it, the field and the pond on one end of it, and the swing they used to have, that eventually Father had a swing installed on the grounds of Abakash. She would climb on it, close her eyes and, pretending as if she was back at Miriam, sing, 'How I wonder what you are . . .' It was all I could do to not reflect upon what I had had to leave behind. I did not miss any swings or any buildings! I missed Runi, I realized. But was it only Runi? No. She was sort of like the pole star, bright as a jewel but too far away. But, of course, that was what made most sense for Runi; it made no sense to drag her beauty down into the dust and grime of our everyday life. What I also missed was the life of habit I had had with those girls, the ones with phlegm in their noses, dirt on their teeth and lice in their hair. The lure of a life of habit is such a strong thing that people, especially the introvert kind, are perhaps terrified of being forced to leave it behind and get used to something new somewhere else. Of course, it did not take time for the grass to get used to a new kind of grass, to form new daily bonds; but when one of those in question was me—grass of a different kind, all curled up and crooked— then things were expectedly different.

In the new school we had to carry our own tiffin. Every night Father would get big slices of fruit cake for school the day after. I carried tiffin to school but hardly ever felt like eating it; kotkoti, fried munchies of gram flour that we used to buy earlier by selling old torn shoes, were far tastier to me. I wished for a change. Perhaps Father believed that fruit cake was the tastiest thing in the whole world but I did not think so! Did I not have even this little independence, to not like something and not eat it?

I was standing in the balcony of the new school that day, holding the railings, the undesired tiffin left behind. There was nothing to see up ahead except for a stretch of infertile land that had been created by filling up a marsh. Suddenly, someone placed their hand on my shoulder. To my utter shock I turned around and found myself face to face with Runi. One look at her and I began taking small steps back, afraid that if I got too close she would be able hear my racing heartbeat and the tremors wracking the hair on my skin. She began advancing towards me, step by step, smiling and talking.

'I'm going to be living in the teachers' quarters of the new school. It'll be so much fun, right? Do you know Rebecca appa, the school doctor? She's my older sister.'

Standing at a safe distance my eyes took in their fill of her, forgetting to answer the question whether I knew Rebecca appa or not. Her sudden appearance in my bleak landscape, like a bright comet zapping across the sky, had rendered me speechless. I had no choice but to acknowledge that if love was strong enough then it could possibly make one's object of desire appear right in front of them. The more she advanced towards me, her arms extended, the more I walked back till my back had gone up against a wall.

'Why are you so shy?' She placed a hand on my shoulder again, the touch sending strange shivers down my spine whose meaning I could not translate. My breath quickened, so quick that I had to cover my mouth with my hands to hide it.

'Aren't you coming for the picnic? Everyone from the school is being taken on a picnic to the zamindar's house in Dhanbari. I want to go. Dhanbari is so far! I so want to go to a faraway place.'

I slowly looked up into her eyes. The sky in her gaze was vast and blue and I wished I could fly in it with my wings spread wide. Her luscious body shook with laughter as she gazed back into my half-open eyes. Who could smile like that except her! I could love her, anyone could love her, from any distance they wanted. But her love for me in return—was it love or was it affection or some form of indulgence—made me extremely awkward. The more she drew me close the more I seemed to curl up into myself. When a giant tree leans towards a blade of grass the insignificance of the latter is only thrown into sharper contrast. I understood fully well that I had absolutely no consciousness of my own self whenever Runi showered me with her love or attention.

What if, on a new moon night, the moon was to suddenly appear and cover everything with her light? What if the moonlight was to sweep me away into a garden of ginger lilies?

I remained standing on the balcony long after Runi had left, as if that spot was the final destination I had dreamt of reaching for a thousand years or so. All of a sudden the dead plants of the new school seemed awash with life, the arches and pillars infused with a new vitality. Even the dry, dusty wind felt like the southern breeze and the grey earth seemed to have turned green at her touch. I wanted to run on the grass barefoot.

The picnic was going to cost ten taka. When I asked Father for the money he calmly told me I did not have to go.

But how could that be! 'No, I must go!' I insisted.

'You must go?' Father snapped. 'Who will make you go if you don't? Is the picnic a subject that you will get less marks in if you don't go?'

He did not give me the money. The girls in the school were already giddy with excitement about the impending trip; I, on the other hand, was writhing in agony like a wounded bird. In the end it was a girl named Ayesha who finally came to my rescue. Offering me a loan since I did not have the money, she lent me ten taka at once without a fuss. With my name finally on the list I joined the rest of the girls early one morning on the truck that was scheduled to take us to Dhanbari. Runi was sitting with the teachers and the girls from the senior classes. Loading up the huge utensils, plates and dishes as well as the ration for the picnic on the roof, mikes blazing, our ride finally set off towards the zamindar's estate. At the picnic I spent most of my time admiring Runi's beauty from a distance, otherwise avoiding her, turning left when she moved right and shifting right when she looked left. But then whenever she disappeared from sight I would look around anxiously to catch a glimpse of her again. Keeping her within the radius of my vision I spent most of my time at Dhanbari on my own, sitting quietly under a tree or on the stairs of the zamindar's house. By the time we returned from the picnic it was well past evening; I got back home and found Father waiting for me on the veranda.

'Why did it take you so long to come back from school?'

'I went to the picnic,' I replied, picking my nails.

Father dragged me to the courtyard and beat me with a branch from the jackfruit tree. It was a rule that when parents were meting out physical punishment one had to be firm and not try and turn away. Having worked out his anger on me he asked, 'Who gave you the money for the picnic?'

'A girl from my class lent me the money,' I whispered, not wanting to cooperate but unable to do anything about it; when parents asked a question one had to answer.

The answer earned me a tight slap next. 'You borrowed money to go on a picnic! What's with this craze? I will beat it right out of you.'

The next morning, before leaving for work, Father tossed me a ten-taka note along with my daily rickshaw travel allowance of one taka. 'Henceforth, if you don't listen to me, if you don't do as I say, I will smash every log I find in the courtyard on your back.'

Soon after the picnic a new event sprung up: a cultural programme. It was decided that people were going to perform whatever they knew or could on stage. In no time numerous girls could be found in various rooms, practising singing with a harmonium, or dancing. There would be poetry-recitation competitions too. Besides, there was a small skit planned as well, based on Tagore's poem 'Pujarini' ('The Priestess'). Some were going to dance to Tagore's *'Aj Dhaner Khete . . .'* and accordingly a scenic backdrop with a paddy field and billowy, white clouds was made with chalk. Enthused by all this, having managed to procure a Hawaiian guitar one day, I too tried my hand at singing, picking a Subir Sen song I had learnt in secret from Chotda's book of notations: *'Eto sur ar to gaan, jodi konodin theme jai'* ('All this music and song, what if it all ceases one day'). When the girls heard me they insisted I perform at the programme too and I had no choice but to comply. On the day of the programme my hands and feet were trembling throughout, but even amidst all this whatever I did manage to play earned me mostly compliments from those in the audience. By then I had developed a reputation of being a good student in my new school. I was a genius in my drawing classes and was regularly called excellent in English, apparently because I had written an excellent essay in my entrance examinations. My Bengali teacher would often say I was a poet.

After the cultural programme was over recruitment began for the Girls' Guide. I had physical training to go through, as well as learning to play the drum tied around my neck while marching. On Victory Day the Girls' Guide performed a dance with sticks on the grounds of the Circuit House. Whatever it was I did, I did it with my face lowered and my eyes downcast in awkwardness. Then one day dance master Jogen Chandra came to school to train the girls for a dance-drama to be staged, a performance of Tagore's *Chitrangada*. He grabbed hold of me and asked if I wanted to play the titular role of the gender-bending warrior princess, but I managed to give him the slip and escape. However, when rehearsals began I got so excited by what I saw that I would go back home in the afternoon and, with Yasmin in tow playing the role of one of my handmaidens, have my own private rehearsals on the courtyard of Abakash, dancing and singing to songs from *Chitrangada*. In my personal trials I was Chitrangada, Arjun as well as Madan. As rehearsals went on in school my performances too continued undeterred at home, with Mother, Moni, Dada, Chotda and Poppy as my entranced audience.

Love

While in his second year of college Chotda requested if his classmate Baby from Netrakona could come stay with us as she did not have a decent place to stay. His request was approved and Baby moved into Abakash with her suitcase. It was arranged for her to share my bed. A table and a chair too were procured for her so she could study at ease. Tall and dark with beautiful entrancing eyes, Baby soon managed to develop a good rapport with everyone in the house. I had never had the opportunity thus far of going to bed or waking up in the presence of anyone who was not a relation. So the entry of an entirely new human being from the outside world into our daily affairs managed to create considerable waves in my otherwise uneventful life. When Baby spoke about her sister Manjuri, how she had fallen from the top of a tree and broken her leg, how she herself had travelled all alone from Netrakona to Mymensingh, or her mad brother who used to sit the whole day with his feet dipped in the waters of the Kangsha and who had one day suddenly gone missing never to be found again, I felt as if the Kangsha was my river as well, just like the Brahmaputra. Manjuri would seem like someone I had known for ages. Sitting beside Mother by the kitchen fire, Baby told us about her mother and how the woman had stopped eating, become sick and taken to the bed after her son had gone missing. She had grown reed-thin in no time. And then one day she had requested Baby to take her to the pond for a bath. She had taken a bath, put on a white saree and gone back to bed, never to get up again. Her tragic story made Mother cry out in despair.

'You are my daughter. From today, I have three daughters.'

In the evening Father would ask her, 'So how are your studies going? You will get a first class, won't you?'

'Ji khalujaan, I sure hope so,' she would reply with her head bowed.

About three and a half months later Baby's stay in the house came to an abrupt end when one afternoon Mother chanced upon Chotda lying on his bed and Baby sitting on the edge ruffling his hair. She exploded in rage at the sight.

'Baby! Is this sort of wickedness you were hiding inside you? You had convinced me that the two of you were like siblings! A snake! I was rearing a snake! You want to fool around with my son?! How dare you?!'

Baby burst into tears and clutched at her feet. She had only touched his forehead, that too because Chotda had complained of a headache. She begged Mother to forgive her, promising her that such a thing was never going to happen again. Mother, however, was not the forgiving kind. She informed Baby clearly that when she turned away from something it was usually for good. Baby left. The one person in the house who remained absolutely indifferent to Baby's departure was Chotda.

His exams were fast approaching—ISC—which he had to pass to get into Medical College. It was a long-nurtured dream of Father that at least one of his sons would be a doctor. And then suddenly one day Chotda did not come back home. A day passed, then two, until finally a week had passed without any news of him whatsoever. Father, driven almost to the point of insanity, went around the city looking for him. He was the civil surgeon in Tangail at the time and every day at dawn he would catch a bus to go to his job— more likely to save his job than anything else—only to return at night. Eventually he put in an application to take time off and look for his missing son in earnest. Mymensingh being a small city, this yielded results pretty quickly. Chotda was soon located but the person that Father found was no longer the person we used to know. Chotda was married. We soon found out what had happened. Chotda had fallen in love with a Hindu classmate of his and married her by posing a friend of his as his legal guardian and witness. It was in that friend's house that he had moved in with the girl when he had gone missing.

Pressing the vein popping on his forehead, Father raged.

'This is a disaster! All my hopes and dreams are now done for! Who instigated him into doing something like this! There are only a few months left for the exams and here I was hoping my son was going to be a doctor. That he was going to become a person of rank and standing. What madness has he given in to! His future is ruined. I had told him so many times not to go around with those friends of his but he never listened. So many times I told him to concentrate on his studies so he could become someone!'

Mother proceeded to pour pitchers of cold water on Father's head; his blood pressure was on the ascent again. Unbeknownst to her, his fluctuating blood pressure had already managed to deal a permanent blow to his heart. All she could do was weep and lament.

'He was my gem of a boy. Who knows where he is, what he is eating! I'm sure some wicked people have put him under a spell, like an enchanted amulet or something. Is he of the age to get married?! Allah, I pray please give me back my son.'

She wiped her eyes and poked Father, rousing him from his stupor. 'Or is it . . . could it just be a rumour?'

'No, it isn't,' Father shook his head in reply. 'It's true. The girl's name is Geeta Mitra, she's a Hindu.'

With the kitchen not functional, all I could do was lie back on my bed and count the beams on the ceiling. Dada had already left for Dhaka to study in the university and I felt terribly alone at home. Dada was not there; if Chotda too decided not to live there any more, then the house was going to become absolutely deserted. Moni was dozing off in the balcony and sunlight was gradually beginning to creep down the stairs on to the courtyard. There was no one to step into the sunlight though. Mother used to make her children stand in the sunlight, scrub them clean and then massage them with mustard oil. Then she would put a few droplets of oil in both ears and some in the navel. This she used to do even with a grown-up Chotda. Chotda used to brush his hair back over his forehead, wear fancy pointy shoes and smile mischievously at our neighbour Dolly Pal, but the moment he entered the house he would be Mother's stammering son again, the one she even had to feed herself.

A Hindu girl, how could Kamal marry a Hindu girl,' she sighed, sitting near Father's head. 'She has come to this house a few times. I did not like her ways. She wanted to take Noman to the movies; when he refused she asked Kamal. It's her habit, hanging around boys. She's very cunning, she's entrapped my innocent boy. I was noticing since the past few days, Kamal was behaving a little oddly, as if he was constantly distracted. If only I had known he had fallen in with that girl! I would have warned him for sure!'

Resting her elbow on the railings of the bed she sighed and went on—

'Only Allah can lead him back now. Allah, have mercy, bring my son back! Would he have even thought of marrying into a Hindu family? My son's a gem, so many renowned men would have lined up to match him with their daughters. I had so many plans for his wedding. Finish your studies, get a job and perhaps then think of marriage! I know he will realize his mistake and come back. After all, to err is human—'

Geeta Mitra was a student of Bidyamoyi too, a doe-eyed girl with an affecting, round face, like a tamarind seed. She used to be a regular dancer in cultural or other events of the school. However, Chotda and she had met while they were students in Ananda Mohun College. One of her aunts, a lady with a limp, used to be our teacher and Geeta had visited our house on a number of occasions. She would come and chat with the two of us, Yasmin and I, promise us that she would secretly take us to the movies and also teach us how to dance. Once, under the pretext of plucking custard-apples, she had climbed a tree and planted herself on its topmost branches. She used to be such a rapscallion that we were absolutely delighted by her. Baby had been different, a homely girl, who could darn and cook and everything; unlike Geeta she had not been the kind to storm about a place.

It had not taken long for the strong-willed Geeta to burrow her way into our hearts. As it was, the gateways to our hearts were so wide-open back then that anyone could just about set foot inside and take over. White satin cloth had been purchased on Eid to make new clothes. Geeta had come and promptly taken the roll of cloth away, informing us that she would make the new garments for us since she had a good hand at stitching, etc. Thus had begun her visits, twice daily, to take measurements with a giant tape. She had taken thirteen days to deliver the garments instead of the promised three; we received them on Eid morning. When I had put mine on, I had found to my dismay that not only was the bust of the robe so tight that it was threating to split at the seams, the length too was such that it resembled the diaphanous robes they wore in the Pir's house. Never had I seen such an odd garment and I remember the incident firmly spoiling my Eid.

On the morning of Eid she had come to the house and made me put my new dress on. Clapping with glee, she had flashed me a rodent-like toothy smile and said, 'Oh, how pretty you are in that dress! Excellent! Come, let me take you to a wonderful place.' I could scarcely wait to see this wonderful new place and in no time Geeta and I had set off on a rickshaw and eventually landed up in a judge's house in Saheb Quarter, a decidedly affluent household where Geeta's friend Ruhi lived. Geeta was supposed to be going somewhere with Ruhi and the latter, a very fair and flat-looking girl, had set about convincing her mother to let her go out. The longer it had taken to convince the mother, the more time the two girls had spent whispering, leaving me stationed there on the sofa like a toy. Around two hours later, when the mother could finally be convinced, Ruhi had slapped on some rouge and kajal and the three of us had finally set off on a rickshaw towards the fantastic place I had been promised. I did not know anything about this place so while the girls had giggled between themselves

I had had no choice but to stay put on Geeta's lap like a little wooden pony. The rickshaw had eventually stopped at a house in Gulkibari; a man with a fox-like face, a stranger I had never seen before, had emerged from therein, led us inside and locked the main gate behind us. It was a desolate house, the property also comprising a large lawn. I had entered the house and realized there was no one about except the fox-faced man. There were two adjacent rooms and the man had taken Ruhi by the hand and led her to the bedroom inside. I had stayed put on the sofa in the first room, like a toy or something, transfixed, watching Ruhi sitting rather close to the man on the bed, so close that I could barely blink, the man falling back on the bed and dragging Ruhi down on his chest. Suddenly he had pushed her aside, sprang up from the bed and walked to where we were. He had pushed a bottle of Fanta into my hand, told Geeta to go sit in the lawn and then walked back to the bedroom, closing the door behind him.

Out in the lawn, I had asked Geeta in a trembling voice, 'Who is that man?'

'Khurrambhai,' Geeta had smirked, 'Very rich. Has a car!'

'He's shut himself in with Ruhi,' I had gulped nervously. 'What if something happens now? I'm scared. Let's go home.'

A luminous smile had lit up Geeta's dark face. 'Sit for a while! Why do you want to go back so soon?'

Hours had passed with me continuously asking to be taken home, writhing in extreme discomfort, until it was finally afternoon. The fox-faced man had continued to bring a steady supply of Fanta throughout but I was no longer satisfied with the drink; I was famished. Edging closer to the gate I had asked in a weepy voice to be let out so I could go back home. Geeta's face too had begun to seem dry by then and she had finally stood up and knocked on the bedroom door—

'Khurrambhai, the little girl doesn't want to stay any more. I think we should leave.'

The fox-faced man had re-emerged, a thick bushy moustache over his lips, shirtless and barefoot.

'Geeta, take a few photos. Come in,' he had said and taken her inside, leaving me waiting at the door.

I had peeked inside and seen Ruhi sitting in the middle of the bed, her head bowed. Her hair, tied previously in a ponytail, was untied and dishevelled. Her lipstick had rubbed off and the kohl in her eyes had begun to run. The entire scene had made me feel terribly sorry for the girl. Had the man taken off her clothes? Had she agreed or had he forced her? Had he threatened her and coerced her? What it was I had not been able to figure out. The man had passed a camera to Geeta and then dragged Ruhi into his arms. Geeta had smiled and clicked, doing it again when he had put his head on Ruhi's lap, and then again when he had pulled her close and put his cheek against hers.

By the time we had left the house that day it was past evening. Geeta had first dropped Ruhi home and then dropped me, explicitly asking me not to tell anyone where I had been. My parents, their Eid spoilt due to worrying over a daughter who had been missing for most of the day, had been livid and I had stood in front of them with a dejected expression and accepted my due punishment. This mysterious Geeta, who had given me such a stupendous day as gift on Eid, was now my Chotda's wife. Chotda was a fairly well-known guitarist in the city. His guitar and the song 'O amar desher mati . . .' ('O my country's earth, I bow to thee . . .') were what Geeta had danced to in college, where it had all begun for them. The same Geeta Mitra who had called Baby a horrible person, who she had asked me to steer clear of. Geeta too had disliked Baby, had insisted Baby not come over to our house any more.

Father was fuming. 'I will disinherit him! He will feed off me, live off me and still stab me in the back ultimately?'

Mother had stopped sobbing and joined in the fray, her voice rising as well.

'He found no one other than that shameless hussy? Her father supplies wood for fuel! That Hindu wood merchant will now become an MBBS doctor's son's father-in-law? The women of that house go to the pond to bathe! They are lower-class people, turtle-eaters, Malauns! We will not be able to show our face in society any longer, our honour and pride are in a shambles. He's blackened the face of the entire family. He's married a dancer, such a shame! Why did I give birth to such a son!'

Mother's tirade was akin to the relentless churning of waves in the familial ocean. Nothing this serious had ever happened in our family before; consequently, Father summoned Nana, Nani, Runu khala and Hasem mama to our place. Dada, Boromama and Jhunu khala too arrived from Dhaka. Everyone was visibly anxious and serious talks were soon held where the children, Yasmin and I, were forbidden to even take a peek. The discussions went on till midnight, their voices so low that despite my best efforts I could barely manage to catch anything of what was being discussed. Although I did manage to catch a few stray words floating in from time to time like fine strands of silk-cotton, it was all too flimsy for me to figure out which way the winds were blowing.

The day after the discussions a terrifying thing happened. Father and Hasem mama nabbed Chotda, brought him home and tied him up in the room where they had all met the day before. Chains were put on his hands and feet and Father kept the key with himself for safe-keeping. His bellows were enough to make the house shake and the trees tremble; the sight of him through the windows, raging and fuming, was enough to make me sweat with nervousness. Yasmin was crying, her head buried in her pillow. Mother was restlessly pacing up and down the veranda, rapidly muttering and counting her prayer beads.

'Tell me if you will leave Geeta or not! Or I will disinherit you,' Father could be heard yelling from time to time.

Chotda remained unyielding. 'Do whatever you want. I won't leave her.'

Father's eyes were about to pop out of their sockets. His shirt, sweaty and wet, was sticking to his body as he stood with his hands on his hips, panting, his blood pressure climbing rapidly.

'You are not allowed to go anywhere any more. Nowhere! You will go to college and give your exams.'

Chotda's voice rose as he replied. 'I didn't want to come to this house. The two of you lied to me and lured me here. I am married to Geeta, let me go. I want to be with her. I don't want anything from you, just let me go.'

'Forget Geeta, or your death is certain in my hands. I will whip the life out of you.' Father's eyes were raining fire.

Father left Chotda with two hours to think about his next course of action, the whole of which he spent sitting up against the wall with his jaws clenched. Periodically, Mother, Nani and Runu khala tried talking him out of the deadlock.

'You're such a good boy, you have always listened to your father. He will forgive you immediately, only if you come back home and get back to your studies, give your exam.

You're going to be a doctor! Yes, you have married her.
Let the girl go back home too and the two of you complete
your education. Later your father himself is going to get the
two of you married, have a big social function as well to let
everyone know. You're still a student. If you leave home now
how will you fend for your wife and yourself? Given your
qualifications as of now you are not going to get any jobs.
So? What are you going to do? Are you going to be a porter,
or a drive a rickshaw? Your father is a well-known doctor,
everyone knows him. Listen to your father. If he disinherits
you, you will not get a farthing of his property. You're a smart
boy, aren't you? Go to the girl and tell her to go back home.
Your father has given his word that when the time comes, he
will let you marry whoever you want.'

Chotda, however, remained inflexible. His only demand
was that they should unshackle him. Father couldn't care less
about Chotda's clenched jaws; he had a reputation for beating
the most difficult things straight. Whatever happened, he
could not bear to let his son gamble away his life and future.
How could he stand by and watch his child jump into a fiery
pit! This was his own son, he had his blood in his veins, he
looked like him! To raise him Father had worked day and
night, just to provide for him. His son, his son was his heir;
Father was determined to get him back. After the stipulated
two-hour period Father returned to confront Chotda again,
the latter still defiant and still in chains and the former
wielding a whip.

'What have you decided? Will you listen to me?' His
voice betrayed neither heat nor ice.

Chotda's jaw tightened further in response. 'Let me go.'

'Oh, I should let you go, should I?! You'll go nowhere
without my permission. You will not go to Geeta.'

'I have only one thing to say, there is no going back from that,' Chotda replied through gritted teeth. 'I will not stay in this house any more, I will be with Geeta no matter what.'

'What will you feed her? What will you eat?' Father asked, with a flick of the whip in his hand.

'That's not something anyone else has to lose sleep over,' Chotda shot back, teeth grating, jaws tight.

Had I been in his place I would have perhaps capitulated to every one of Father's demands by then. Who could have imagined being trapped under a tiger's paw and snarling at the beast itself! It was Father's turn to tighten his jaw, his eyes fiery with rage. The whip swung through the air with a screech, like a ravenous tiger jumping on a deer. It seemed to hit me, it seemed as if I were the only one beginning to bleed under its assault. As if the skin had peeled off my flesh, and the flesh as well, to reveal the bones underneath. I shut my eyes, waiting for the whipping to stop. But it did not stop. Mother, Nani, Boromama and Runu khala silently walked out of the living room, some leaning against the balcony pillar and staring out into nothing, some pacing without even knowing why, some clutching their hair without realizing when they had done so. As if they were all dead, they had just risen from their graves and did not know where they were headed. They did not notice each other either, an impenetrable darkness stretched out in front of them, like a dark forest lying ahead where only the swishing sounds of a whip could be heard.

Unable to bear it any longer Mother ran back inside the living room and, fighting to be heard over the combined sounds of the whip as well as Chotda crying out her name, screamed, 'He's going to die. Do you want to kill him? You want to kill my son, don't you?'

Chotda was bleeding under his whip; Father bellowed, 'Yes, I will kill him today! He doesn't deserve to live.'

'Let him go wherever he wants to!' Mother pleaded through tears. 'There's no point beating him, he was always the stubborn one. That Malaun girl is now dearer to him than his own family. Let him go, let him go to her.'

However, Chotda was not let go. He was locked in his room and new locks were installed on the door, the keys of which remained with Father. The latter issued an edict that Chotda was not to be given any food. Neither was he supposed to be let out to go to the bathroom or something; he was to stay in captivity till good sense prevailed. Barred inside his own room, Chotda tried breaking the doors and windows but the nine feet by five feet entrances, sturdy as if the wood had been smelted from iron, remained unbending. His groans could be heard throughout the night; they succeeded in keeping us, a family of ancient animals in a haunted mansion, awake in our beds, our heads burrowed inside our pillows. Late in the night, I cannot recall exactly how late, Yasmin whispered to me, 'Bubu, I can't sleep.' I turned to face her. 'I can't sleep either.'

Our sighs swirled in the room and gathered into mist, blurring vision and making it impossible to discern the windows, the entrance or the furniture bathed in the golden glow of the lamp from the balcony. The darkness came and settled on my hair, on my eyes and on my chin.

After four days of fasting, Mother managed to sneak in some food for Chotda through the iron bars on the window. She herself had not eaten for those four days and finally broke her fast only after she had fed him. Father remained outside, ear to the door, hoping for some gesture from within, driven by captivity and hunger, that could be taken as a sign of capitulation. When no such sounds emerged, Father issued a second stern dictum: the kitchens were no longer functional. And how were the rest of the people in the house supposed to survive? By having muri soaked in water, of course! He also made sure to let us know that anyone sneaking food into Chotda's room was going to be beaten up as well. Despite his warnings, something or the other ended up being passed through the bars of the window of Chotda's prison. I was quite certain that Father knew about this and only pretended that he had no idea what was happening behind his back. He extended his leave and decided to stay at home longer so he could hasten Chotda's surrender. The latter was already showing signs of starvation, his cheeks hollow, the skin of his neck and shoulders stretching across his bones, a skeleton holding the bars of his window and groaning.

Two tigers were in mortal combat and we were merely silent helpless spectators. The battle raged on for fifteen days.

In the end it was Father who had to beat a retreat. Chotda had to be let go.

After Chotda was gone Father clutched the two of us, Yasmin and I, to his chest; so tightly that it seemed his ribs would pierce our flesh.

'The two of you . . . give me your word that you will finish your education and become someone. Promise me that you will.'

We nodded to assure him we would.

'My two daughters are now where my dreams lie. Promise me neither of you will become like your brother. Promise me.'

We nodded to assure him we would not.

'I did everything I could to ensure my children are brought up well. I had so many dreams for Kamal. Such a brilliant student, with those star marks in his matric exam. He was my pride. Now all my pride, all my dreams have crumbled. The two of you are my final hope. It's with that hope that I must live now. Promise me you will let me live! Promise me you will finish your studies.' His voice had become hoarse as he finished.

We nodded to assure him we would.

'No, I did not want to hurt my son. Did it hurt me any less to do that to him! To make him starve? It was my one last attempt to change his mind. I pleaded with him but he didn't listen to me. So I beat him, but he still didn't listen to me. You will listen to me, won't you?!'

We nodded to assure him we would listen to him. His tears were making our clothes damp as he held on to us. That was the first time I saw my father cry.

But the two of us nodding to assure him we would do something and Father accepting that promise happily was not something that was to be; Father was just not that kind of a person. He declared to Mother that the atmosphere of the house had been irretrievably damaged.

'I had bought such a huge house just so my children could have a good atmosphere for their studies. Everyone with a room to themselves, no chaos, no commotion. I had stopped my children from mingling with the other children of the locality so they could concentrate on their studies in peace. Nothing worked,' he sighed as he fell back on the bed. 'What will I do with this house now? I will sell it off! Behind my back Noman wasted all his time with his friends and did terribly in his exams. Kamal has chosen to destroy his life for a girl. The girls too will go astray if they live in this house.'

All Mother could do was wordlessly watch the pained struggle of someone who had slipped and crashed on his way

up the ladder of success. She had prayed each and every day
after reading her namaz, hoping her son would turn away
from the non-Muslim girl, that he would become pious and
read the namaz himself, that he would find his faith. But
none of her prayers had worked; her son had not even looked
back while leaving.

Within two days of Chotda's leaving Father packed our
books and clothes in two individual suitcases and took us to
live in boarding schools, me in the hostel of Model School
and Yasmin in Bharateshwari Homes in Mirzapur. Neither
of us dared utter a word of protest. As we were being taken
away Mother was standing at the black gate, still like a stone
statue, or a withered rose petal that I know would have fallen
off at the slightest tap.

I was not yet thirteen back then; I had never stayed
anywhere without my mother before. Mother used to tie my
hair, feed me when I had to eat, sit by my side through the
night to nurse me when I had fever. She would keep aside the
biggest mangoes, guavas, custard-apples or green coconuts
from the garden for me, her oldest daughter. She made me
dresses with embroidered flowers and bell sleeves. When I
could not sleep she would tap a rhythm on my back while
singing me a lullaby, singing to the moon to come and douse
her Raju with sleep; Raju was what she fondly used to call
me sometimes. Leaving her behind, leaving my bed behind,
the hopscotch grid on the yard, the field where the other
girls and I would play gollachut, I was suddenly consigned
to spending my days on the single bed assigned to me in the
girls' hostel of Model School where my father had left me.
The other girls of the hostel were expectedly surprised to see
me there.

'Why are you here? You live in this city, don't you?'

I could only stare at them, I had no answers to their questions. I was like a strange new animal that had been imported to the zoo. The other girls saw the horns on my head and the horns on my stomach and could do little but purse their lips and laugh. I did not wish to tell anyone how my Chotda—back when we were in the house in Ishwargunj where Yasmin was born, the house where lines and lines of ants could be found crawling all over the walls—used to crush the red ants with his fingers and exclaim, 'The red ones are Hindus.'

Once when I had killed a black one by mistake, he had been so angry. He had swiftly landed two massive blows on my back and told me, 'Why are you killing the black ones? The black ones are Musalmans! Pick the red ones!'

The same Chotda, my black-Hindu-ant-killing older brother, got married to a Hindu girl and moved out, abandoning his studies as well as his family in the process, and irretrievably breaking the family apart.

Seven days after my arrival at the hostel Mother came to visit me and put in an application with the superintendent, asking to be allowed to take me home. Unfortunately her application was turned down since the official documents had only Father's name as legal guardian, leaving her no choice but to turn back in tears.

The top floor of the hostel building was where the principal, Wabda Saheb, lived. The ground floor had been transformed into somewhat of a hostel. On most afternoons Father would come and visit, bringing sweets, biscuits, candies and lots of other goodies. He would hand them over to me and immediately ask, 'How are your studies going, my sweet?'

Eyes downcast, I would nod and assure him it was going well.

'There are other girls in the hostel, aren't there? Girls of your age?' He would ask in a gentle voice.

I would nod and say there were.

'Stay here and study. After school, come back to the hostel, wash up and sit with your books. There's nothing else to do, right? I have brought you here for your own good. If you don't understand now why that is, then one day you surely will. Fathers always want what's best for their children, don't they?'

I would nod and say they did.

It made me want to burst into tears. To hide them I would look up at the sky, towards the sun, so Father would think it was just my eyes watering for staring at the sun for too long and nothing else. I did not wish to let him understand just how much I wanted to go back home. I was not allowed any other visitors except him; not even Mother was allowed to see me. All I wanted to do was run away from the place! But the huge moustached guard sitting at the gate made escape impossible. Dr Rebecca had shifted to the teachers' quarters of Medical College so Runi had had to move in with her as well. If she had been there perhaps things would have been easier. Or would they have been easier? I cannot say for sure.

In the afternoons, after school got over and we were all fed and rested, some girls would go out and play badminton while others would sit around and gossip which of the masters or mistresses were married, who were divorced, who lived on their own, who was in love with whom. I understood only bits of what they discussed. I did not get a lot of it and I did not want to either. What I failed to fathom was how they managed to gather so much information about what was brewing in the hearts and homes of the teachers. I could not do it at all and had to pass my time watching the girls play or hearing them gossip. In the evenings one had to sit in front of one's books; the superintendent usually went on rounds to ensure all the girls were studying. My tears would trickle down on the pages of the book open in front of me and every night the words would get fuzzier and unclear. Every night I had to sleep alone on my bed, there was no one to coax and lull me to sleep. What had I done to deserve being exiled from my own home? Chotda was the one who had had an affair but I was the one being punished! I was left with no doubts that what Father had done was wrong.

I had seen Dada fall in love too, albeit silently. About three days after moving to Abakash he had fallen in love with a girl from the neighbourhood called Anita. One day, while walking on the road, he had spied her standing on her roof, a bright girl with a halo of dark tresses framing her face. That was it, he had fallen in love. Six months later when Anita and her family had moved to Calcutta for good, Dada had wept and begun writing poetry. This had stopped for a while after he met Sheela, his friend Farhad's sister. There used to be two Farhads, one thin and the other fat, and Sheela was the former's sister. A tall girl with a betel-leaf-shaped face, according to Dada she looked just like the film actress Olivia. Over time his room had come to be covered in photos of Olivia cut out of film magazines, in his books and copies, under the tablecloth, beneath his pillows or his mattress, everywhere all one could see was her. If Yasmin or I were to find any photos of her anywhere we would instantly bring them to him. I remember watching Dada stare at those photos for hours, comparing how Sheela's chin was similar to Olivia's, as was her nose and her eyes. When she laughed, Sheela too had dimples on her left cheek.

This had resulted in Dada pushing aside his old notebooks, finding fresh ones and starting to write poetry again with renewed vigour. He had also begun listening to love songs by Hemanta Mukherjee while he was by himself. He had pooled together his daily rickshaw fare for college as well as his lunch money to buy himself a violin, which he learned to play from Jamini Roy. He would play the most plaintive tunes on it, thinking about Sheela as he did. Sheela was yet to fall in love with him, so far it had only been one-sided.

It was not his violin that was going to sway Sheela though; that was going to happen one day because of his poetry. A doe was going to look a bull in the eye and ask, 'Where did you learn to write poetry? This is quite beautiful.'

The bull was only going to smile in response.

'Why do you stare at me so much?' the doe was going to inquire.

The bull was only going to smile in response again.

'You walk past this main road so frequently these days that my brother keeps wondering why you are visiting Kachijhuli so often?'

The bull was only going to smile in response.

'It's no one's business why you come here! It's not as if Farhad owns the street! You walk past as often as you wish to. You have other friends in Kachijhuli, right? Visit them too!'

The bull was only going to smile in response.

'You want clothes made for your mother and sisters, right? Why don't you get the material one day, I am quite good at stitching and stuff.'

The bull was only going to nod in response.

'It's so hot now. It's probably a little breezier on the roof. You must be feeling hot too?'

The bull was only going to nod in response.

Despite being an MA student in the psychology department of Dhaka University, much of my Dada's psyche was going to remain fixated on Khachijhuli in Mymensingh while the science part would remain suspended, like a bat or a monkey, on the fig tree in the campus. It was going to make him cook up excuses for holidays to return home frequently. To go meet the desolate doe under a red silk-cotton tree in Khachijhuli.

'My father has fixed my marriage somewhere else,' the doe was going to sigh one day.

'With whom?'

'Whoever it is, it's not you.'

'Oh!'

'Baba isn't well. He's afraid he's going to die so he wants to get his daughter married off and be at peace.'

'What's happened to him?'

'Whatever it is, he's fixed on the marriage.'

'Oh!'

'If you go to him with an offer for my hand, I don't think he will turn you down.'

'Oh!' Seeing the doe cry the bull was going to inquire, 'Why are you crying?'

'Don't you know why I'm crying?'

When he would nod and confess that he did not know why she was crying, the doe was going to chide him accusingly, 'I thought you were a student of psychology. You know nothing about what is going on in my mind.' The bull was going to get all bothered and out of sorts.

Dada was first going to mention Sheela to Mother quite casually; she was beautiful, she was getting married soon, she was going to look very pretty in red, she was an excellent cook, she knew how to sew and darn well, she was going to take a lot of care of her in-laws, she was going to have lots of beautiful children, etc.

'One of your friend's sisters is very beautiful and a good girl. That's good? So what's really the matter?'

It was going to take Dada some more time to fess up to the real matter. After hedging around a bit more he was finally going to admit he wanted to marry Sheela. Mother was going to broach the topic in front of Father with the lightest of touches, mixing it with a spoonful of sugar to help it go down. And yet, that too was going to seem bitter to Father. Then finally one day, after having avoided it long enough, Father was going to ask to meet the girl.

The bull would go to the doe and tell her, 'You must come to the house, you've been invited for a feast. Father wants to meet you.'

The doe was going to smile bashfully.

'I feel so happy! You're going to be my wife.'

The doe was going to smile bashfully.

'After meeting you Father is going to go your house to talk about our wedding.'

The doe was going to smile bashfully.

'Don't wear bangles or earrings or make-up. Father doesn't like them. And tell him you had a first division in the matric exam, with star marks. Rather, don't say that. What if you get caught! You're studying for your IA, working very hard so you get first division and will continue your studies after getting married. If he asks what your aim is, tell him you want to teach in a college.'

The doe was going to smile bashfully.

She was going to come home and find herself sitting in our living room in Father's company. Dada was going to be in his room, out of sight, sitting on his bed and shaking his legs out of nervousness, too embarrassed to come out. Mother was going to cook vermicelli in milk, set up a tray with tea, biscuits, sweets and vermicelli pudding and place it on the table by the sofa for her. They were going to eat and talk and a smile of satisfaction was going to flash across Father's face. When the time would come for her to leave, he was going hail a rickshaw to see her off himself, waving at her from the black main gate of Abakash. Mother, clad in a new saree, her lips red with paan, elated beyond measure, was going to run up to Father and gush, 'She looks like Madhubala, doesn't she?!'

'Truly.'

'She seems like a good girl,'

'That's true too.'

'The boy is of marriageable age. The sooner the better!'

Father, in his customary shirt-pant-tie-shoes, bespectacled and curly haired, was then going to make a pronouncement. 'I'm not going to get my son married to this girl.'

The judge could be swayed, but never the judgement.

Two months later Sheela was going to get married off to a pot-bellied, moustached, five-feet-two-inches tall man, twenty-three years of age between the two of them.

The doe was going to be locked up in a cage.

Dada had cried, but no one got to know he had cried. Jhunu khala, on the other hand, had not cried alone. She had cried loud enough for the whole neighbourhood to know. She had given up food, given up on taking showers and smashed every last glass utensil in the house against the wall. She had even tried hanging herself from the rafters using her dupatta but before she could succeed in doing it Hasem mama had managed to break the door down and stop her. An Ayurvedic doctor was consulted who had prescribed an oil to cool her head. The maulvi from the mosque too was summoned to blow enchantments on her face meant to cure her. When none of this had worked, she was sent off to Dhaka to live in Boromama's house.

Runu khala and Jhunu khala were nearly the same age and everyone in the neighbourhood knew how close the two sisters were. When the chanachur-seller would pass by the house he would call out their names together, enticing them to go out and sample his wares. The sisters laughed together, cried together, sang and danced together, went gathering fruits and flowers together, besides sharing the same bed as well as all their secrets with each other. People used to say they were like twins. Then one fine day Runu khala had vanished from home, vanished as if she had disappeared. After an extensive city-wide search we had found out she had eloped and married a boy called Rashu and gone with him to his house in Begunbari. Jhunu khala had heard the news and exploded into a maelstrom of tears, her despair spilling over like waves and sweeping across the house, the yard and the entire neighbourhood. Why was Jhunu khala so devastated? Rashu had been her private tutor, he had had nothing to do with her sister Runu. Runu had not sat in front of him and read the covert messages in his gaze, had not heard the pounding of his heart in his chest. Only Jhunu khala knew how Rashu's toes used to inch towards her foot under the table, how his hands would secretly tangle with her own. Only she knew who she used to make garlands out of shiuli for, why she used to stand in front of the mirror every afternoon and why she used to line her eyes with kohl. Everyone knew about the master who used to come home to teach Jhunu khala but no one had any inkling about how much time they spent actually studying and how much in unrelated activities. No one had been allowed to disrupt them or cause any commotion while the lessons were on. Only Runu khala used to go into the room at some point every day to serve them tea and biscuits, that was the only instance of any interruption during the lessons or whatever they were doing.

So if Rashu was to suddenly marry her younger sister Runu, was it a surprise that Jhunu khala had tried to kill herself in despair! Men were animals, as Jhunu khala used to say. Two days after the maulvi had administered his enchantments, we were sitting by the pond when Jhunu khala, her feet immersed in the water, had told us how falling for a man's promises was almost certainly doomed to be a disaster.

'They are worse than pigs, they will lick whatever they come across. None of them have any morals. Today they will tell you they love you, tomorrow they will repeat the same words to someone else.'

Jhunu khala had a cascade of dark hair that fell past her bottom, all matted from lack of care, eyes dark from the bags underneath rather than any kohl, and fair skin pale and dreary like dead grass. Among Nani's four girls, Fajli khala was an eighty out of hundred, Jhunu khala a fifty, Runu khala a thirty and Mother . . .

That was how Dada used to rank their beauty, like marks received in school.

'So how much is Mother?' we would ask.

'She's a big zero,' Dada would reply, sitting on a chair and swinging his feet, his pencil between his teeth.

'You and I are the same, you know,' Jhunu khala had said to Gnetu's mother. 'Your man hurt you, mine hurt me. If there is truly an Allah, He will not tolerate it. They will be judged by Allah Himself,' Jhunu khala had declared, the newly ordained hermit whose beauty had earned her fifty per cent marks from Dada.

'What is Jhunu discussing with Gnetu's mother for so long!' Nani would grumble unhappily from the window seeing the two of them sitting so close. 'Jhunu can't keep anything to herself, who knows what she will say!'

Gnetu's mother had sighed, as if from the very core of her being. 'Allah doesn't do justice. Allah is very partial. Gnetu's father beat me, burned me and threw me out. He got married again. But he's still happy. I am the one who's unhappy. I have no father I can go to. My two brothers abuse me at every turn, accusing me of being responsible for why my husband abandoned me.' Her hands had remained frozen in mid-air, the burn wounds on them visible.

With her chin resting on one knee Jhunu khala had gone on. 'I don't want to live in this world any more. Then I think, why should I die alone? I would rather finish them off first before killing myself. If I'm not happy, why should they be happy either!'

Darkness had crept up the narrow road and slipped into the yard of Nani's house. A half-moon had appeared, seemingly sleeping on the still surface of the pond, wrapped in a quilt of water hyacinths. Gnetu's mother's charred hands were asleep in the folds of her saree. Jhunu khala did not really want to go anywhere. All she wanted to do was to remain sitting beside the pond, beneath the date palms all night and let the dew drench her matted hair. She no longer needed to gather shiuli off the dew-drenched grass within

the folds of her saree early in the morning; there was no one
for whom she had to make garlands any longer. She did not
have to wait for anyone any more every afternoon with her
hair braided with red ribbons and her eyes lined with kohl.

She had felt completely empty on the inside. She had run
to her room and brought out a handful of papers, stinking of
naphthalene, letters Rashu had written to her that she had
carefully hidden away inside her trunk among her clothes.
While the moon was still sleeping peacefully over the pond
and darkness was hanging like bats from the date tree, she
had set the letters on fire.

'Come,' she had said to Gnetu's mother, 'let's warm
ourselves up a bit. It's getting quite cold.'

Ash from the burning pile was floating in the air, some of
it settling on Jhunu khala's matted hair. Gnetu's mother's face
was glowing red in the fire. Fire made her want to boil rice,
to inch closer to boiling rice and take in its fragrance. One
of the dark bats of the date palm seemed to leapt abruptly on
her from above.

'I stick around for food, for sustenance. I tolerate their
abuse and their torture only for that. Hunger is such a thing
that it knows no limits. I've never traded in emotions with
anyone, that's something that best suits rich people. We
don't have emotions, we only have a hungry belly. The one
who feeds is the one I consider master.'

Jhunu khala did not want to listen to her tales of hunger
any more. She did not feel hungry at all; in fact, the thought
of eating made her want to throw up. An arid desert had been
taking root within her soul bit by bit. She could have been
happy with Rashu even under a tree. Looking at his eyes used
to make her forget about hunger and thirst. Even drowning
to their death together would have made her happy.

The fire had gone out leaving the last letter only half burnt. Jhunu khala had remained sitting in the darkness, holding the charred piece in her hand, badly wanting to read it again. She had been sure it was the letter where Rashu had confessed to loving her more than life itself.

Before being sent away to Dhaka, one day Jhunu khala and I—no else ever got to know about it but us—had found our rickshaw dropping us off in front of a yellow two-storeyed house in Jubileeghat. Jhunu khala had led the way while I brought up the rear. There was a plaque on the outside of the house: Dak Bungalow. Jhunu khala had knocked and as we had stood outside Room No. 12 of Dak Bungalow, I had noticed little droplets of sweat glistening on the tip of her nostrils. The door had opened to reveal a familiar face with a long droopy moustache falling past the chin, a reed-thin figure that resembled a tree-dwelling ghost: Jafar Iqbal, Nani's neighbour who used to live just two doors from her house. He had pulled her inside with him and closed the door, leaving me to stand outside and stare at the Brahmaputra. I had spent my afternoon looking at the waves breaking on the surface of the river and the boats rolling by with the boatmen singing bhatiyali songs. Even when the sun was going down, a giant egg yolk setting in the Brahmaputra and bathing the western sky in red, I had remained standing where Jhunu khala had asked me to as if in a trance.

Just as the sun had set, the doors had opened and Jhunu khala had re-emerged. She had placed her palm softly and lovingly on my cheek.

'If someone asks where we were, tell them we went to visit a friend of mine.'

Walking out of the Dak Bungalow and hailing a rickshaw she had spoken again.

'What if they ask which friend? Where does she live?'

I had stared at her expressionlessly, waiting for her to supply the answer herself.

'Tell them it was Fatema, from Kalibari. No, not Kalibari. Tell them Brahmopalli. Is that all right?'

I did not have to spell it out to Jhunu khala whether it was all right. Perhaps she had understood that whether she warned me or not, given how rarely I talked about things, I was definitely not going to be talking about that day to anyone.

The Return 1

Another four months were to pass before Mother could bring me back home from the hostel. How that happened was quite the incident as well; for someone who was not even allowed to see me, it was as good as being gifted the forbidden fruit. Mother used to often meet the super of the hostel and burst into tears in front of him, lamenting about how Father was planning to marry again, how I had been sent away from home for that exact purpose. There was a conspiracy afoot. Father was planning to sell off the house and move to a new one with his new bride. Neither of her sons were with her. If the daughter was at least home then she could fight her errant husband and stop him from selling the house or remarrying.

Eventually, Mother's tearful stories succeeded in melting the superintendent's heart. The daughter was restored to the mother, four long months after she had been taken away. Yasmin too was brought back home from Mirzapur.

With her daughters on either side, Mother sat waiting anxiously for Father's return.

Father came back home and was greeted with the sight of us; it was as if he had seen a ghost. Seeing his eyes turning red, jaw tightening and teeth gnashing was enough for me to wilt in fear. Yasmin, cowering, tried to hide her face behind Mother.

'I gave birth to them,' Mother squeaked somehow, 'I have a say about them too.' It was directed at the room in general, no matter who it landed on in the process.

Father did not utter a single word. He did stop sending rations and groceries to the house after that day. Mother would get us food in paper bags from Nana's shop and then grumble loudly, her grievances directed at the air like before.

'It's all because he wants to get married. Can only do it if the girls are not here. I won't tolerate it as long as I'm alive. He had come to the city a destitute. It was my father who had given him money and saved him.'

She would pace and mutter to herself. At least that was what she pretended to do, since it was clear everything was directed at Father. Not that she stood in front of him, looked him in the eye and said anything. She usually did it from the room next to his or from the balcony, loud enough so he could hear without expending any effort.

Next, Father stopped giving us money to pay the rickshaw while travelling to or from school. As a result we stopped going to school altogether. Mother was determined as well to see how long he could go without paying for our education, convinced as she was that it was not going to be possible for him to stay mad or stubborn about this one thing at least. When three days had passed without either of us going anywhere near school, Father was left with no choice but to break his silence on the matter. Having taken his customary cold shower early in the morning and getting dressed, he called me, cleared his throat and asked, 'So? Is that it? Done with your studies?'

I had nothing to say. I did not need to decide anything about my studies. Father was there to do just that.

'If that is so,' he continued, raising his gaze towards the ceiling, 'then tell me directly right now. I don't have to worry about anything in that case. Your brothers have already informed me that they are no longer interested in pursuing their education. I send Noman money every month. And now he tells me he isn't appearing for his exams this time, he's going to do it the next time! And your other brother, well his life is over anyway. If you two want to go the same way then tell me. I don't have to waste money on sending you to school any more in that case.'

My impassive gaze had begun to stray to the grass growing tall in the courtyard, the mossy sides of the tube-well, a stray crow up on the branches of the guava tree. I was not used to speaking in front of my father. The lesser I spoke the better, the more sedate I appeared the more it served to reassure him. Such were the rules that he could keep saying whatever he wished to and we had to keep our heads and eyes lowered and listen to everything he had to say. If he wished he could draw me close and pet me, or slap me right across the face, but it all had to be borne without complaints. So all his talk about letting me follow Chotda's precedence if I so wished was just that, nothing but talk. If I was to admit that I did want to follow Chotda's footsteps, that I did not want to study in school, etc., he was hardly going to let me do it. He would have skinned me alive!

'Why aren't you going to school?' His voice was like the beating of drums, a sound so startlingly harsh that it sent a shiver running down my body and my gaze snapped back from the tail of the crow on the guava tree. The raised voice meant he wanted a definite answer. He knew the answer already but

I had to repeat it to him nevertheless. Just to ensure he knew it was his fault and not mine that I was not going to school, I raised my voice as high as it would go in front of him and said, 'I don't have money to pay the rickshaw.'

'Why don't you have money? Mother's pets the both of you are, aren't you! She's getting you food from elsewhere too! So can't she arrange for money to pay for the rickshaw too?'

As he finished he flung two taka at me; the money sailed through the air and fell on the floor. I wanted to leave it lying there, just where it had been thrown. But beyond my feelings about the matter was Father, standing in front of me and seething at the remarkable lack of reaction on my part. Unable to help it I bent over and picked up the money. I had seen Father lose only once, to Chotda. I did not know for sure if this was another such an instance but it was definitely clear that he had silently capitulated and accepted our return. Not that he said he had accepted it in as many words, we only knew he was no longer going to drag us back to the hostels. While that was definite, he also did turn the house into a veritable prison after this incident. The windows from which the roads could be seen were permanently boarded up. Bullock carts full of sand, bricks and cement were brought and masons were deployed to make the walls surrounding the house double their original height, like prison walls, so that all contact with the outside world ceased to exist. The roof was made out of bounds as well; if we were to be found there Father would drag us downstairs by the throat, warning us that he was going to break our legs if we ever went up there again. The place for us to sing and dance in the rain, a place where we could play houses or lean back against the railings with a good book, or simply stand and keep watch over the goings-on in the neighbourhood, our beloved roof soon became a forbidden place. I found the space within which I could move around freely suddenly shrinking in size but I had no idea why it was happening. The roof was from where I had been gradually learning about the outside world. While strolling on the roof in the balmy breeze, words would gradually crowd together in my head, fine powdery words, like rain. I used to string those words together in my heart and make garlands.

Once it was made out of bounds for us, the roof only served to stoke my obsession with it further. As soon as Father would leave the house in the morning I would run up to the roof. Then later, when a sound at the main gate would signal his return, I would run downstairs like the wind and park myself in front of my study table like an innocent child. The more the walls surrounding me closed in, the more maddening became the irrepressible urge to demolish all barriers. I could sense there were two facets to my nature, one deep within me and one that was visible on the surface, one of them inquisitive and the other apathetic.

It was only a few months later that I understood why Father was behaving the way he was. He was afraid that I was going to fall in love with some wastrel somewhere and run off with the guy. As a result my life became restricted within the strict confines of my home and my school. It was at such a time that Ratan came into my life, ushering in a tide of joy at his wake for a short while. Ratan used to come from a village, now a town, called Elenga in Tangail. He used to sleep in Dada's room and every evening he would gather us around to play Chor–Police. The game revolved around small chits of paper with 'Police', 'Chor' (thief) or 'Dacoit' (bandit) written on them. He would throw them at us to catch. Whoever got 'Police' had to guess which of the others in the group were thieves or robbers and if we failed to guess correctly he would jump up and yell 'Dabba!', his word for 'Zero'! Ratan's father, also a doctor, was Father's friend and the boy was always welcome at our home. And rightly so! When Father had been going through a difficult time, long before I was born, this friend had helped him financially. Ratan was a year or two older than me. He would run around the house, a naughty smile on his lips, his shirt askew and hair unkempt; he was like one of us, or at least he behaved so. He would turn up, grab the gamcha and head to the washroom. Once done with his bath, making his already fair skin appear even fairer, he would brush his hair in a fancy manner and walk into the kitchen asking Mother what she had cooked that day. Mother was very fond of Ratan's mother Bulbul. She would sit him down to eat and ask him if his mother was still as beautiful as before; she did this whenever he came to our house. Mother used to often talk about what a beauty Bulbul was; I had never seen her talk so animatedly about any other beautiful woman. It was Ratan who, by playing Chor–Police or Ludo with us or by regaling us with card tricks, somewhat managed to heal the wound of being banned from going to the roof. On what was going to be his last visit, the day he was leaving for home, he came and placed a folded note on my table, swatted me over the head one last time and said, 'Take care! Goodbye!'

Ratan did not walk, he was like the wind. When the wind had blown over just as it had arrived, I picked up the note and realized it was a letter. Wherein he had confessed how much he loved me, how his life was going to be completely futile if I did not love him back. He had signed off with a farewell and as I read his words I could feel my throat dry

up and a frisson of fear radiate through my heart. Folding
the letter carefully within my fist I ran to the bathroom.
There I unfolded the note, by then wet with sweat, and
read it again. My gaze fell hungrily on the one word: love.
And it was addressed to me! The very thought made me
shiver again. Had anyone seen him leave the note behind?
It was going to be a disaster if someone had, even more so if
someone was to ever find the letter. With disaster snapping
at my heels and breathing down my neck, the safest option
was to tear the letter to shreds and be done with it. But
I did not want to destroy it. I wanted to keep it, wanted
it to live, hidden away somewhere secret and safe, inside
a history book, under my pillow. While I did safely stow
away the crumpled piece of paper, I felt no surge of love in
my heart for Ratan because of it. Every bit of love that I felt
was for the letter alone.

It was not too long before Father discovered the letter.
One day, while I was in school, in the middle of going
through my books and copies to assess how my studies were
going—how much of the books I had read and made notes,
what I had written in the copies, what maths I had practised,
etc.—he came across the piece of paper. He did not speak a
word about it to me but he did write a letter to his friend in
Tangail at once, telling the latter that his son was no longer
welcome in our house.

It hardly made any difference to me, I told myself.
Nonetheless I could not help feel bad for Father's friend,
whom I had never seen. How insulted he must have felt, I
wondered, and it made me cringe on the inside; as if I was
the one to blame for the whole thing. As if I was the one
entirely responsible for Ratan writing the letter to me, as if I
was the one who had sinned.

While Father was thus occupied with concocting numerous secret schemes to keep me sheltered and protected, one fine day he suddenly gathered us and, with a deeply anxious look on his face, said, 'Things have become so expensive! From now on we eat rice only once a day. The other time we will have rotis.'

Rotis? Instead of rice? What was this new game he was playing?

With a fair bit of burn in her voice, Mother quipped, 'He must have got married again. Has to feed the new wife. Wants to cut corners here so he can manage that one!'

Mother was quite wrong though. There were hundreds of beggars on the road, the number rising so much every day that I heard the rickshaw-pullers discussing how hordes of people were coming in like the tide from the villages where there were no crops and no food to eat. While travelling on a rickshaw I would stare in amazement at the crowds of dispossessed refugees everywhere. People with empty plates and utensils running from the banks of the river to Notun Bazar, eyes jutting out of their sockets, ribs threatening to break through skin, stomachs caved in, a pageant of skeletons from which some of the outliers had fallen behind, panting by a drain somewhere. Some would stand in front of the big houses and scream for rice. They came to our black gates too and all they wanted was rice—leftover, fermented, spoilt—whatever. Seeing them one day, just back from school and well fed, I ran to the kitchen to get them some food—a few handfuls of rice was all they desired—only to stop short at the sight of a huge, sturdy lock hanging from the rice drum.

'Ma, give me some rice! Those people are begging. They look like they haven't eaten in days,' I hollered anxiously at

Mother who was in the middle of namaz. She finished her prayers, bowed, kissed her hands and folded the prayer mat. Then she turned to me and said, her face listless, 'There's no rice.'

Mother never used to turn away beggars. Giving them food was always a thing in our house. Extra rice had to be thrown away or during summer it tended to go bad overnight, so beggars used to be often fed paanta-bhaat. Even that was not there any more.

A few days later, while having lunch, having finished the rice on my plate I asked Mother for another helping, licking my fingers as I made the request. I was always the one who had to be force-fed my meals. Since I didn't want to eat Mother would tell me stories. She would mix rice and fish, make round balls out of it and place them around the edge of the plate like a small garland of food and tell me that each one of those was an animal, a tiger, a lion, an elephant or a bear.

'Now quickly gobble down the bear! See how afraid it is of you?! Okay, now the elephant!'

I always ate because of the stories and Mother had numerous ingenious ways of making me eat. Perhaps I could be reading something intently and she would suddenly come to me with food and say—

'Quickly, open your mouth, see this is so nice—'

When I used to realize what she was up to I would try and drive her away but she was always determined to make me eat something or the other. She would slice up mangoes, pineapples and watermelons, arrange them neatly on a plate and leave it behind on my table with a fork. I was the one who always used to get up from meals with leftovers on her plate. But that fateful day in 1974, as I sat licking my fingers hoping for some more rice, Mother informed me there was no more.

What was it, I wondered! Were we suddenly poor? I was asking for rice but was not getting any and that was nothing short of unbelievable in our house. Why were even the beggars not being given alms? Father was having rotis for both his meals, as was the case with Mother and the maid. Rice, of which there was already precious little left in the drum, was reserved only for the two daughters of the house.

Pressing the veins on either side of his forehead Father sighed, 'Famine has come to our land.'

The number of beggars on the streets continued to rise. Unable to find rice they took to visiting the houses to beg for the starch. One day, what seemed like a walking skeleton found its way to our gates. Barely seven or eight, the boy looked so terrifying that I remember turning away in fright. He stood there at the door, unable to even beg for anything, his voice weak and barely audible. I ran to Mother and implored her to give him something to eat, whatever, my share of the food if required. Mother called the boy in and gave him some rice. As he was eating with his spindly and skeletal hands we sat and watched him struggle to swallow; he had almost been on the verge of starving to death. I had seen want before, but never the kind of acute want like this that could reduce a human being to such a state. It was as if lack of food had made his throat close up. So much food would go to waste, thrown away for the dogs, cats and crows to eat and here people were dying from hunger.

That night at dinner, as she chewed on her roti, Mother said, 'There was a famine when I was young. They would drop sattu [gram flour] from aeroplanes that we had to run and gather. We never got rice.'

Snapping out of his stupor Father joined in. 'How could you have got rice?! There was none! People had money but there was no rice in the markets. Millions of people died of starvation. I had heard there were heaps of the dead on the streets of Calcutta. You know the white core of the banana plant, many of us survived on that. So many people in our village sold off their daughters, husbands sold off their wives, all for a little rice. Who knows if this famine will be like the one in the '50s,' he finished with a sigh.

What if we ran out of rice? What would happen? Were we not going to have anything to eat? Were we going to starve and shrivel into a skeleton like the little beggar boy Israel? I was assailed by these terrifying thoughts. Something similar had happened when a rumour had been spread from the Pir's house that Allah was sending His Dajjal to test the faith of the people of the world. The hideous Dajjal, immense machete in hand, was going to decapitate the ones who did not have faith in Allah. I had been so afraid that every time I closed my eyes I could almost see the frightening figure, unsightly teeth bared, naked and huge as a mountain, slicing off my throat with his blade and severing my body into five parts, the courtyard awash with blood as well as my pitiful cries for my parents to come and save me. I could see myself dying and the apocalyptic figure laughing over my corpse. Back then I used to shut my eyes tight, and wound like a spring, pray to Allah to give me some faith. Mother had taught me that firm belief in the phrases 'Allah was one and only' and 'Muhammad is the Prophet of Allah' was a sure way of earning faith. Unable to find any recourse I would repeat the phrases ad nauseam. Faith used to be a fairly mysterious entity at that time; I mostly had to believe what Mother told me to believe, without seeing or understanding, much like accepting the existence of ghosts and djinns or the fantastical, speaking-through-his-feet Foting Ting, things I had never seen but only heard about. So if this incredible Foting Ting had been the one who could award faith or despatch a Dajjal to cull the faithless I would have probably chanted his name as well. Mother had told me to go sleep in Nani's room, telling me how much my uncles loved me. When Sharaf mama had forced my clothes off me it had not seemed at all like love. The fact that I had no choice but to believe in what she asked me to was perhaps the sole reason why I had faith in things like Allah, the Prophet, ghosts and djinns in the first place. Had there been a choice I doubt I would have been so easy to convince just because someone was telling me to. Like how they used to teach in school that the air around us had gases! Sometimes it felt as if I was being coerced into believing things I had not seen with my own eyes. For instance, if someone would have barked at me and told me there was a horse flying above me in the sky, I would have perhaps seen that as well. Like how I saw the skeletal shadow of the famine on my own body.

'You all would waste so much rice before, do you remember?' Mother's words interrupted my thoughts. 'Even a single grain of wasted rice upsets Allah. Do you now see how valuable it is? See how people are dying without it!' She placed her elbow on the arm of the chair and tilted her head on her palm. 'My boys must be starving.' 'I send Noman money regularly, don't worry,' Father tried to placate her at once. The one Mother was really worried about, however, was Chotda, there was no one to send money to him. We did not know how he was or even where he was. As Mother began softly weeping for her missing child, Father shot a 'It's getting late, go to bed' at her and headed off towards his bedroom.

Morning revealed a new crowd at the black gates of
Abakash. Mother went out and distributed the starch she
had been collecting every day among them. In the afternoon
Israel turned up at our door again and was given rice to eat.
Rallies marched past, shouting slogans demanding food,
clothes and the right to a life worth calling by its name.
Workers of the Communist Party were rallying on the road,
singing and going to people's houses, spreading a red cloth
and asking people to donate.

'Give us some rice. The poor are dying, help us save
them.'

One such rally turned up at Abakash one day; men with
red cloth tied around their heads. One of them called out
to me.

'Go call one of the grown-ups. Tell them to give us rice.'

Hair standing on end, I ran inside to Mother. 'Give them
rice. There are people outside. We have to give them rice.'

'Give them rice just because they want it? What will the
two of you eat?'

'Many people have given! There's a lot of rice in that
cloth, come see. They're calling you.' I held her hand and
pulled.

Standing behind the door Mother called out to the men
outside. 'Yes, what do you want?'

One of the men came forward. 'Just some rice, Ma.
People are dying because they don't have anything to eat.
We are students, we are going around from door to door
asking for rice that we can give to them. Give us some rice.
Whatever you can, however much you can.'

Some Will Eat While Some Go Dry,
It Won't Fly, It Won't Fly!

The voices of the other men rang out in unison. I, already trembling with nervous energy, nudged Mother. 'Give them rice, Ma! Break the lock and give them rice.'

'Your father will kill me,' Mother said in a hushed voice.

'Let him! But still give them rice. Let's go break the lock.' I was desperate.

Mother was getting visibly uneasy at the sight of so many people who had suddenly appeared. 'Only if I could send word to your father! Now how do I handle these people!'.

The black gates were wide open. Boys from the neighbourhood were gathering outside, hoping to catch a glimpse of what was happening. Mother hesitated, unsure of what she should do. Unable to contain myself any longer I picked up half a brick from the yard and went and slammed it hard on the lock hanging from the drum used for storing rice. Three strikes, then the fourth and the lock broke. The huge, sturdy lock.

The drum was half full. I gathered up rice in a gamcha and ran to the men outside. Mother stood watching, shocked into silence by what I was doing. Their demands met, the men marched out of Abakash singing. I watched them leave, my gaze awestruck, a strange and comforting sense of happiness filling my heart gradually. As if a proud, steadfast, indomitable version of me was slowly bursting forth from within, a me that was fiercely brave and full of dreams. I looked this new version of me up and down and came away surprised. Was this really me, or simply nothing but an eager adolescent girl carried away by the sight of a group of young men one afternoon!

Her face ashen, Mother bolted the door close and stumbled inside. 'Your Father is going to end you today.'

'I get thrashed every day,' I laughed at her warning, 'how is that anything new?'

Mother had always said communists were bad people. If that was true why were they going around collecting rice for the hungry poor? Was it wrong to save people from starving? They did not believe in Allah, but neither could they be accused of committing a sin. Rather they were taking care of helpless people, trying to feed the numerous hungry people like Israel who were wallowing by the road somewhere. I wanted to join their group, singing and going from house to house collecting rice. I wanted to remain hungry till the famine had passed. But it hardly mattered what I wanted. Even if I wanted to I could not cross my boundaries. All I could do was wait for Father to come home and whip me. The whip he had bought for Chotda, which was still under his mattress.

Father came back home and his gaze went straight towards the rice drum, just as I had expected it would. I had expected he was going to pick up the broken lock, the one that was still hanging limply from the holder. I had expected him to bellow in anger and the house to shake from the sheer force. I heard my expectations playing out as I had imagined them; I remained in my room, barely able to breathe. I imagined Father reaching under his mattress for the whip, the one that was going to bloody my back very soon. I could almost sense the pain already, could feel my back arching like a bow from the assault, could almost anticipate the terrible pain that was going to cascade down my spine soon. The house trembled under Father's roars. The blood in my veins was frozen from fear, hollows for eyes and my gaze stony, nothing but a roomful of darkness stretching all around me. Within myself I was flying away, like a feather airborne, swept away somewhere, where I had no idea. I was naked like the white Meerabai statue on the courtyard of the Rajbari

School, naked because I had done that to myself. I had no relations, no friends, I was all alone. The world was not for me, I was rising above it and attaining nirvana.

All of a sudden the house went quiet, as if it was abandoned, always had been. Everyone must have slithered into their caves to escape the fearsome roars. I sat waiting for my call from across the Pul-e-Sirat, where my sins were going to be weighed. I was convinced I had committed no sins. For the first time it was a belief I had formed of my own volition. Trying to toughen my body, still curved like a bow under the assault of an imaginary whip, I prayed for faith, in myself, to take hold of me. I kept repeating to myself what I was going to say, what I had read in books about giving food to the starving. Why when the men had come asking for rice, I had given it to them.

Mother's voice was clearly audible from outside. 'Oh, why are you screaming? Can't you speak a little softer? I broke the lock. The girls were crying from hunger.'

'Why? Didn't you give them rice for lunch? Didn't they eat?'

Mother's soft reply floated in from the direction of the veranda adjacent to the kitchen. 'It wasn't enough. You measured out rice for them. I wanted to eat some rice too, how can someone survive on rotis alone! I had some from their share.'

'How dare you break the lock? Why didn't you send me word?' His voice was yet to come down.

'How could I have? Was there anyone at home to send word with?' Her accusation was laced with a trail of anger.

Father's ravings stopped, rather abruptly. Just as it did, the silent house seemed to stretch and wake up from its slumber. Soon the cave-dwellers were out too, seeking light.

Pots and pans could be heard clattering by the tube well, as well as Mother's heavy, plodding gait on the veranda. Once Father had left for work again, Mother could be seen taking the path beneath the bael tree and heading towards the main gate, her stomach oddly distended beneath her burqa.

This was to soon become a regular thing. Mother's oddly distended belly hidden underneath her burqa as she disappeared around the bael tree. Trailing her like a shadow one day, I found her noiselessly opening the front gate and hailing a rickshaw and then taking a left turn from the crossing ahead. Right was the Pir's house, Nani's as well. So why was she headed left? Later, after she was back, I asked her the same question, my narrow gaze fixed on her.

'Where did you go Ma? The rickshaw took you left. Who lives that side?'

'Mind your own business,' her voice quivered with irritation. 'Don't talk so much.'

That was how Mother was. If she did not like something it usually made her angry. And it was not just any anger! Once, on my quizzing her about what was it she had taken that day to the Pir's place stuffed in a little bundle, she had slapped me so hard that I had spun around and hit the iron grill on the window.

Although she refused to tell me at first where she had gone in the opposite direction, a few days later she came up to me herself.

'Do you want to know where I go every day?'

'Yes!' I jumped at the opportunity.

We set off on foot. Past Golpukur and then Mrityunjoy School, into a lane just ahead that housed a slum. There, in a six-by-six makeshift thatched house I found Chotda and

Geeta Mitra. Inside, Mother brought out a few canisters from under her burqa, the biggest one containing rice.

I was blindsided by the scene unfolding in front of me.

'Beware! Not a soul must find out about this,' Mother warned, her eyes fiery.

'I won't tell anyone,' I gulped.

'Afroza, get on with the cooking. There's dal at home, isn't there?' Mother was speaking while she arranged the things she had brought with her.

'Who's Afroza?' I asked her.

'She's converted. She's now called Afroza.' Mother sounded quite ecstatic about it.

Afroza was sitting on the small bed, the saree pulled over her head like a veil, a dry-faced Chotda beside her. Besides the bed there was a clay oven in one corner of the earthen floor and a few basic utensils.

Where was that whistling boy with the eccentric hairstyles! Looking at Chotda's dry face I felt a rush of affection for him. He was in such a rundown house! I could not help but feel immensely guilty. When he was being abused I had remained in hiding like a worm, mouth tightly shut. Could a person even think of putting another person in shackles and beating them up! These were things only our father could have made possible. None of us had been able to do anything for Chotda except shed tears in secret.

'Chotda, a number of letters have come for you.'

'Hmm,' he grunted while stoking the fire in the clay oven.

'Cottonda was passing by the other day. He asked me where you were, but I didn't tell him anything.' I spoke louder this time.

Without a word Chotda finished lighting the oven and placed water on boil. With unpractised hands he proceeded to push in more fuel wood into the oven. It was a scene that I was frankly not used to witnessing. I noticed he had no interest at all in the guitar teacher Cotton or the letters that had arrived in his name. I also noticed how much he appeared to have changed over the past few months. He opened the cans Mother had brought with her to see what was inside: rice, cooking oil, spices, some cooked chicken. Obviously delighted at the sight he nonetheless pursed his lips to stop the smile that was about to break out and went on fiddling with the fuel wood, as if it was the most important job in the world at that moment. Was he very hungry? Earlier too he would get hungry but back then he used to pay scant attention to such basic needs. He would roam around the city and come back home to still more addas, most of the time simply letting his lunch remain uneaten on the dinner table.

I kept staring at his self-conscious features as it had been a while since I had seen him. Edward VIII had abdicated his throne for the sake of love. Chotda was somewhat similar; he had given up the luxuries of a soft mattress in favour of a dusty bed, all for love. I came to be convinced that their little shanty despite its many shortcomings was overflowing with a certain kind of wealth, not the material kind but a very different variety altogether. It was not something one could explain, it had to be experienced. Not everyone could forsake their desire for material wealth, very few had the fortitude to voluntarily choose renunciation. Chotda had written a letter to Dolly Pal wherein he had claimed that he was willing to spend his life under a tree with her by his side. He had shared the exact same sentiment with Geeta as well, in a thirty-two-page letter. The shanty they were in was akin to living under a tree. It was only Chotda who could possibly dare to take such risks! He did not care about wealth and standing! He had broken off all ties and emerged a liberated man, free from anyone's discipline or coercion, free from someone dictating when he should come back home or when he should study. Seeing him I too wanted to break free. I was beginning to feel invisible chains wrapped around my body, much like the ones Chotda had physically been tied with.

After the secret renewal of their relationship, on the afternoons when Father was away at work, Chotda began to visit us, Geeta Mitra tiptoeing in behind him with her head covered. Mother would quickly pull them inside, firmly shut the doors and windows so that not a soul discovered them there, and feed them. On their way out she would stuff their bags full of rice, dal, oil and other rations. Yasmin and I had to stay on guard during the whole time and watch out for Father in case he returned home early, unannounced. Chotda would drift from one corner to another like a cat, pick up the odd radio, clock or record player and remark that he needed them. Or he would keep searching the room for something, under the mattress, in the drawers of the cupboard or on the bookshelves. Each time it would seem it was his first visit to our house, the way he would rifle through things with undisguised wonder in his eyes. Seeing him roam around the house gladdened my eyes. All I wished was for him to live with us again just like before, find him sleeping with his head on the table, the pages of his book wet with drool, or standing on a low wooden stool outside in the sun and scrubbing himself with a loofah. Like how it used to be with him, fancy hair flying in the wind, guitar slung across his shoulders, a whistle on his lips as he knocked on the door at night, every night.

By and by Chotda began clearing out his things: his guitar, clothes, tin trunk, etc. One day I found the radio missing, soon after the clock was gone too. It was all I could do to pretend that I was not noticing what was happening. To ensure no one noticed the empty table on which the radio used to be I deliberately heaped a pile of books and magazines on top of it, a colourful calendar taking the place of the clock on the wall. Yasmin too went along with the subterfuge, pretending as if she too did not notice the things that were going missing from the house. As for Mother, she would ask time, for instance, by telling me to check my wristwatch, deliberately pretending as if she had never been used to glancing at the clock that should have been on the wall. The three of us, Yasmin, Mother and I, went about our daily lives as if we were blind, none of us asking any questions to each other and earnestly hoping Father would not look around for the radio to listen to the news or glance at the wall to check the time. In case a search was to be conducted I decided I was going to suggest that it could have been the work of petty thieves, and I also knew that Mother and Yasmin were both similarly mulling over plausible responses. One day, having just returned from school, I was greeted by the sight of Chotda, having taken off the sofa cover, in the middle of tying the big record player in a bundle in it. Pretending as if I had not seen what he was up to, I had just about started humming to myself and turned towards the calendar, when Mother burst in abruptly and spoke to him in a hushed voice—

'Don't take that. Your father will be furious!'

'It doesn't play well. It needs repairs. I'm taking it to the mechanic,' Chotda replied, in a voice that could melt stones.

When you are being consumed by both regret and longing, you can feel hurt but you cannot be angry. In the end none of us could say anything to him. Chotda finished packing the record player, huge and made in Germany, and took it away, bent over in half by the weight of it. Days passed but we heard nothing about any repairs. Neither did anything he had taken away find its way back to us. Nevertheless, we knew if taking something that used to be so dear to him gave Chotda even a measure of contentment then we were fine with it; ultimately it meant some atonement on our part as well.

One afternoon, finally proving my long-standing anxieties right, Father came back home while the two of them were still there. It felt like my body was freezing in fear. Chotda and Geeta scurried inside the nearest room at the sound of his footsteps; the sound of the bolt sliding home from within rang out like an explosion. Had he heard it?! Knowing him, who knew how far he was going to go along its trail! While my frozen body was slowly starting to go numb, Mother parked herself by the door they had chosen and began speaking, her words directed at me. As if she had closed the door herself, as if there was no one inside. What she spoke about hardly mattered, inane things like why had I not washed up and eaten yet, even though I was already done with all of that, or how she was getting late for her Maghrib namaz, despite the fact that the sun was still up. Whenever he dropped by the house at an odd hour, Father would typically first check up on what everyone was up to, to make certain that we were all studying, that no one was on the roof, that all the doors and windows were shut. If everything turned up fine he would approach my table, shower upon me a series of adages attributed to various wise people and then leave to go check patients again. That day it felt like he was at home far longer than usual, as if he was roaming from one room to another quite unnecessarily, each passing moment stretching as long as eternity. No sooner had his shoes screeched through every room of the house and stopped in front of the fateful door than Mother spoke—

'Do you want anything to eat? Should I give you something?'

The question had no context, it was way past lunch time and way too early for dinner. Without answering Father pushed the door to go inside. It was locked from within, all the family members were accounted for, so who was inside? It was not an unreasonable question, despite the fact that it felt so to us. Whoever it was inside, why did it matter to him! Could he not have assumed it was I who was inside, just as I was also outside with everyone else! As if by magic! The way P.C. Sarkar used to do it, or Houdini, with the boxes they used to lock themselves inside only to suddenly appear outside the locked contraption, as if by magic.

Father banged on the door again and called out—

'Who's inside?'

Mother silently moved aside; there was nothing for her to guard any longer. My cold body suddenly wanted the release of a toilet. The smell of burning curry was wafting in from the direction of the kitchen. Yasmin was bent over her books as if she was made of stone, silent and unmoving. None of us could conceive of a single way in which the flame of Father's singular and irrepressible interest in the closed door could be snuffed out. He was the sort of person who never rested until he had seen something through till the very end, even if solving something meant giving up on food and rest. No one was quite willing to answer his question as to who was inside, even though he kept repeating it.

What was the need of so much scrutiny? The dog, the cat and both the daughters were where they were supposed to me, the former two on the veranda, the latter at their study tables. No one was on the roof, all the doors and windows were shut. Mother was at home as well, not as if she had packed everything away and left to go see the Pir. The house was as it was meant to be, not a hair was out of place. So why was Father bellowing for no reason?

I was hunched over geometry; for all intents and purposes I was struggling with a particularly difficult problem. Neither did I have any thought or time to dedicate to who was where, nor had I heard him yelling. Keeping up the pretence that I had not noticed what was happening I got up and ran to the washroom; the geometry problem tangled inside my head could only be untangled by pouring water on it. Shutting the door behind me, I heaved a sigh of relief. I felt acutely aware that I did not possess either the daring or the strength to weather what was about to happen in the house. So it was best that whatever had to happen happened in my absence. Escape, however, was easier to hope than achieve. Soon enough there was a loud banging on the bathroom door.

'Open the door! Open it!'

As soon as I stepped out Father pounced on me like a cheetah. 'Who's inside that room?'

All I could do, seeing him so livid, was hold my breath and remain rooted to the spot like a convicted criminal. As if it was all my fault, the locked room and everything inside. Secure within his grasp, Father dragged me across the veranda demanding an answer to his queries, threatening violent retribution otherwise.

In the end it was my dark, wiry-haired, stub-nosed Mother who stepped in as my saviour. Whisking me away from his hold she finally answered him, with frost dripping from her words—

'Kamal has come with his wife. She has converted.'

'Who? What did you say? Who's here?' Father shot back hoarsely.

'Kamal. Kamal's here.'

'Who's Kamal? I don't know any Kamal,' Father thundered, running to the closed door. The whole house reverberated with his roar, 'Ask them to get out of my house at once! At once!'

I was still rooted to the veranda. My limbs were beginning to go numb again.

Father's wrist was pointing at the direction of the entrance. Holding his wife's hand Chotda shot out of the door at the back and began running towards the black gates.

Periods

I was changing out of my school clothes when I noticed my white pyjamas were stained with blood. Why? Did I get hurt somewhere? Where? How could that have happened? There was no pain! Then? I was overcome with terror. There was so much blood, it seemed I was going to die!

I ran to Mother, who was picking cauliflowers in the kitchen garden, hid my face in her embrace and burst into tears.

'Ma, there's a cut somewhere in my body. It's bleeding non-stop.'

'Where are you hurt? Where?' Mother pried me away gently.

'Here.' My fingers began to inch beneath my navel.

'Don't cry,' Mother said, soothing me softly.

'Get Dettol and cotton quickly,' I began, wiping the tears trickling down my cheeks.

Mother laughed and assured me, 'Don't cry. It'll be all right.'

I was bleeding and my mother wasn't worried at all! She picked up two cauliflowers and took me inside. Locating my wound, she put Dettol on it but did not dress the wound like she normally would. Rather, with a smile on the corner of her lips as she began to wash the sand from her harvest, she said to me, 'You're a big girl now. These things happen to big girls.'

'These things? What things?' I said with a splash of hatred directed at her smile.

'This bleeding. It's called getting your periods. It's called *hayez*. It happens to girls every month. It happens to me too,' she laughed again.

'Yasmin too?' I asked at once, alarmed.

'Not yet. It will happen when she's big like you.'

Suddenly one afternoon, just like that, I had grown up! Mother spoke again.

'You're no longer a child. You can't go out and play like children any more. Stay at home like big girls do. Don't run around, be restful. And don't go in front of men.'

Mother tore up one of her old sarees into strips, folded some of them together and handed the wad to me along with a pyjama string. Then she began rather solemnly, the hint of a smile having slipped off her lips—

'Tie the string tightly around your waist and tuck both ends of this folded pad in on either side. It will bleed for three days, might even go on for four–five days. Don't be afraid, it happens to everyone. It's very normal. If the pad gets soaked through with blood, wash it, put it out to dry and wear another one. Do it in absolute secrecy so that no one finds out. These are shameful things, not things you tell other people.'

I was terrified. What strange occurrence was this where I was going to bleed, that too every month! Why were boys exempt from it, why was it just for girls! And why did I have to go through it! Was Nature just as partial as Allah? All of a sudden I began to feel like I was a grown-up too, just like

Mother and my aunts, that I was no longer the age where one played with dolls and such, or even fooled around in general. I was of the age where I had to wear a saree, learn my way around a kitchen, learn to tread lightly and speak softly. I was a grown-up; someone had held me by the throat and banished me from the field where we played gollachut and the court that had been drawn for hopscotch. I was not who I used to be, I was a different person, a terrifying version of myself. In the blink of an eye, like a feather adrift in the wind, whatever little independence I had left was taken from me as well. Was it all a nightmare? Or was Mother telling the truth? What if it was indeed all a bad dream and I was going to wake up and discover that things were just the way they had been before! Why could it not be like that? At least that was what I desperately hoped for, that this bleeding was a false alarm. That it would turn out it was nothing but an accident, some hidden wound bleeding inside my body, for the first and final time. That I would be able to return the torn bits of the saree to Mother and tell her I was healed.

I banged my head against the wall of the bathroom but felt no pain. The body was merely a vessel, to carry one's bleeding heart around. Sorrow was gathering in my heart, pebbles and stones piling up to form a peak. The folded wad of torn strips she had handed to me were still held within my fist; my hand held my fate, my dreadful, biased fate.

Knocking on the door of the bathroom Mother whispered—

'What is it? Why are you taking so long? Do as I told you and come out quickly.'

She would not even let me cry to my heart's content! Would not let me hide my face in shame and weep, would not let me turn pallid with mortification or curl up in pain and anxiety. I felt terribly cross with her, with everyone in the house too, as if I was a victim of some nefarious scheme of theirs. I was the one who was disposable, the one who was putrid, whose entire being was laced with calamity. This blemish too was mine to bear. How was I supposed to hide such an infuriating thing? How was I going to walk or run? What if someone found out I had a wad of cloth underneath my pyjamas that was soaked with blood? I felt nothing but disgust for myself, enough to want to spit at my own body. I was nothing but a circus clown any more. I was no longer like the others; I was different and terribly so. There was a disease hidden deep inside me, a sickness that was incurable.

Was this what they meant by growing up! To me it seemed nothing had changed, I was still how I had always been. I still wanted to run out to play, but Mother had expressly forbidden me from doing so.

'Don't jump, don't run, you are no longer a child.'

If I were to venture out she would yell out to me at once—

'Come inside. The boys of the neighbourhood are on the roofs, staring.'

'So what, Ma? Why is that a bad thing?' I would ask in a listless voice.

'You're a big girl now. It's a problem.'

I never managed to learn from her what the problem was. Gradually, men who were not family became a forbidden thing in my life as Mother completely immersed herself in her new game of shielding and hiding me from the world. When my uncles came to visit with their friends I was ordered to go inside and remain there, just so none of the men would catch a glimpse of me. In time it seemed I was becoming untouchable. Once, while searching for keys in her cupboard, when my hand accidentally brushed against

the copy of Quran kept there, Mother descended upon me
in a flash—

'Don't touch the Quran Sharif when you are impure.'

'How am I impure?' I asked bitterly.

'During hayez the body becomes impure. It's forbidden
to touch Allah's book during that time. Neither can you
perform the namaz or keep roza.'

I knew dogs were considered impure; I learnt women could
become impure too at times. Performing the ritual ablutions
of *ozu* worked to purify everyone except menstruating
women. It was a rotten pond I had been consigned to and
from the tip of my toe to the top of my head everything was
caked with dirt. It was all so sordid that it made me want
to throw up. I was disgusted, above all with myself. While
washing the bloody cloth all I wanted to do was hurl my guts
out; I was sure that being possessed by a djinn would have
been a far better alternative to what I was going through.
This dirty, impure thing had to be pushed into some box in
some crevice of my soul, and the box buried under earth that
no one walked upon.

I was afraid to walk, afraid to even stand up, afraid that
at any moment the folded pad was going to slip out and, to
my utter obliviousness, slip off and reveal itself to the whole
world. I was constantly terrified that everyone was going to
find out everything, that at any moment the room was going to
be awash with dirty blood and the sound of mocking laughter.
It was my own body that was out to demean me, making me
drown in filth in broad daylight, day in and day out.

Even with the sun beating down hard all afternoon I
could no longer take my top off; my breasts were gradually
beginning to take shape. Blood was relentlessly flowing out
of my body. In absolute wretchedness, I took to bed.

On the third day of bleeding out I was still in bed, exhausted and traumatized, when Father noticed my state and charged at me like a raging bull—

'What is it? Why are you lounging about in bed till so late? Get to your studies at once!'

Somehow dragging myself to the table I managed to collapse on the chair. 'What is it,' Father growled again, 'why are you so slow today? Have you gone weak? Don't you eat?'

Yet again Mother appeared as saviour. She took Father aside to the next room to talk. It was the one on the left and through the walls separating the two rooms I could overhear a whispered conversation, the words edged with a silent searing flame that was enough to set my ears aflame. The letters in the book open in front of me were becoming fuzzy, the flame gradually spreading to my books, copies and stationery and the heat brushing against my face.

Coming back to the room Father walked up to the table, placed his hand, or perhaps his chin, on my shoulder and told me it was all right for me to rest if I wanted to.

'Go lie down a little. You can study later. Go, go to bed. The body needs rest as well, of course it does. That doesn't mean one should sleep or laze around like Kumbhakarna the entire day. Don't you have a lazy brother already! Noman! He could not finish his studies simply because of his laziness. Now he studies psychology or something. What rubbish! As if he will rule the world with it!'

Picking me up from the chair he put me to bed, sat down by my side and, while gently rubbing my head, continued—

'You must understand that as far as children are concerned I only have two daughters now. The two of you are very close to my heart. I depend on you and you provide me hope and strength to go on. If I can make something out of the two of you I will find some measure of peace. But if you hurt me there will be nothing else for me to do but kill myself. If you feel too tired, take a breather. Then when you feel better again, get up and go back to your studies. The human body is very resilient, it can take a lot. I have not kept you wanting for anything in life, just to make sure that you can channel all your efforts into your education. As a student your only focus should be your studies. Later, when it will be time to work you must be ready for that too. And then when it's time for you to retire, retire from work that is, you can choose that as well. Everything has a system, isn't it so!

As he spoke his rough fingers were stroking and tucking the hair at my nape. Father was a back-brush kind of person; he hated locks of hair flopped over the forehead, hated it for himself and for me as well. Physical displays of affection for him meant tucking someone's hair back; it was something I had seen him do before. Could his hands have been any more callused? His rough fingers were on my back; let alone a gentle petting, it was as if he was scrubbing off my skin.

It did not sit well with me that since I had had my periods I could no longer play outside; instead I had to stay at home and feign seriousness. As a child I had always dreamt of being big enough to unbolt the door myself. Now when I could easily bob on my toes and do it, the bleeding forced me to grow up all of a sudden, so much and so distant from everyone else that I felt terribly afraid. When I was eleven Mother had banned shorts for life and forced me into pyjamas she had made herself. When I turned twelve she ordered me to start carrying an *odhni* or a stole as my legs were growing, as were my breasts and everything had to be kept covered. If I failed to do these things I was told people were going to call me a shameless hussy. Shameless women were not regarded very highly in society and only the girls who managed to retain their shame succeeded in earning good marriages. Mother hoped the same for me, that I too was going to marry well. My friend Mamata, herself a bookworm, had got married a while back. I had asked her if she knew the person she was marrying and she had admitted to me that she did not. The groom in question had arrived on an elephant, the entire city had been witness to the spectacle. The dowry he had taken was considerable as well: nearly seven *bhori*s of gold, thirty thousand taka in cash, a radio, a wristwatch, etc. He had whisked Mamata away on his elephant and taken her home. Mamata's sole purpose henceforth was to take care of her husband's family. Her studies were over and surely the elephant-rider was soon going to cure her of her interest in reading as well.

Hardly had I managed to recover from the shock of my periods when someone from the village, a hawaldar, turned up at our house with a giant rohu fish to ask for my hand in marriage for his son. Father heard his offer, returned the fish and turned him away, telling him to leave the house immediately without uttering one more word.

'Is what you're doing right?' Mother made her displeasure evident afterwards. 'Won't you get her married? She's old enough now. This is the best age for it.'

'Only I will decide when my daughter needs to get married,' Father interjected, stopping her in her tracks. 'You don't have to meddle in this. My daughter is studying, she'll become a doctor. Not an MBBS like me but an FRCS doctor. I don't want to hear anything further about her marriage.'

Eavesdropping on their conversation, all the anger I had reserved for my father evaporated immediately. I wanted to make him a glass of lemonade myself; he must have been very thirsty. However, without being summoned by him, it was not in my nature to approach him or offer him anything. Try as I might I could not break rank with habit.

It soon became evident to me how excited Mother was about me growing up. One day she handed me a black burqa she had purchased from the bazaar.

'See this, darling, I bought this burqa for you. Wear it and see if it fits.'

'What did you say!' I exclaimed in indignation. 'You want me to wear a burqa?'

'Yes! You're all grown up now! Big girls have to wear the burqa.' Holding the burqa against me she proceeded to check the measurements.

'No, I will not wear a burqa,' I declared stonily.

'You're a Musalman! Allah Himself has talked about the importance of Muslim women observing the purdah,' Mother argued in a conciliatory tone.

'Let Him! I will never wear it.'

'Fajli's daughters wear it all the time, so nicely too. They are such good girls. Aren't you a good girl as well? If you wear the burqa people will say you're such a decent girl.'

As she spoke she was softy stroking my back, a move that never failed to melt all my resolve. But that day I was determined; I could not let my resolve waver. I needed to learn how to say no. And that's what I kept repeating to myself silently: NO!

'No!'

'You won't wear it?!' It was obvious she had lost her patience.

'I said no!' I repeated, jerking away from her reach.

The hand that was hitherto stroking my back now landed with a hard whack.

'You're going to Jahannum. Mark my words, you're going to Jahannum for sure. I can't say I trust your ways. Despite so many visits to Naumahal you still haven't begun to see it. Can't you see, right in front of your eyes, girls your age or even younger than you, they are all wearing it. So pretty they look! They keep their fasts and offer namaz. But the older you get the more you are refusing to do these things. Jahannum is in your destiny.'

Even if she were to skin me alive I was determined to not don the burqa. Instead I stubbornly went and sat down to study. Which meant sitting at the table with books spread open in front of me, all the words concealed beneath the massive wings of a vulture that was tormenting me. I could hear Mother's heavy gait pacing the veranda, my room being adjacent to the interior balcony. Perhaps hoping to make me hear, she was speaking aloud—

'That one's a sneaky little devil. When you see her it seems she hardly knows a thing, that she always listens to everything her parents tell her. But no! She argues with me! Do any of the others do it?! How dare she! If I had beaten her up like her father does then she would have listened. Some people just can't learn a straight lesson—'

Every time she did try to teach me the not-straight lesson I had the distinct feeling she was no longer my mother but a demonic witch. So ugly she would appear then, not one bit like the woman who had fed me, sung me nursery rhymes and sat by my side through nights when I had been ill. I was beginning to crumble into dust; and anger was congealing everywhere, in my bones, in my flesh and in my blood like tiny flecks of diamond.

I wished at times I could drink poison and end it all, once and for all. The world was a cruel place where it was far better to die than be born a woman. I had read in a magazine somewhere, about a girl suddenly becoming a boy. I often desperately hoped that one day I was going to wake up and find I had turned into a boy. That there would be no strange mounds of flesh on my chest and I could wear threadbare shirts whenever I wished. I could roam the city, go to the movies, have a smoke or two and finally return home late. The largest piece of fish was going to be reserved for me, because I was the son, the future of the family. Sons could do no wrong. No one was going to tell me to wrap stoles around my chest or force me to wear a burqa. No one was going to have a problem with anything I did, going to the roof, standing at the window, visiting friends or going out of the house whenever I wished to.

But who was there who could turn me into a boy! I had no such power myself. Which meant I had to pray to someone for it happen. Since everyone usually prayed to Allah, what if there was someone else who could help me! Perhaps I could pray to any of the 33 crore gods and goddesses that the Hindus had. But would they listen to me, I was not a Hindu! I had prayed to Allah often and finally come to a conclusion that He just did not have it in Him to give me what I wanted. It was all bogus. So instead of praying to anyone I confessed my desire to myself, kept repeating to myself that either I had to die or I had to turn into a boy. Father used to say everything was possible if you wanted it hard enough. I too put in every shred of earnestness I could muster in my heart, everything within and without, the account of all manner of deeds, good or bad, as I willed myself to transform.

Phoolbahari

My yearning to become a boy died the day when, still in thrall of my desires, I found Phoolbahari's mother standing at our door. She looked gaunt and ghoulish; I learnt she had been grievously ill with jaundice and had barely survived thanks to the prayers and cares of pirs and fakirs. But such was her sorry state that no one wanted to employ her any more. Desperate, she had been begging for food from people's houses for a while. When she came and sat down with a heavy thud on the veranda of the kitchen, and then later when she had to hold the pillar and heave herself up, it appeared she was too tired to carry the weight of life any longer. Looking at her it dawned on me how life was exactly like that from time to time; a huge weight fell on one's shoulder that one often did not wish to carry as a burden down a long trail.

Back in Nani's kitchen Phoolbahari's mother used to grind spices, with a grating sound of stone grinding against stone: *ghoshh ghoshhh ghoshhhh* it went. As she was leaving I could suddenly hear the sound from somewhere, as she dragged her feet laboriously down the path under the bael tree. Who knew where she was going; neither did I run after her to find out. Where in the world could she have even gone! In an instant the sound of grinding spices took me back to the broken threshold of another kitchen from another time, where I used to sit and stare at Phoolbahari's mother bent over the mortar and pestle, grinding away. She would come early in the morning and start the chore, getting done sometime around noon. Turmeric, chilli, coriander, cumin, onions, garlic, ginger, there were seven things she had to grind, which someone from Nana's shop used to come with a big container to take away. In the afternoons she would do it again, the entire afternoon. Seeing her I used to have an uncontrollable urge to grind masala, like her, swaying to the rhythm of the work. I had even asked her once to give me some so I could try my hand at it. She had laughed out at the offer, her paan-stained blackened teeth flashing as she had, and told me it was a very difficult task and I would not be able to do it.

Phoolbahari's mother and my mother were nearly of the same age; she used to formally call me Aapa because I was her master's daughter. I had no business grinding masalas, that was the work of the underlings whose hands were always dirty because of the hard and often revolting work they had to do. It was as early as three that I had learned to spot the difference between us and them. So Phoolbahari's mother, despite looking older, was beneath me in station. Not the kind whose lap you could clamber up on, who you could touch or whose food you could eat. I had learned that the underlings were not supposed to sit on the chairs or the sofas; it was preferred if they could stand, and if they could not and had to sit or lie down then the floor was the only recourse. They were meant to be at the beck and call of their masters, willing to carry out any and every order without further ado because such were the rules meant for the lower classes, the underlings.

One day, my eyes fixed on her stained teeth, I had
suddenly asked a question—

'What is your name?'

Perhaps the first time I had asked the question it had
slipped into the spices and been pulverized; I had waited but
received no answer. That very afternoon, again sitting on the
threshold, I repeated the question, my voice a touch louder.
Nearly everyone was in the middle of their post-lunch siesta;
the sneaky cat was sleeping beside the oven.

'What is your name?'

Stopping, Phoolbahari's mother had looked up from
the mortar and pestle, her forehead, nose and chin beaded
with perspiration. Beads of sweat on the tip of the nose
meant imminent romantic attention from one's husband,
or so Runu khala used to say. Phoolbahari's father had
passed away ages back and there was no one to shower any
sort of attention on the mother. My second question had
not sparked a black-teeth-baring smile any more; instead
the smile had pursed her lips and pushed her cheeks into
forming two tiny dimples as if she had betel nuts in her
mouth—

'I don't have a name. People call me Phoolbahari's
mother,' she had replied finally, her calm gaze resting on my
curious one.

Laughing, my eyebrows dancing in mirth as if I had
caught her in a lie, I had persisted—'What was your name
before Phoolbahari was born?'

'I did not have a name,' she had said again, wiping her
face with her saree.

'So what did people call you? What did your parents
call you?'

'My parents?' she sighed, 'They have been dead for years.'

'That I understand, but when they were alive did they not give you a name? Like I have a name. Nasrin.' I was explaining it to her as a schoolteacher would.

Resuming her work on the spices she had said again, 'No, I did not have a name. They called me chit, girl, monkey, whatever suited.'

I was so amazed that I had remained transfixed, watching her swaying form, as if the grating noise was happening inside my head rather than on the mortar and pestle.

'Do you know, Phoolbahari's mother has no name.' I had informed Mother of my recent discovery just as I would tell her about a fallen stack of bananas or a broken branch of the fruit trees.

'Hmm—'

Mother had not appeared the least bit surprised that someone her age did not have a real name. I could scarcely understand why she seemed so dispassionate.

'Ma, how can a person be without a name?' I was forced to look away from the book in front of me to vent the question that was clogging my mind.

'Don't jabber so much. Read out aloud,' Mother had snapped at me.

Ever obedient I had gone back to my books promptly—

He who people talk about is everything, he who beats his own drums is not.

Education is the path to prosperity.

Always speak the truth.

'Phoolbahari, do you know your mother has no name?' I had whispered to the girl while we were studying. She did not seem surprised at the revelation either, as if it was the most natural thing in the world that her mother had no name. Rather, she had looked at me with a certain expression in her gaze, as if assessing me to figure out if I had any hidden agendas behind my interest.

'So what if she has no name? She does not and that's it. What's in a name? How does it matter if a poor person has a name or not?' Her jaw had tightened as she answered.

Mother used to often say that Phoolbahari was way too headstrong. That she spoke like a boy, with a voice that seemed to be emanating from a cracked bamboo. It was true. And her words had plunged me headlong into thought. So the poor did not need names! Perhaps she had been right. The poor did not attend school, so they did not have to enrol names in registers. They did not own property, so there were no wills or legal documents with names. I realized it was possible to survive without a name, although only for the poor. Not just a name, the poor could survive without warm blankets, fish and meat, shoes and sandals, clothes, soap and oil, etc. The more I thought the more I could not help but feel terrible about Phoolbahari and her poor unfortunate mother. While I was thus occupied, Phoolbahari had soaked a rag in a bucket of water and begun wiping the floor clean, on her haunches, a beedi stuck behind her ear that she was going to smoke once she was done. No one in the house had any objection to her smoking. While women from genteel families were forbidden to even touch such things, the lower classes had to encounter far fewer embargos of this nature. Of course, if it was a man he had the right to do whatever he pleased, irrespective of his social standing. Her appearance—tall and dark, pock-marked face and beedi on her ear—was very familiar to me. Taking breaks between chores she would plop down on the floor and take drags from her beedi. I had noticed those were the times she appeared the happiest.

'Can you read the alphabet?' I had directed the question at her hunched frame.

'No,' she had replied while wiping the floor.

Scribbling the first alphabet on a piece of paper I had held it up in front of her—

'This is A. Say A.'

'A,' she had replied, work forgotten, eyes sparling with interest.

'And see this, here, it's your name Phoolbahari.' I had held up another paper in front of her.

She had looked at it with amazement, as if it was a picture of some far-off country somewhere that I had shown her, something she could hardly recognize. If Mother had been home she would have screamed about the girl not working; since she was not home Phoolbahari could squat on the floor and ask me, 'Is that my name, khala?' The headstrong girl's face was alight with the smile of a cute young miss. I wanted to teach her the alphabet so she could write her own name.

'Why do you call me khala? I am so much younger than you.'

'Oh god, who will I call khala otherwise? You are rich, big people. So what if you are younger than me! If the person is higher in station then you can't call them by their name, even if it's a baby in question. We are poor, that is what's written on our foreheads.'

Laughing, I had placed my palm on my own forehead and shot back, 'Our foreheads look the same! Do poor people have crooked foreheads?'

The young girl's smile had widened, 'I don't mean the actual forehead! I meant our destiny.'

Sighing, she had dipped the rag into the bucket again, drained the excess water and proceeded to wipe the rest of the room along with the threshold.

'After my father died, our destinies too went up in flames. Now we have to slave in people's houses for food. We are not meant for studies.'

'You don't have a father? When did he die? How?'

'A bad wind took him,' she had replied, without raising her head from her task.

'Wind! How can someone die of the wind?' My voice had betrayed my surprise.

'A djinn, khala. He lost the ability to use his limbs and took to bed. That was it, he never got up again,' she had sighed again as she finished with the threshold. The thick saree she wore was torn at the knee; except this one she had just one other saree, a green one that was in worse condition. I was sorry for her; I could not shake off the feeling. Her chores done, Phoolbahari had got up and left, leaving me staring at her departing back, a storm raging inside me at the news of the man who had been killed by the bad auspices of a djinn. Later, I had verified from Mother that it was indeed true: a djinn's 'wind' blowing at you meant the risk of losing one's motor functions.

These sorts of businesses with djinns and ghosts were undoubtedly very strange. Only Sharaf mama had seen a ghost ever, I never had. Sometimes I hoped to at least get a glimpse of a witch's glamour but that too eluded me, despite spending days with my eyes fixed on the darkness of the bamboo grove outside the house through a tiny hole in the window.

Within a week of my conversation with Phoolbahari a djinn's deadly wind had struck Gnetu, taking his right leg with it. His mother, traumatized with grief, had come straight to Nani's house in tears. She was not allowed to see him. She had tried visiting but her ex-husband had chased her off with a broom. After the talaq she had no rights over her son, irrespective of the fact that she had given birth to him. So everyone had sat around and watched her cry, some on the bed, some standing by the door, some outside under the mango tree or by the tube well. Jhunu khala had made a few shushing noises of distress then turned and gone inside, her braids swaying. Nani had gone on making paan. Abruptly, with a mighty roar, Tutu mama had asked Gnetu's mother to get lost; he hated the sight of feminine tears. Biting down on her saree to stop herself from crying, the woman had had no choice but to walk away; no one had noticed that I too had stood up to follow her. The path underneath the bamboo grove ought to have been pretty scary but I had felt no fear, neither was I afraid that the djinn could catch hold of me next and take away my hands and legs as well. I was careless, reckless, unmannered and wilful. Gnetu's mother had kept on walking, heading towards the railway track, with me on her trail like a shadow. She had reached, sat down on the rail line and kept weeping. I had picked up a few pebbles and began to throw them at the rails, the stones hitting the metal with successive clangs. The woman had stopped and looked up to find me standing behind her, hair uncombed, feet dirty, teeth unbrushed.

'Don't cry, please. And move from there. The train will be here any minute. Gnetu will hack his father to death one day and escape to you, you'll see.'

This term, hacking to death, was something Mother had threatened Phoolbahari with one day when the latter had fallen asleep while cooking catfish and ended up burning the whole lot. Then again, after finding Razia Begum's letters from Father's pockets, Mother had similarly wanted to hack the former. The very thought that Mother might attack

Phoolbahari, or Razia Begum for that matter, even though
I had never actually seen the latter, made me feel as if they
looked like Jhunu khala; I felt terrible for them. On the other
hand, I had no difficulty imagining Gnetu hacking his father
to death. I barely flinched imagining their courtyard awash
with blood, just like I had barely felt any fear while following
Gnetu's mother through the bamboo grove in the evening
that day.

Around five days after Gnetu's death the djinn's wind
found its next victim: Thanda's father. Pulling the shutters
on his famous jalebi shop, the man took to the bed and
soon began to cough up blood. Despite the maulvi visiting
from time to time to blow enchantments on him and holy
water from the pir of Sharshuna being fetched for him as
well, nothing could be done to stop the blood. A djinn's
wind meant certain death. Thus convinced, the family gave
up all hopes of him surviving in favour of waiting for the
inevitable. When the news reached Father he decided to
pay the man a visit himself. Turning up at the slum where
they lived, he checked the ailing man's pulse, pulled down
his eyelids to check his eyes, examined his tongue and then
advised the man to get tuberculosis medicine from the shop.
The medicines worked and much to everyone's surprise,
Thanda's father managed to overcome the djinn's evil and
recover. Within a week he reopened his shop and settled
back into his business. When such a thing happened right in
front of my eyes I had no more occasion to give credence to
things like djinns or their magic. Neither did Father himself
seem particularly moved or surprised by Thanda's father's
recovery, as if it had not been anything remotely unexpected.
It sort of convinced me that had Father made an attempt he
could have perhaps saved Gnetu as well.

Thanda's father used to be a distant uncle of Phoolbahari, although he never accepted the relationship in public. One day, while smoking her beedi, Phoolbahari had told me—

'He has a shop, he has money. Now he no longer wishes to accept us as relations, because we work in other people's houses. Poor people have classes among them as well.'

Thanda's mother had told everyone that it was the pir of Sharshuna's charmed water that had cured her husband; Phoolbahari was convinced otherwise.

'It was Nana's medicines that did the trick. Everyone says a djinn's touch is fatal, no one survives it. This one survived, didn't he?' Phoolbahari was generally not persuaded by things people said. Whenever she spoke her dark neck would tense and straighten.

During the famine of 1950, after Hasem mama was born, Nani had had two more boys in quick succession. Both of them had fallen victim to the djinn's evil and died. Thanda's father's close encounter with the djinn had immediately reminded Mother of those tragedies. The boys had been having loose motions, they had stopped breastfeeding almost entirely. The local witch doctor was summoned and he had declared it was the work of a djinn that used to inhabit the berry tree in Sahabuddin's house. Nani was advised to keep leather and iron at her person at all times, two things that djinns avoided. She used to take the leather and iron with her even if she had to go to the bathroom or the kitchen. To avoid any possible way the djinn could possess her and get to her children she used to cross over a burning fire and pat herself down with a broom before entering the house, just to ensure no traces of the evil entity could cling to any part of her body. However, despite all her efforts neither of the baby boys had survived. Later, when it was Mother's turn in the nursery Nani made a series of arrangements, including ritual cleaning with the fire and the broom every time she stepped out of the room for something, all in order to protect her grandbabies from the djinn. Seeing Mother perform these rituals after I was born, Father asked her what they were about. Mother insisted these were necessary things ones had to do to protect a child, or run the risk of an infant getting possessed, rejecting milk or dying of a fatal dysentery.

Their children, the four of us, grew up perfectly fine and healthy. None of us gave up on milk as children; even if we had dysentery it was nothing fatal. None were possessed by a djinn either. Mother would claim this was because she had chanted the holy verses of al-Anam repeatedly to ensure the protection of her family and her children. She would say this to everyone, even Father, although he hardly ever paid any heed to her claims.

After Thanda's father got well, incidents in the slum involving the djinn's ghostly wind saw a sharp downturn. The few stray cases that did crop up were easily handled by Father. He prescribed people medicine or referred them to hospitals as required from where they managed to came back fully cured.

Soon after leaving our house Phoolbahari fell ill. This time around no one claimed it was because of a djinn. Rather, most were of the opinion that Allah had finally done something truly worthwhile. She was a shameless girl who used to walk with a heavy gait. It was best if she got sick and died. Or so said the imam of the masjid, the day he came by to tie an amulet on Thanda's father, who had fully recovered by then. When the news of her illness reached me I wanted to go visit her. Instead I got my ears boxed by Mother who reprimanded me for wanting to wander around all day.

I never got to visit Phoolbahari. After she got better one day I heard she had been married off to some old toothless git from her slum, a septuagenarian who already had three other wives. For her wedding her mother came to Nani for money. I saw Nani taking out five taka from a knot in her saree and giving it to Phoolbahari's mother. Two–three taka were gathered from the rest of the house to buy a red saree for the bride while two hundred taka were given to the groom as a wedding gift. To me it seemed Phoolbahari was suddenly so very far away. I was no longer going to find her sitting on the veranda of the kitchen smoking her beedi, we were no longer going to spend hours chatting. Phoolbahari was no longer going to have to work as a maid in other people's houses. She was only going to cook for her husband and walk to the pond, a pitcher at her waist and her head covered, to fetch water. This new version of Phoolbahari seemed too incongruous to me. It worked best for her when she used to walk in that ungainly manner. One day when some of the local boys had called her mother a whore while she had been walking past them, she had turned around and slapped one of them across the face. I had stood there watching the scene with unfiltered admiration in my eyes, not even noticing when I had let go of the helium balloon I had been holding.

Before she passed under the bael tree and disappeared amidst the soft hues of the falling twilight I heard Phoolbahari's mother speak, 'The husband killed her. He choked her to death. I don't cry, what's the use of crying! Will she come back if I cry? Allah will deliver justice.'

The giant python had slithered out of the charmer's basket and was approaching me with its maws wide apart. A strange mute agony was gnawing at me, tearing me apart into a hundred pieces, grinding my own pain into fine dust within my heart. Like the mortar and pestle I could hear the grating noise—*ghoshh ghoshhh ghoshhhh*—deep within me.

Poetry

'Khudar rajye prithibi godyomoi, purnimar chaand jeno jholsano ruti.'

'In a hungry land the world brims with poetry, the full moon as if a charred roti.'[1]

Boromama had recited these lines standing in the middle of the courtyard awash with moonlight. Kana mama, hearing the tall claim, had stopped in the middle of a tale of Sohrab and Rustom that he had been narrating, sitting on a low stool nearby, and asked with a laugh, 'Who is so hungry that they want to eat rotis! Ask them.'

'Thousands of poor people die of starvation.' Boromama had replied, his wooden slippers slapping against the steps as he clambered upon the porch.

Making sure no one could hear me I had whispered—

'Get me the moon rotis. I will have some and distribute the rest in the slums.'

But Kana mama was not so easy to deceive—

'Has everyone become a poet! Who wants to distribute food among the slum-dwellers? Who is it?'

I had covered my mouth and kept quiet.

I used to have the bad habit of making impromptu rhymes. Mother could be teaching me a poem—the palm tree stands tall on one foot, above all others—and I used to change it and say something else entirely. The banyan tree stands on five feet, spreading its seven arms out! In school when I would be asked to recite a poem, instead of the actual one my made-up ones would crowd inside my head.

'Hey, honeybee, why do you prance away, why do you not tarry a while.'

While reading these lines one evening under the light of the kerosene lamp, sitting on the veranda back when we used to live with Nani, I had seen Kana mama approach and changed the rhyme a bit.

'Hey, Kana mama, why do you walk away, why do you not tarry a while!'

'Because I have to tell stories and I have to find children for that. I have no time to waste.'

'What is all this? This is such a terrible habit of yours, making fun of the poems you are supposed to study,' Mother had screamed at me from inside.

On the occasion of Bengali New Year the naughty girls of the school would give nicknames to the other girls. The list was put up early in the morning; no one knew who made it or put it up. All of us would crowd around the poster to read the names. On one list I found I had been named 'Cracked', on another 'Greenhorn'. Dilruba, the most beautiful girl in class, had been nicknamed 'Slut'.

'They have nicknamed you "Slut". What does it mean?'

Instead of replying her eyes filled with tears. I felt so bad looking at her that I edged closer and placed a hand softly on her back. I had heard Mother use the word while abusing our

maids but I did not yet know what it meant. Feeling bad for
her and sitting so close to her, just like light dispels darkness
before dawn, awash in her light I felt myself blooming like
a lotus. That mournful New Year afternoon Dilruba and I
became friends. She would tell me stories of her plants, her
birds and suchlike and hearing them I would imagine these
characters in my head leading certain kinds of lives. The day
I finally visited her house and saw them for real, while I did
have some stray conversations with them, there seemed to exist
a stark difference between how I had imagined them and how
they really were. The fictional ones seemed closer to my heart
than the real ones. So when I would meet her vine, instead of
asking it how it was doing I would ask Dilruba the question.
And Dilruba would describe to me how the vine had not got
better, no medicine man or doctor had been able to do anything
to prevent it from dying, from shrivelling and drying into a
piece of thread. Everyone had told her to throw the dry thread
hanging in the room into the water; some had asked her to hug
it tightly to her chest. Finally, someone had taken the plant in
their arms and kissed it, and behold, the vine had opened its
eyes and smiled, apparently having survived its ordeal.

Whenever Dilruba told stories it seemed she was no
longer part of our world. During such moments I would look
into her eyes and although her gaze would presumably be on
me, it would be quite apparent that she was entirely absorbed
in something else.

One day Dilruba showed me a notebook full of poems,
ones she had written herself. While flipping through the
pages I found myself stopping at a poem named 'Grass'.

Grass,
Will you take me? And the little flowers, will you take me
    too? To play?

As I have spent my days in useless quests,
I give you all I have,
Just touch me once, even if it be a mere trace.
I have come to you at an odd hour,
But if you turn me away,
If you cast me into oblivion,
I will keep returning to you
To lose myself a hundred times over.

'Dilruba, will you teach me how to write poetry?' I was bent over the poem 'Grass' as I asked.

Her perfect face and her slender, pink lips were framed by a mop of curly locks that was tied into a bun at the back of her head, a few wayward locks escaping the bind and brushing against her forehead, neck and chin. She seemed very familiar, as if I had seen her somewhere before, had witnessed her unruly hair too. It struck me as a familiar image, wanting to learn how to write poetry and Dilruba not telling me if she was going to teach me, like I had already lived that moment once previously. As if I had sat beside such a lonely girl somewhere once before, with someone who had looked just like her. There had been a notebook full of poetry open in front of us then as well and an open window too, beyond which had stretched a desolate meadow upon which the sky had been rolling around.

Dilruba spoke lesser than even I did; she was much more shy than I was. When the other girls would be running about on the grounds, she used to sit by the window and stare at the sky in the distance.

'You can't teach someone to write poetry. Keep staring at the sky, you will find you want to cry. If you can cry a lot, you will be able to write as well,' she told me, her voiced touched by warmth.

Since she did not pay much attention in school, she had to often stand in class holding her ears as punishment. Sometimes she had to leave the classroom as well. She would simply stand outside on one foot and resume staring at the sky. She felt a strange love for the sky and I felt dazed looking at her. In that haze I would walk beside her, speak to her, put my arm around her shoulder.

But since I did not feel like crying when I looked at the sky, I could not write poetry like she did. Rather, having found a torn paper packet on the school grounds one day, I imagined Dilruba's face and scribbled on it—

I will ask you out to play, Dilruba.
Do you know how to play gollachut?
One afternoon, like a ball from the sling,
Shooting into the unknown, far away somewhere.
Across the seven seas and thirteen rivers,
Will you come with me?

Dilruba smiled sweetly as she read the lines on the torn paper packet. I had never seen her smile like that. Perhaps Runi used to smile in such a manner, or perhaps not exactly like that but somewhat similarly. Someone with a smile like that did not need to speak, that's what Rabindranath had written and rightly so. In front of Runi I had been shy as a feather but that was not the case with Dilruba. With her there it was a different world that I was building up, a world of wordplay. Dilruba wrote on her notebook—

I will go wherever you want me to.
I will lose myself.
All I ask is you come close,
With just one promise, with love.

That's all I knew, how to love. Our love gradually deepened, both of us losing our way in each other's eyes, across the seven seas and thirteen rivers. Of course, it was all in our hearts. Neither Dilruba nor I could disappear from our society and our families. She was like the poems she wrote, a quiet pool in a remote forest somewhere. The water of the pool was blue like the sky above and often a leaf would drop on the surface, like a raft for Dilruba to float on, only for her.

One day, to my utter astonishment, Dilruba informed me she was soon getting married; her father had fixed a match for her.

'No,' I cried out, looking at her pale face and grey eyes, 'tell them you can't do it. Tell them you don't want to get married.'

Dilruba flashed a wan smile at me, like someone with a burning fever does. From the next day she stopped coming to school. I was left alone all of a sudden, so alone that I sat in the emptiness she had left behind by the classroom window, a long time after school, past the last bell. I was watching the sky and searching for her. Who knew, perhaps she had been upset and gone there! For the first time staring at the sky made me want to cry.

A couple of days before her wedding Dilruba came to Abakash to see me. Perhaps to truly lose herself with me, somewhere in a remote forest across the seven seas and thirteen rivers. Somewhere in her dreams, far away from the cruelties of the world, a place where sad girls could find wings and take flight to play hide and seek with the cloud maidens. As she was walking in through the black gate I was at the window, my unabashed gaze transfixed on her perfect face; it seemed as if she was floating instead of walking down our dreamy garden. I was still at the window when she left; she did not get to meet me that day. Father turned her away from the gate itself because he did not manage to find a reasonable explanation as to why a young girl had abandoned her studies in the middle of the afternoon to go wandering about. He asked her name, where she was from, the reason why she was at our home, etc., before turning upon her with a fiery gaze and pointing her towards the direction of the black gate.

'Enough with your stories, get out right now! You bad girl!

The bad girl left, the slut. I did not know at that time that I was never going to see her again. That soon she was going to be married off to an old stranger and forced to sacrifice her poetry and her education at the altar of domesticity: grinding masalas, chopping onions, cooking, feeding and yearly pregnancies. Truly, I did not know it then.

And I was left to watch the sky in her stead, weeping ceaselessly and writing poetry. Hating this world and this society. Hating my invisible prison and the unseen shackles on my limbs. Feeling as if my wings had been clipped and I had been locked in a sturdy cage for eternity.

Or perhaps there was a cage hiding within me, ready to bundle me up inside it every time I tried taking flight.

Mubaswera Lay There, White . . .

One Thursday night, all of a sudden, to the utter astonishment of her family members, Mubaswera passed away. I had met her on the occasions she had visited us in Abakash or whenever we had gone to the Pir's house. We had even played houses together on our courtyard and roof. Since playing houses had not been allowed at their place we used to re-enact the fight at Karbala with Mubaswera as Hasan and Muhammed as Hossain. Since nobody wanted to play Yazid and Muawiyah, they were shadowy figures who received feigned kicks and punches. I used to be the sole spectator of their war games.

I was never friends with Fajli khala's children; they seemed too distant to me. They did not speak in the tone or language we used to speak in; their speech was more non-Bengali, heavily inflected with Urdu. They had begun keeping their fasts and offering namaz from when they were five years old and, by the time they were ten, the girls had all taken up burqas. They did not go to school, did not run on the fields, never left their house alone, all because their elders had told them that doing these things would make Allah angry at them.

When Mubaswera was around fifteen, Abu Bakr's steel factory had become part of the Pir's property. Abu Bakr

379

himself had signed over the factory to Pir Amirullah, with
Allah as his witness. Crowds of people had begun gathering
before the Pir, like ants, from wherein the Pir had chosen his
favourites, the most devout worshippers of Allah whom he
employed in his newly acquired factory. By that time Tutu
mama and Sharaf mama had consigned their studies to the
pits and completely devoted themselves to the service of the
Pir. Fajli khala too was decidedly elated at having managed
to turn her brothers away from worldly pursuits towards the
path laid out by Allah. In no time my two uncles had given
up wearing pants and shirts in favour of kurtas and pyjamas,
adopted the fez cap and stopped shaving. To uproot the
last vestiges of worldly underpinnings from within, they
took to taking special advisory services, *nasihat* they were
called, in the small rooms of the Pir's house with the girls
Humaira, Sufaira and Mubaswera. Obviously, safety was
the prerogative of Allah. Once when I walked into one of
the services by mistake I was roundly reprimanded by Tutu
mama and turned out. I had caught a glimpse of him lying
in bed with Humaira sitting beside him, her hands stroking
his chest as part of the service. That was how the service
worked, alone in a dark room, stroking the man's chest, that
was what Mother had told me. Mubaswera had been allotted
to conduct the services for Sharaf mama. This was not a
service meant for just anyone, this was for the betterment
of their own uncles! It was during such a service that a djinn
allegedly took possession of Mubaswera. And this was a
different kind of djinn altogether, all it wanted to do was
sit under a tree by itself and cry. No one knew why that was
so, just that Mubaswera did not wish to eat, always felt as if
she was going to throw up and was no longer interested in
her fasts and prayers, all she wished to do was find a tree to

sit under. Eventually, the services had to be stopped as the erstwhile bubbly girl, once so intent on her imaginary war games, took to bed. Before any arrangements could be made to exorcise the djinn from inside her she went down with a terrible fever. Enchanted water was administered, Quranic verses were recited but nothing could bring the fever down. Fajli khala sat by her head, putting cold compresses on her forehead; she was burning so hot that the compress could be seen giving off steam. Soon after Mubaswera began experiencing breathing trouble.

'I don't know what to do,' said Fajli khala, 'call a doctor now.'

'Doctor? The charmed water is not working, will a doctor be able to do anything?' exclaimed Musa, Fajli khala's husband who was from Medinipur.

'Doesn't matter, there is no harm in trying. Allah is the Lord, He is the one who will decide, medicines are but pretexts.'

When the call came Dr Rajab Ali grabbed hold of his bag of medical supplies and set off towards the Pir's house to treat the girl. It was around twelve thirty at night at that time.

He found Mubaswera on a white bed, gaunt and skeletal after a week-long fever, her tongue, eyes, nails, nearly all of her, white. Pale, ashen.

The doctor duly checked her pulse, measured her blood pressure and listened to her heartbeat. He then asked the room to be cleared for ten minutes, telling the family members to come back in a while. He proceeded to administer an injection and, despite the lines creasing his forehead, the doctor declared that he was going to wait and see what happened.

The doctor did not take his fees, it was something he never did when it was a family member he was examining.

Mubaswera was found cold on her bed the next morning, dead. Fajli khala wept silently; in their house people were not allowed to cry loudly if someone died. Death was an inevitable thing so what was the point in crying! Besides, death meant being reunited with Allah. Keening for someone who had received such a glorious fate meant causing Allah displeasure. Rather, the dead had to be bid farewell with a smile. Every time Fajli khala's voice attempted to rise with her grief, Zohra, the Pir's eldest daughter, would leap at her and cover her mouth—

'Shame! What are you doing, your daughter has gone to Allah! Pray for her, bhabi! See, what divine light frames her face! She must be headed to heaven. Allah has taken back what was His, crying will be considered a sin! If you want to shed tears you can go ahead, but don't make a single sound.'

Keening for someone was a major sin, a gunah-e-kabira. Fajli khala had no choice but to comply, stuffing her stole into her mouth to choke her grief.

Ma was at home, thinking about Mubaswera and crying when Father returned and informed us that the girl was dead.

'If they had treated her before she might have lived. By the time I reached, there was hardly any time left.'

Mother wiped her tears and snot with her left hand and sighed audibly—

'How could she have lived if she had not been given life? This was all the life Allah had given her. She must be destined for heaven. Apparently she was crying out Allah's name before dying.'

Father took off his shoes and pushed them under the bed, tucking his socks inside the shoes. There was a crinkle on his forehead. As he was taking off his shirt he spoke—

'She was pregnant.'

'Who was?'

In the next room, to their left, my snooping ears had begun to ring.

'Who else? Your sister's daughter. What was her name, Muba . . . Mubaswera,' Father said as he hung his sweat-soaked shirt on a hanger.

'She was not married. How could she have been pregnant? How could you say such things about such a pure girl? Your tongue will fall off, I'm telling you.' Mother began to weep in earnest.

Father pulled the lungi up over his pants, bit down on one edge of the yardage with his teeth, slipped his pants off, put them on the rack and then proceeded to tie the lungi firmly around his waist.

Mother was pacing up and down the room, through a crack in the door I could see their feet. Hesitating, Mother's feet finally turned and went closer to Father's. Both pairs of feet were bare; Mother's was dark, soft, the big toe missing its nail from some previous illness, Father's was fair, pale from being covered by socks for long stretches. The four limbs were very close. Father's toes were bunched together, his feet hanging off the edge of the bed. Mother walked up to him and then walked back again.

'She must have tried to abort the baby with some root or something. It had become infected, septicaemia.' Father's voice was cold.

'No, it's a lie. Your tongue will fall off. Allah will pay you back for these allegations.'

Mother's voice was laced with fire. A door shut with a thud.

Stray words from the other room were reaching me, crushed as if in a mortar and pestle; I could barely put them together and make any sense of it.

Death was beginning to seem like the most natural thing to me. There I was breathing, the very next day I could be lying dead and cold on a white bed. The limbs that were still moving would cease to function, the dreams I was still dreaming would disappear, everything would vanish with death. Mother used to say the *rooh*, or soul, floated away to Allah, leaving the body behind on earth. It was the soul that was everything. How did the rooh fly, was it like a white dove? Mother had said the soul was invisible, it could not be seen. There were so many such invisible things in the world.

After Mubaswera's death Sharaf mama too turned away from the path of Allah, perhaps because there was no one to give him his nasihat lessons any longer. Donning his pants and shirts again, he renewed his commitment towards the material world. For a while he did preserve a few blood-stained rags and pads as mementos in a trunk in his room.

The Return 2

Having left his MSc course at Dhaka University, Dada moved back home in Mymensingh with a new job in an overseas medical company. He returned and declared—

'I have taken this job for Ma's sake. There's no one to take care of her in this family. No one gives her any money. I don't want her to face these hardships any longer.'

With his first salary Dada bought her four sarees; he also put in an order for gold bracelets.

Mother fell over the sarees and wept. She had long stopped wearing sarees but she wore the ones he bought for her, continuing to weep as she pleated. She was looking strangely beautiful. Hugging Dada tightly to herself she spoke through her tears—

'Don't buy anything else for me, darling. I don't need anything. Please save, so it can be of some use to you in the future.'

The ever browbeaten and bullied woman seemed to have suddenly learnt to straighten her spine. Her own son was earning money, she no longer needed to beg a philanderer for money. I had never seen her so exuberant, so full of life. Maintaining relations with a kafir was a sin, having convinced Mother of this fact Fajli khala had taken her to the court to sign divorce papers. Mother had signed the papers as well but Father had taken one glance at them, made a sound of disgust and torn them up. She hated living under the same roof as an apostate but despite having claimed time and again that she was going to leave, she had never managed to take that final step. Had she not left because she had nowhere to go? Or had she stayed behind for the sake of the house, the garden that she had carefully taken care of herself, as well as a strange sense of attachment with the people? I could never tell for sure what it was.

'My gem of a son has come back a graduate from the University. I can barely contain my excitement.'

It was a line Father had repeated often through gritted teeth ever since Dada's return from Dhaka. He had sent his graduate son to the University for a master's degree but two years later Dada had ultimately returned home with the same BSc certificate from Anandamohan College that he had left home with. For Father death would have been a better alternative to such an outcome.

All Dada could do was play dumb like a fish and swallow all of his insults.

Having returned home Dada made arrangements to settle down in his old room, moving Chotda's bed outside into the veranda. Surprising, the move did not sit well with Father. Screaming the house down on everyone he ordered Dada to put the bed back to where it had been.

'The person whose bed this is, where are they going to sleep if they come home? Put it back exactly where it was.'

'Will Kamal ever come back?' Mother sighed, 'I've heard he has moved elsewhere, to Islampur or somewhere like that. Who knows how he is, what he gets to eat—'

The comment served to incense Father further.

'What do I care what he eats or not? Let him starve and die! Let him suffer! What can I do? You're the reason behind all this. Don't speak! The kids have turned out this way because of you.'

Moving to stand in front of him, her spine stiff, Mother raised her chin and said—

'Why should I not speak? How much longer do you want me to keep playing dumb? I don't survive on someone else's money. My son earns now, he gives me money, clothes, all that I need. I am not responsible for any man any more. You're the one who beat him up like a monster and drove him out! What is the point now of keeping a bed aside for him? What?'

'I will see what the point is. You don't have to understand it.'

Dada bought a book of poems by Rabindranath that he would often recite from in a deep voice and ask me to do the same. I read one poem after another, with Dada correcting my pronunciation from time to time, telling me how much I should emote and where, where to stress or where not to, where to pause and where to speed up.

'If you cannot put your heart into it, don't read poetry.'

He began organizing evenings of poetry reading, just for the two of us, wherein we both were the participants as well as the audience, with Dada acting as the judge. Under Dada's tutelage a new chapter in my life commenced. He gave me a red notebook he had received from a medical company; in it I started writing a couple of poems every day that I would show him for approval. Some he liked, some he loved and for some he would simply say, 'This is shit, not poetry.'

The notebook was soon making the rounds of the girls at school; when one finished reading it another would take

it home and often a month would pass before I could lay my
hands on it again. My poems were becoming a craze among
the girls. Reading a poem of mine called 'Free Bird', Dada
remarked ruefully one day, 'If only *Pata* had still been in
circulation. I would have had this poem published.'

Not just poetry readings, we started storytelling sessions
as well. He would read one, then I would follow suit. Some
lines he paused over, applauded loudly and reread two–three
times; watching him I would do the same. Our sessions
would go on unhindered till it was time for Father's return.
Sometimes we had musical sessions too. When asked I usually
sang two lines in my tone-deaf voice and then stopped; Dada
would continue bellowing like cattle in his equally atonal
style. When Yasmin joined the fray she was the only one
who could properly sing. Dada told Yasmin he was going to
buy her a harmonium.

Dada also bought a music player and some afternoons
he would entirely spend listening to music. One day while
listening to '*Muchhe Jaoa Dinguli . . .*' ('My faded past keeps
calling me back . . .) I found him crying; he had not noticed
when I had entered the room silently.

'Dada, you were crying?'

'No, no, why should I cry?' he replied wiping his tears. 'I
wasn't. It's nothing.'

Dada had been crying. Had he been crying about Sheela?

The incident remained in my thoughts, that Dada was
hiding some secret pain in his heart. That he would sit
alone and cry about someone very near to him and about
his faded past.

I was sitting beside Dada by the window. Lilies had
bloomed in the garden and their beautiful fragrance was
wafting inside. Outside, Dulal went by playing a mouth-organ.

He walked so fast that it seemed he was running; be it morning, noon or night the sound of the mouth-organ was enough for anyone to guess that it was Dulal. He never spoke to anyone, never waited for anyone. He would only run, as if he had some very urgent business to attend to. In reality, there was nothing. People used to say Dulal was crazy.

'Is Dulal actually mad?'

'I don't think so,' Dada replied.

Sighing suddenly, Dada stood up and his face broke into a smile, as if the sun had emerged from behind a veil of clouds. 'Go, set the chessboard. Let's see who wins today.'

Seeing him smile put my mind at ease and I set about doing as he had asked. Having learned to play chess from him, I had been consistently beating him at our games. Pulling the wool over my eyes he would always try to tamper with the pieces; before we sat down to play I warned him repeatedly not to cheat.

Despite that I caught him cheating on two occasions. After a couple of hours, once I had locked his king in a checkmate, he turned over the board deliberately. I began screaming that he had lost. Pretending as if he did not know what I was talking about, like an innocent child he countered—

'What have I lost? Where? Show me where I lost! You lost!'

Pulling his most innocent expression he completely refused to accept his defeat. I had made such a bad move that he had been unable to tolerate it and had turned the board over, that was the excuse he gave. Not for a moment would he accept that I had won or that I played well.

In school I was developing a reputation of being a good student. I would always be among the top three girls.

Nevertheless, Father refused to accept that I was good. He was convinced I was slacking, or else why was I not the top student! It never ceased to irk me.

Mother, I noticed, was intent on keeping Dada appeased. Dada liked crumbly fried dried beef so she would cook it for him. If he said he wanted to have savoury patties she would immediately make arrangements. The moment the skies would get cloudy or there was even a short spell of rain, he would ask Mother to make khichdi and fry hilsa fish. Mother would immediately set about mixing dal and rice. Her visits to the Pir's house started becoming more infrequent.

My affluent Dada soon came to be regarded as an important member of the household. He took us to Chitrarupa Studio one day for a group photo. He himself started having pictures taken in various poses that he would file in an album. Some he had blown up and framed. He would ask me, 'What do you say, don't I look like a hero?' I had to accept that it was true, he did look like one. I had noticed that Dada was truly very handsome. He also had two of my drawings, one of Rabindranath and the other of Najrul, framed and hung on the wall, telling anyone who came home that I had painted them.

He bought me brushes and colours and encouraged me to keep painting. While painting I would imagine growing up and going to an art school. The music teacher back in PTI School had told me I was destined to be a great artist. No matter what I drew, Dada would admire and say, 'Good that I had taught you to draw when you were a child. Would you have been able to draw so well otherwise?'

One day I told him about my secret desire to go to an art school and become an even better artist. Dada pursed his lips and said, 'Father will kill you if he finds out. He will not let you become an artist. He will say artists remain destitute.'

Not just Mother, Dada bought clothes and shoes for me as well. He also took us to the movies, something I soon became obsessed with. I would incessantly badger him to take me and from time to time he would say, 'Fine, write an application to me. I will see if it can be approved.'

So I wrote applications addressed to him beginning with 'Dear Sir . . .' and signed off with 'Your obedient servant . . .' They were all copied essentially from language books, like the 'Write an application in English to the manager' type of essays, from where I would replace the asking for money bit with asking to be taken to the cinema. Often, even after receiving the application, Dada would fail to reach a decision, much to my utter impatience.

'You have no patience,' he told me once. 'I hate it when people get so impatient. Once I had gone to watch a film with this friend of mine called Iqbal. We used to call him a White Elephant, he was that fair and that fat. On reaching the theatre we realized that the show was already sold out. Iqbal was adamant that he had to watch the film, no matter how, even if we had to buy our tickets in black, which meant paying thrice the price. I tried convincing him that we should come back the day after but he just would not listen! He was determined to go for the matinee show on that very day. In the end I gave him one tight slap across his face. Ever since he has never displayed any impatience with anything in front of me. You're like Iqbal, you have no patience at all.'

I loved Dada, just as I envied him too. He could go wherever he wished to, do whatever he wanted. He bought a motorcycle and was soon roaming around the city on it, often going off to other cities as well: Tangail, Jamalpur, Netrakona.

I badly wanted to go as well, step outside the boundaries around me. Dada told me he was going to take me to Jairamkura to see the hills, the Garo hills.

While I began to grow impatient waiting for this promised trip, Dada kept postponing the date from one month to the next. Nevertheless, I refused to give up hope that early one morning, long before anyone would wake up, we would be off to the hills, somewhere far away where I was going to lean on the silence around me and watch the dew falling silently.

A few months after Dada's return Father got transferred to the Mitford Hospital in Dhaka and the news of the transfer immediately managed to put him in a cranky mood. Handing over all the responsibilities of looking after the house and the family to Dada, Father soon left to join Mitford. He would come back home every two days, arriving around midnight by train from Dhaka, and barely spend the night before setting off for Dhaka again at dawn. He had been appointed a professor in the jurisprudence department of Mitford where he had to teach students and also perform autopsies. Back home the person who was perhaps the happiest about him being transferred was me. That was the age when I was just starting to sprout wings.

One afternoon I was overcome by an urge to wet my feet while walking along the shore of the Brahmaputra. The river was so close to where we lived but I had never been allowed to visit. When I was little the excuse had been that I was too small to go anywhere alone, for fear that someone was going to put me in a sack and kidnap me. Or Foting Ting was perennially standing by the river, speaking through its feet and ready to eat me. When I was old enough the excuse changed to girls my age should not be out on the road.

Without letting anyone catch wind of what I was planning, I set off for the river that afternoon with Yasmin in tow. Mother was asleep, Dada was out, Father was in Dhaka and there was no one to hold us back. I was no longer afraid of Foting Ting, so why should I not have gone? So I did. My dreams, amassed in droplets over ages, were by then as great as a river, dreams of walking by the Brahmaputra and sitting on its shore with my feet submerged in the water.

I was walking along the shore of the Brahmaputra, my hair was flying, as were the ends of my dress, and the wind was rushing past my ears with a whistling sound. In the sweet afternoon sunlight the sand beneath my feet was glistening. Just then, just at that very moment, my utter elation with my surroundings was punctured as if by a poisoned arrow in the form of a young man coming from the opposite direction. Even before I could make sense of what was happening, with no fault of mine and without having done anything to him, he pinched me hard on my breasts and on my buttocks as he passed me by, laughing as he did. His friends, all boys of his age, were standing at a distance clapping and laughing. As if my body was not my own but something they were casually allowed to have fun with! The Brahmaputra was everyone's river, mine included. I had just as much right as anyone to stand on its shore. What right did they have to abuse me? My hands curled into fists; I wanted to attack the boys, skin them alive. But I could not, neither could I take one step towards them.

'Let's go home, Bubu,' Yasmin whispered in a trembling voice, 'I'm scared.'

Returning home from the Brahmaputra seething in rage, I was met with the sight of Mother and my uncle Aman sitting very close to each other and talking.

'How are you, sweetheart?' Aman kaka asked me.

I fixed him with a piercing gaze, walked to my room without a word and shut the door behind me. Then I broke down into tears, crying pitifully for all my helplessness. But I did not let anyone see that I was crying, just as I did not let anyone realize that my deep-rooted anguish was drawing me further down into its murky depths.

'Why was Aman kaka here?' I asked Mother later.

'He wishes to walk the path of Allah,' Mother smiled sweetly. 'I'm giving him nasihat.'

'Don't help him too much. Don't you remember how Mubaswera died giving nasihat?'

Either my voice was so low that Mother did not hear me, or she was too engrossed in something else to even try and listen.

After this day Aman kaka would come home every day in the evening and he and Mother would go into her room and talk in hushed voices. During that time the door to her room remained closed from within. One day I pushed the door open and went in, only for Aman kaka to leap off the bed; I could see Mother through the mosquito net.

'What are you doing in the dark, Ma?'

'Aman is having a lot of trouble with his wife. He's not been doing well, so he comes to me to talk about his sorrows and feel a little lighter. I have been trying to convince him to turn to Allah.'

'I'm hungry. Give me rice.'

That was said just for the sake of it. Usually Moni made arrangements for me whenever I was hungry.

'I have a headache,' Mother replied, irritated. 'I'm resting a little. Won't all of you let me have even a moment of peace!'

I walked out of the room to the veranda outside and drew in a deep breath. I was having trouble breathing remembering the sight of them sitting so close to each other. It made me anxious to think that the man who had undressed the seven-year-old me was perhaps doing the same to my mother in the dark.

Aman kaka's regular visits at odd hours did not fail to catch Dada's attention either; neither did he not notice the former's odd and skittish gaze.

A Nest of Termites

One half of Mother's wooden cupboard was filled with books, the other half with clothes, unfolded, just sort of stuffed in together. The first half had books on the Hadith, copies of *Maksudul Momenin* and *Niamul Quran*, a book of poems by Pir Amirullah called *Minar*, a copy of *Tazkirat al-Awliya* and an English book called *Who Am I?* Amirullah knew English as well and Mother would often tell me how erudite her huzur was and what fluent English he could speak. Whenever she spoke of him her eyes would glow.

The Pir must have studied about the material world, that's what I always wanted to ask her but never managed to. Asking such a question would have been a transgression. Mother had no interest in having debates regarding Allah and the Prophet. It was the same with Pir Amirullah as well. She was happy if I dutifully nodded and agreed with whatever she had to say. Since I was her child it was my duty to please her, or so I had been taught. Keeping her happy meant getting spared from being slapped or thrashed or punished in some form or the other. It also meant being served extra helpings of fish or meat during meals. More than being pampered with food, it was the prospect of deliverance from being thrashed that largely tipped the scales regarding keeping my mouth shut. Mother was of the firm opinion that those who did not believe in the Quran or the Hadith were not true Muslims and such people were destined to burn in the fires of hell. There was no special treatment in this, it was all quite straightforward. With Allah things generally were like that, always straightforward. No namaz or roja, you were going to burn in hell. No burqas for women, you were going to burn in hell. You mixed with strange men, you were going to hell. You did not put water after peeing, you were going to hell. Laughing out aloud meant inviting hellfire, just as crying loudly did. It was all about hellfire! I wanted to ask Mother why people were so afraid of fire, especially given our day and age. In cold countries people kept fires burning in their homes throughout! Circus acrobats had entire routines revolving around fire. Even fire injuries were curable. So why did Allah insist on scaring people with fire! There were so many other terrible ways to torture people, none of which He seemed to be interested in! Bad people like to cause bodily pain, while the clever ones target the mind, especially since the latter is more effective in causing anguish. Allah did not seem particularly clever to me. Instead he seemed like a mean person, much like Gnetu's father. At times Allah resembled Father who always wanted me to do as he wished and subjected me to physical punishment if I refused. The only difference between the two was that Father wanted me to pursue a formal, worldly education while Allah wanted his subjects to concentrate on the Quran and the Hadith. With both, I felt the same amount of distance. So I was happiest when Father was not at home, while with Allah, since He was unfortunately formless, any mention of Him served to make me uneasy. With both it was their absence that I preferred. I felt torn between the two, barely able to hold on to my sense of self, a dissected corpse in a morgue.

Whenever he was happy with me, Father would get me lots of sweets or freshwater fish like rohu and katla of which he would insist I have the best portions. Allah too was known to feed people—whoever He wished to feed—to their hearts' content. The best game, grapes, wine and so much more. In heaven there are supposedly beautiful girls, their bodies blushing pink, who serve people alcohol. Nana used to say the food there is so fragrant that the burps are aromatic as well. Whether fragrant or not, burping was something that I just could not tolerate. And how was someone even going to smell someone else burping! Let's say the person who was going to be fragrantly burping was Nana and the person smelling it was Gnetu's father. Clutching the book of Hadith laws that I had been reading to my right, I imagined placing the two characters on my left. They were going on burping and smelling. I was surrounded by it all, the imaginary duo, the termites in the book I was holding, as well as the words in it. I was there and yet I wasn't! No one was burping but I could sure imagine they were. The termites and the words were real, but they could just as well have been imaginary like the burping. Not even in my imagination did I want anything to happen to them.

The book containing the Hadith was infested with termites. Our house was damp and books left unopened for even a couple of days ran this risk. Overcome with rage at the sight of the fat white bellies of the insects I flung the book at the floor, crushing a few of them in the process. With one eye on the crushed insects and one on the book, I could make out the words together on the open page—

'Everything in the world is a commodity and the most valuable commodity is a woman of good character.'

I was half-lying on the floor with my chin resting on one hand, the other hand on the book open in front of me, the hallowed words therein stained by termites.

'If I were to command anyone to perform sajda then I would have commanded the whole of womankind to prostrate themselves in prayer in front of their husbands.'

'If a wife ever tells her husband that she dislikes something he has done then the fruits of seventy-years' worth of worship would be nullified for her. Even if she had earned those seventy years of blessings after keeping roja during the day and dutifully offering her namaz at night.'

'A husband is allowed to beat his wife on any one of these four occasions: if the wife refuses to dress herself prettily and go to him when he asks her to; if the wife refuses sex; if she forsakes ritual ablutions and offering namaz; and if she goes to visit someone without her husband's permission.'

'The wives who can be in accord with their husband's second marriage without any displays of envy will be rewarded by Allah with benedictions comparable to that of martyrs.'

The termites from the book were beginning to crawl all over my body, as if they wished to eat me instead. The entire house was infested with termites and wheat weevils. The weevils nibbled on wood with soft ticking noises through the night and the termites silently munched on the books. They did not even stop before consuming the grand axioms of the great prophet Hazrat Muhammad. Were termites Muslim! Surely they did not have religion! They could eat a Saradindu Bandopadhyay omnibus just as well they could eat the Quran or the Hadith.

After Dilruba school books had become my closest companions. In no time I was through with most of the books in the library: Bankimchandra, Saratchandra,

Bibhutibhusan, Rabindranath, I read whatever was available, sitting on the roof or on the stairs leading up to it, at my study table or in bed. The moment Father would be back I would hide the extracurricular book and replace it with something I was supposed to be reading, mainly to keep it propped open in front of me for the sake of appearances. Then later, after everyone had gone off to sleep, I would get up, stealthily switch on the lights again and get back under the mosquito net with the book I had been reading earlier. Beside me Yasmin would be fast asleep. From time to time Mother would say—

'What is all this rubbish you keep reading? Don't you remember how abruptly Mubaswera died? Why can't you take Allah's name for a change!'

Everyone has to die at some point. There was nothing I could say to her in reply. Mother's commands and advice hovered over my head like the high summer sun, threatening to burn me to ashes.

I had been warned how there would be no way to save myself on the Day of the Judgement if I had no faith in the words of the Quran and the Hadith. However, I never had a clear idea as to what the Hadith were. After getting to know what they were, I had no interest in delving into their depths. One knew what to expect in an open latrine, there was no reason to expect to find precious jewels in it. I shut the termite-ridden book and kept it aside; it seemed as if the book too was burping, as if it too had feasted on the food of paradise. Hearing the sounds of Mother's footsteps I hurriedly put the book back in its place on the shelf. She did not even know that termites were silently devouring her book, busy as she was with Aman kaka's nasihat sessions. Every night I had been hearing the evidence of those in the hushed whispers and stifled giggles coming from Mother's dark room. I decided not to tell her about the termites. They were hungry, it was best to let them eat. Getting rid of them was not my responsibility.

What I could not understand was why I had to take recourse to Allah's name, only because Mubaswera had died. I did not want to take Allah's name. Allah and such things all seemed made up to me. It was all written by some unlettered man, perhaps even someone like Sharaf mama. Or perhaps someone like the boy who had groped me on the banks of the Brahmaputra. If the Hadith were the utterances of Muhammad, then it seemed he was a lot like Gnetu's father, a cruel man. I saw no difference between Allah and Muhammad.

Despite having kept the book back it felt as if a million tiny termites had somehow managed to find a way inside my soul; they were silently nibbling away at all my letters, my words, my sentences and who knew what else.

That afternoon Gnetu's mother came over. I almost could not recognize her at first, even though she spoke in her familiar broken voice. Mother was sitting on a chair in the veranda; she had her prayer beads in one hand, which she was counting, but she was also listening to the poor woman. Counting the prayer beads involved intense focus on reading the associated prayers. How could Mother manage to do both together? Perhaps because she had two minds, one meant for Allah and the other for the world. Besides, her world was rather small and it was perfectly easy to take an entire round of it twice a day. Gnetu's mother suddenly stopped and began to lift the bottom of her saree; Mother's fingers moved faster on the blue beads in her hand. The more the beads moved, the higher the saree went, almost in tandem, until

the woman's entire leg, right up till her thighs, was visible.
It was burnt in several places. Mother glanced at the wounds
and made a sound of distress. It was not Gnetu's father who
was the culprit this time but another man called Safar Ali,
someone she had married around two years ago. The man
had taken a burning log and burnt her. Why? Because he was
her husband and had every right to do whatever he wanted
with his wife! At least that was the answer I formed in my
head. Gnetu's mother and my mother both agreed that Safar
Ali was a cretin and a scoundrel.

I wanted to tell my mother that whatever Safar Ali had
done was in perfect accord with the Quran and the Hadith.
I turned the words around in my mouth, testing them, before
finally gulping them down. Were the words eaten up by
termites? Who can tell! Gnetu's mother was there to ask for
a job as a maid in our house. There was no way she could get
married again with burn wounds on her body. No man was
falling over himself to provide for her. Mother, her fingers
moving on the beads much slower than before, told Gnetu's
mother that she already had a permanent maid and did not
require the services of a new one.

Mother's legs were moving, to the rhythm of some odd
tune perhaps. Perhaps somewhere within her a secret tune
was playing. Like how peacocks dance! Just that Mother kept
her wings folded during the day; bringing them out only at
night. Sitting on the threshold I could see Gnetu's mother's
darkening face through the gap between Mother's legs. In
the gathering dusk the blue beads in Mother's hand were
glowing like feline eyes. Even though she could not employ
her Mother insisted the other woman eat something, at least
some dal and rice, before leaving. Sitting at the threshold, I
looked away from the burnt leg and suddenly said—

'What would happen if you keep her? Would the Mahabharat become impure or something?'

'Isn't it impure already?' Mother replied without a shade of emotion in her voice.

Gnetu's mother was still sitting in the veranda, like the stump of a felled tree. Possibly a hundred mosquitos were hovering around her, some landing on her limbs occasionally to feast. It was possible the burnt skin could no longer feel anything. All that remained was hunger, deep in the gut, like it usually happened with the poor: everything went away, family, society, loved ones, possessions, everything except hunger. I imagined myself in her place, wondering what would I have done if I had been her.

Instead of waiting for someone to toss me some dal-rice I would have got up and walked away, without glancing back even once. I would have walked past the bael tree and out the black gate, kept walking till I was moving faster than the wind. Much like the 'mad' Dulal in our neighbourhood, without waiting for anyone or anything. Dulal used to play the mouth-organ, but I would have had nothing to play. Neither would I have needed it, the anguish suppressed in my heart for ages would have been music enough. A fire would be threatening to burst out of me. Not something that could burn me, since much of my soul had already been reduced to ashes; neither was there any skin left on the bones to singe. No, this fire would have been more about embers from my burnt skin spreading to other things. On reaching Safar Ali's house he would have been surprised to see me. He would have come at me again with a burning log from the oven; but even before it could touch me he would have burst into flames, bellowing and swelling flames, blind and all-encompassing. The fire would have danced on Safar Ali's

body, on the burning log in his grasp. I would have waited to
see him burn; only that would have been able to satisfy me.

The fire they had fuelled inside me for so long would have
swollen fourfold. I would have set off again, faster than the
wind like Dulal. The fire would have shown me the way to
Gnetu's father's house, right till the courtyard where echoes
of me writhing in agony could still be heard. Agony of the
talaq, of being discarded in public in front of a courtyard full
of people.

I took a deep breath. Gnetu's mother was still sitting
like a tree stump on our veranda. Mosquitos were spinning
above her like a top. Staring at her cringing body I stopped
imagining myself as her. Instead I imagined myself as
Gnetu's father's new wife, an adolescent girl, being tortured
by him with a machete. A bleeding and screaming me was
writhing on an open courtyard and the people gathered there
were standing and watching silently, propped up on their
elbows, hands behind their heads, an audience during the
climax of a film in a theatre. And suddenly, to their utter
shock, I was snatching the machete away from my assailant
and striking him with it, peeling away his skin and rubbing
salt on the wounds. The people in the courtyard were yelling,
they were calling me insane, downright crazy.

Ha! Crazy!

It was Mother who had threatened Moni with that
fate—that she would peel her skin and put salt in the
wounds—when the girl had forgotten to clean and de-vein
the prawns properly one day. Aman kaka had wished to eat
prawns cooked in coconut milk and the partially cleaned
prawns had made him sick. Mother had been livid and she
had threatened Moni with this punishment. Moni had been
terrified, having taken the threat literally. I had as well, had

even asked Moni what happened when one peeled the skin and put salt in the wounds.

'It burns so much,' Moni had exclaimed, her face going blue at the thought.

Wiping her scared tears away, for the next couple of nights I had tried comforting her with whatever our bodies could think of. In the middle of the night I had wordlessly moved my hand away from her and silently willed Moni to go away from there and forget all about those unfortunate days. Had wished for her to go somewhere far from our house, find a place of her dreams where she could take her mother and younger sister, somewhere near a lush field full of grain. Had hoped to tell her that if she could find a place by the river she should see how the sun sets in the water, what a brilliant hue the sky takes on then. It would have surely made her happy.

In the end Mother had not carried through with her threat and Moni's skin had been spared. But there were a few people who, deep in my heart, I wished to torment like that. Like Sharaf mama and Aman kaka. And from that day Gnetu's father as well. But wishes were all I had; often I could not help but feel that there was not much I was capable of actually doing. There I was, a spindly girl that a storm could toss about, what strength did I have to dissent! Then again, the thought would cross my mind that at least the desire to do something was there.

After the War

1.

The Hindus of the neighbourhood were slowly returning to their abandoned houses. They were coming back to their country from refugee camps in Calcutta, to the homes they had abandoned before the war. All their things had been robbed in the meanwhile. The empty courtyards that the pariahs and mongrels used to sleep in were suddenly full of the chatter of people. With my chin resting on the railings of our roof, I could see them returning. As if a tide had arrived on the Brahmaputra, as if flowers were suddenly blooming all over a desolate garden. None of the returned seemed to perturbed by their missing things. They were happy simply to have got their homes back. Some houses had already managed to organize kirtans, etc., and women were ululating and lighting evening lamps. A graveyard had seemingly come back to life.

Around a week after their return, a group of muktijoddhas marched into the house through the black gate, guns on their shoulders, followed by fifteen–sixteen people from the neighbours, most of whom we recognized. I greeted them with a smile but none of them were in a mood to reciprocate, as if they were our mortal enemies. They walked from room to room, yelling loudly about stolen goods, telling the people who had come with them to pick up whatever they thought were their stuff.

The familiar faces from the neighbourhood took turns in taking away a number of our things: bronze utensils, a brass pitcher, chairs and tables. Mother had been putting oil in the sewing machine. The container remained in her hand as someone came and casually picked up the machine and walked away. Both Mother and I were left standing in shock.

After they were gone Mother sighed, 'Wages of sin! What can I say.'

It was meant for Father, I knew. After returning from the village Mother had noticed some new things in the house and asked him about them.

'Did you buy these? If you did, why did you buy old stuff? What use will this broken old drum of molasses be?'

Father, in the middle of tucking the socks he had just taken off inside his shoes, had not replied.

'Or did you take these from the Hindu houses?' Mother had asked in disgust.

Father had not replied to that either.

The drums had surprised me as well. It had been difficult for me to imagine that Father had nicked those things from someone else's house. This was the person who had given refuge to a Hindu boy called Pradip during the war. The boy, rechristened Alam, had stayed on in our house after the war and Father had employed him as a cashier in the pharmacy. And this very same person had become greedy over things the Hindus had left behind! Back in '71 Dada, Riyazuddin and Imaan Ali had been living with us as well. Perhaps they were the ones who had done it.

Since I did not dare ask Father any questions, I had ended up asking Dada.

'Were you the ones who robbed the things from the Hindu households?'

Dada was seated on an iron chair watching the ducks and chickens in the yard. As if those birds were the most fascinating things in the world and no human being or their queries could catch up to their appeal. When I had broken the spell and repeated my question he had replied—

'The Biharis were bringing everything out on the streets and burning them. We had gathered some things from the road and brought home.'

'Who had? Had Father done it too? Tell me!' I was not about to let Dada go without an answer.

'It was us,' Dada had replied while throwing wheat at the ducks and chickens.

The answer had done little to reassure me.

On returning home, when he received the news of the raid on our house, Father went out and stood in the veranda, hands folded and elbows resting on the railings. Seeing him like that I wanted to believe he was repentant. I wanted to see his remorseful face. I had only ever heard the yelling, only ever seen the proud man. So much pride was bound to make someone inhuman.

After Dada returned home I informed him about the raid, 'They have taken away all the things that were looted.' I informed Chotda as well. A pall of gloom seemed to descend over the house. Father remained stationed on the veranda.

Mother's voice finally shattered the silence, her words uttered from a careful distance so Father could hear.

'What was the need of stealing a drum of rotten molasses? Allah always punishes those who sin. In the middle of this

I lost a bunch of my things. My sewing machine! I had saved money and bought it myself.'

When times were meant to be bad, they could get really bad. The day after the raid security personnel of the Rakkhi Bahini apprehended Dada from the road. These forces had been formed by Sheikh Mujib after Independence to put a check on terrorist activities. They were stationed at various places and could apprehend anyone they were suspicious of and beat them up. Even someone like my Dada who had no involvement in anything whatsoever. Father went to get him out but returned empty-handed. After torturing him for fifteen days when the Rakkhi Bahini found no evidence that he was involved in any terrorist activities, they let Dada go. After returning from their barracks Dada became a vocal critic of Sheikh Mujib, even going as far as telling people that things had been better under Pakistani rule; at least the roads had been safe.

Even those who had been supporters of Sheikh Mujib were soon beginning to chatter: What sort of government was this that was using the Rakkhi Bahini to assault and oppress innocent citizens!

2.

The murmurs continued for a few years. Unrest among the people continued to rise as well. Sheikh Mujib formed a political party called Baksal and prohibited all other parties.

'What sort of government is this that lets its people die in a famine because they have no food?' Father said one day.

Bearded men wearing fez caps materialized out of nowhere and began to clamour that such an Independence was of no value. The country needed to be put back under Pakistani rule. Boromama sighed and said he did not know which direction the country was headed.

'The government is doing things that did not happen even when Pakistan was ruling us. They are celebrating Shab-e-Baraat in Banga Bhaban with so much pomp. It never used to happen back when this was East Pakistan. Mujib attended an Islamic conference recently. Russia helped us so much during the war and here Mujib is bent on making Bangladesh a part of the Islamic world. The government is even saying things against India. Would we have become free if India had not sent its forces?'

I understood very little of politics. The only thing I knew was that I liked listening to Sheikh Mujib's 7 March speech whenever it was played on the radio. I would get goose-bumps from excitement. 'This struggle is a struggle for Independence, this struggle is a struggle for freedom,' this was not just a slogan but a verse that could make the blood boil. In our music classes we would sing '*Joy Bangla, long live Bangla!*' It was not merely a song, it was something greater, something that sent a jolt through the heart. Every few days pandals would be built in the neighbourhood for music and dance programmes. Every time they would play something on the mike I would be off to see it. Boys and girls would play the harmonium and practise singing and dancing. They all looked so beautiful and their songs always managed to shake me to the core. Like it used to happen while listening to Khudiram's songs. Kana mama used to tell us Khudiram's stories, how a young boy had bombed a British Governor-General and embraced death, all for the sake of freedom. I wanted to be like Khudiram, as courageous and as devil-may-care.

Then suddenly one day, quite abruptly, something happened that plunged the city into uneasiness again. People gathered on the roads to talk as if the world was about to come crashing down on them any moment. Some had radios stuck to their ear, faces dry, eyes threatening to pop out. What was the matter again? The days of sticking close to the radio for news had come to an end back in '71, so what had happened again! Whenever things in the country were tense in any way everyone tended to switch on BBC radio for news. No one had too much faith on our own broadcasters. Father too did as expected. I was asked to turn the knob of the radio to try and catch BBC, a big responsibility I felt very proud of having been given. Father never ordered me to do anything except studying, I was never usually asked to participate in anything else. Earlier it was either Dada or Chotda who were asked to turn the knob while I had to stand apart and watch. But that day Dada was away on a work trip to Sherpur for a couple of days. Chotda was not even living with us any more. Hence, the responsibility fell on me. I had almost found the BBC channel when Father asked me to stop. Words could be heard over the ether, broken fragments of half-truncated news.

Sheikh Mujib was dead.

Not just him, nearly his entire family had been shot dead by assailants at his house on 32 Dhanmondi. How could it have happened? How was it possible? Father sat down heavily, pressing the veins on his temple. Chotda, had he been home, would surely have sought refuge in the veranda with his lips curled. Dada would have said, 'His two sons Sheikh Kamal and Sheikh Jamal had caused so much trouble for so many people in Dhaka University. They used to carry pistols! They had gone too far, how much could people tolerate!'

Mother was pacing the room uneasily and speaking from time to time.

'What sort of inhuman thing is this? They killed his sons, daughter-in-law, even his young grandson Russel. What had they done? Such brutality!'

'Will the country become Pakistan again?'

I asked as if my parents had all the answers. Obviously it was not so. Mother went on, 'They wiped out his entire family under the cover of darkness. Allah will judge them.'

Baba was still sitting holding his temple. Early next morning two men from the neighbourhood came to see him. Makhanlal Lahiri and M.A. Kahhar, Munni's father. Sitting in the living room and sipping on tea they carried on a complicated conversation about the future of the country. Eavesdropping from behind the door I could only partially understand what they were talking about. The grown-ups never included me in their conversations. Was it because I was too small or because I was a girl?

Looking at Mujib's photo on our wall, his forearm outstretched in the middle of a speech, I felt terribly sorry. The man had been alive just the day before! It was almost unbelievable. 'Joy Bangla' was no longer playing on the radio. It worried me, made me have nightmares that there was going to be another war and we were going to have to run away on bullock carts again. Again there were going to be cannons on the city streets and random innocent people were going to be shot dead. Someone was again going to flash a torch over my body, a cold snake was again going to enter my flesh and find its way into my bones and blood.

The world had changed overnight. It was no longer fine to take Sheikh Mujib's name or sing 'Joy Bangla'. I was having trouble breathing. Time and again Father's comments about our uncertain future were drifting in from the direction of the living room.

The next day when Abu Ali, an employee in the pharmacy who had been Father's right-hand man, stole two lakh taka and ran away, Father repeated his lament about our uncertain future again. Mother, on the other hand, was of the firm opinion that such was the just fate of a miser's money. Allah did not tolerate wealth that had been saved by causing distress to one's wife and children.

'The money goes one way or another. So many times I told him, my mother lost everything she had in the war. And it got robbed from this house, didn't it? I asked you to help her but you did not listen to me twice. Now see what's happened to your wealth. This is divine justice.'

The nation was in a tense state but that did not stop Riyazuddin and Iman Ali of Madarinagar from coming to Father time and again for money; they were going to buy land. Mother sat them down in the kitchen and served them mounds of rice, with just a tiny bit of dal and some roasted dry peppers on the side. She made beds for them on the floor without mosquito nets and they got bitten till their faces were swollen.

Baba would return home at night and ask, 'Did you feed them?'

'Of course I have! They ate so much!' Mother's reply would be pungent with the sting of potent garlic oil.

My education continued as before, with books not meant to be read hidden underneath course books. Father continued to dream that his daughter was going to study and become self-reliant. I continued going up to the roof in secret. I liked watching some of the boys of our neighbourhood: someone with wavy hair, someone with dimples or eyes dancing with laughter, or lips curled coquettishly. The boy-watching would get over around evening when I would come downstairs. Inside the room it was impossible to know whether it was the full moon or the new moon, whether there was moonlight or it was pitch-dark. My relationship with the moon became nearly non-existent.

Mother's visits to the Pir continued as well, just as Aman kaka's stealthy visits to our home under the cover of darkness. Mother kept putting in her body and soul into his nasihat sessions. A suitcase full of her clothes was kept packed and ready under the bed. She was determined to go visit Allah's holiest site at the soonest: Mecca. To that end she kept requesting the Pir to recommend her name in the first batch of devotees. It dawned on me over time that I was no longer going to die if something were to happen to her.

Meanwhile, Father got transferred from Mitford back to Mymensingh again. He joined the Medical College as a professor, his job entailing beating idiots into the shape of good doctors. In the afternoons he would check patients in Arogya Bitan. Over time the crowd of patients coming to him gradually grew to a considerable number.

After her talaq with Chakladar, Razia Begum frequently sent missives to Father.

None of us knew where Chotda was, whether he was alive or dead. Father kept his bed made where it was, hoping he was going to come back one day.

Dada kept making furniture at home and roaming the city in search of a pretty girl with a round face like a betel leaf whom he could marry.

Amidst all this I kept growing up.

Glossary

aqiqah: Islamic tradition related to childbirth where an animal sacrifice is made, usually one for a girl and two for a boy, and the meat distributed among the poor and orphans.

bhuna: Traditional mode of cooking protein in Bangladesh where the spices are slow-cooked in oil with no addition of water.

chomchom/
chamcham: Bengali sweet, fried and soaked in sugar syrup.

Chanachur
chomchom: Sweets made of milk, flour and cream and dusted with coconut or mawa (dried whole milk) flakes. Originates from Porabari in Tangail, Bangladesh.

Dajjal: The Islamic variant of the Antichrist.

danguti: Also known as 'tip-cat', this is a South Asian amateur sport, popular especially among children.

dozakh: In Islam, a place of judgement and punishment after death; in many ways analogous to notions of 'hell'.

hadiya: A gift or offering made out of goodwill that, when given sincerely, is considered one of the highest forms of worship.

hadudu: A variation of kabaddi and the national sport of Bangladesh; the Bengali word for kabaddi

Iblis: The Islamic variant of the idea of Satan, who was cast from Paradise by Allah.

Israfil: The Islamic counterpart of Raphael, the archangel of music, whose trumpet is supposed to announce the end of days.

janamaz: Prayer rug or mat used by Muslims during namaz.

khoyer: Also known as *catechu*, this is a dye, tannin and astringent from the acacia tree, which is widely used in the subcontinent for making paan.

marfoti: Also known as 'murshidi', these are devotional folk songs that primarily evolved and flourished because of Sufi saints.

nakshi kantha: A century-old hand-embroidery tradition of Bengal, essentially quilts of everyday use made of old cloth and thread work, comprising a signature running stitch and various patterns, designs or even entire pictorial narratives.

paanta-bhaat: Leftover rice soaked overnight in cold water that partially ferments and is eaten with accompaniments during summer. Though the dish is fairly common, oftentimes it is a fixture in kitchens for the working-class or lower-income households.

pir:	A master or spiritual guide, sort of like an elder.
shaora:	A Siamese rough bush or toothbrush tree, associated in folk culture of Bengal as the preferred dwellings of spirits.
talaq:	divorce of the irrevocable kind.
tasbih:	Ritual utterance of short phrases or prayers while counting on a set of prayer beads.
wudu:	Ritual ablutions in Islam.

Notes

The War

1. The Bangladesh Liberation War or Bangladesh War of Independence ('Muktijuddho' in Bengali) of 1971.
2. My youngest uncle, my mother's youngest brother, who was younger than even me at the time.
3. *'Amader Chhoto Nodi Chole Enke-Beke'* ('Our Little River Winds Along') is a poem by Rabindranath Tagore that is traditionally taught to every child in Bengal at some point when they begin their education, be it at school or at home.
4. A guerrilla resistance movement formed by nationalist Bangladeshi soldiers and civilians during the Liberation War; the freedom fighters who were part of the Bahini were called *muktijoddha*.
5. The national anthem of Pakistan.

Birth, Aqiqah, etc.

1. A Bengali primer that has been used by all Bengali students at the start of their education, to this day.

2. The Bengali word for kidnapper is *chheledhora*. *Chhele*, or kid, is also the Bengali gendered noun for a little boy.
3. The term 'Ma', while meant for mothers, is often used as a moniker for little girls too, with numerous examples in Bengali of fathers referring to their daughters as 'Ma'.

Growing Up

1. An iconic song by Rabindranath Tagore, it was written on a full moon night ('a*aj jyotsna ratey*') in a train en route to Calcutta. Tagore was returning from Munger after receiving news that his youngest son had passed away.
2. Her father and her brother.
3. A Mohammed Rafi song from the 1960 Hindi film *Kala Bazar*.
4. Bengali film actor and star whose career spanned nearly three decades, starting from the 1950s. He was extremely popular and was considered a matinee idol of his time; he remains a cultural and cinematic icon to this day.
5. Term of endearment, used here for his older sister, my mother.

Mother

1. A popular Bengali proverb.

Pirbari 1

1. Song by Rabindrantha Tagore, roughly translates to 'Come, darling sisters, let us hold hands and dance around as we sing.'

2. From *Al-Fatiha*, the first surah of the Quran. This is the second line.
3. From *Al-Ikhlas*, the 112th surah of the Quran, the one that declares the absolute oneness and singularity of Allah.
4. Almost literally 'Me! Me!'

Faith

1. There is no god but Allah, [and] Muhammad is the messenger of Allah.
2. I bear witness that [there is] no god except Allah; One is He, no partner hath He, and I bear witness that Muhammad is His Servant and Messenger.
3. Ayat al-Kursi, or the Throne Verse, is the 255th verse of Al-Baqara, the second surah of the Quran, and one of the most widely known and utilized verses in the Islamic world.
4. Talaq or divorce of the irrevocable kind.

Poetry

1. Iconic closing lines of the Bengali poem 'Hey Mahajiban' (O Great Life) by poet Sukanta Bhattacharya.